GRAPHIC DESIGN + ARCHITECTURE

A 20TH-CENTURY HISTORY

First published in the United States of America by Rockport Publishers, a member of Quayside Publishing Group
100 Cummings Center
Suite 406-L
Beverly, Massachusetts
01915-6101
Telephone: (978) 282-9590
Fax: (978) 283-2742
www.rockpub.com

Library of Congress Cataloging-in-Publication Data

Poulin, Richard.

Graphic design and architecture, a 20th century history : a guide to type, image, symbol, and visual storytelling in the modern world / Richard Poulin.
    pages cm

Summary: "This innovative volume is the first to provide the design student, practitioner, and educator with an invaluable comprehensive reference of visual and narrative material that illustrates and evaluates the unique and important history surrounding graphic design and architecture. *Graphic Design and Architecture, A 20th Century History* closely examines the relationship between typography, image, symbolism, and the built environment by exploring principal themes, major technological developments, important manufacturers, and pioneering designers over the last 100 years. It is a complete resource that belongs on every designer's bookshelf"-- Provided by publisher.

 ISBN 978-1-59253-779-2
 1. Design--History--20th century. 2. Visual communication--History--20th century. 3. Communication in architecture--History--20th century. 4. Architecture and society--History--20th century. I. Title.
 741.609'04--dc23
 NK1390.P67 2012
                                    2012021721

ISBN: 978-1-59253-779-2
Digital edition published in 2012
eISBN: 978-1-61058-633-7

10 9 8 7 6 5 4 3 2 1

Design: Poulin + Morris Inc.

Printed in China

GRAPHIC DESIGN + ARCHITECTURE

CONTENTS

I
PRE-20TH-CENTURY INFLUENCES

II
THE MODERN AGE 1900–1950

III
THE POSTWAR WORLD
1950–2000

IV
THE BEGINNING
OF THE 21ST CENTURY

INTRODUCTION

For centuries, graphic design and architecture have coexisted in the built environment. Although each discipline speaks in its own unique language, each has historically attempted a dialogue with the other. Architecture speaks of form, space, and purpose, celebrating human continuity and offering experiences that both function and inspire. Graphic design—typography, image, and symbol—communicates the subtleties of time and place and tells cultural and visual stories, clarifying a building's purpose and echoing its architectural message.

Mankind has been telling its collective stories and histories by marking cave walls and inscribing buildings for millennia. Animal drawings at Lascaux, cuneiform writings in Mesopotamia, Chinese calligraphy, and Egyptian hieroglyphs all demonstrate how early mankind expressed themselves by drawing and writing on the places of significance in their lives. These early forms of visual communications or graphic design conveyed beauty, integrity, and above all—permanence.

Our need to dedicate and consecrate places is clearly the beginning of the integration of graphic design in the built environment. Classical inscriptions, figurative murals, and ornamental surfaces have long been a part of architecture and have influenced our understanding of typographic form and graphic style and their visual representation in the built environment. Buildings and public spaces coexist with billboards and signs, patterned and textured facades, and informational and wayfinding signs to effect an overall experience with the public. Graphic design has become integrated with the built environment in shaping not only cities but also the lives of their inhabitants.

At the intersection of the history of art and architecture, long before the design discipline was defined by its current name, environmental graphic design, seminal examples of twentieth-century graphic design arose in our built environment from the cultural, social, and economic climate of their time. Environmental graphic design is a vital part of our visual heritage, appreciated for its practical uses and enjoyed for its decorative appearances. Urban streetscapes, office buildings, museums, convention centers, airports, public parks, shopping malls, and entertainment centers all have been transformed by the use of environmental graphic design. This design discipline has evolved not only by its technical improvements but also by its integral relationship over time to art, architecture, and cultural movements.

For example, the meetinghouse signs and identification markers of American Shaker communities; Russian constructivist wall murals lining the streets of Moscow during the Bolshevik Revolution; the great white ways of Times Square, Piccadilly Circus, and the Las Vegas Strip; the festive and celebratory graphics of the 1984 Los Angeles Summer Olympics; the provocative typographic walls of the Vietnam Veterans Memorial in Washington, D.C.; and corporate identity and branding of the American marketplace after World War II all responded directly to the social constructs, political upheavals, and economic needs of the times. Additionally, prevailing artistic movements directly influenced and inspired other groundbreaking design benchmarks such as Hector Guimard's art nouveau entrances to the Paris metro, Otto Wagner's decorative building facades in Vienna, Edward Johnston's typography for the London Underground, Peter Behrens' integration of graphic and architectural form for Allegemein Elektricitäts-Gesellschaft (AEG), supergraphics by Barbara Stauffacher Solomon for Sea Ranch, and Robert Venturi's transformation of the ordinary into the extraordinary by applying decorative imagery to conventional buildings. Innovators and visionaries such as Frank Lloyd Wright, Georges Claude, Walter Dorwin Teague, Charles Eames, Margaret Calvert, Donald Leigh, Alvin Lustig, Walt Disney, Paul Rand, Alexander Girard, Dan Reisinger, Deborah Sussman, and Thomas Geismar have all transformed our built environment with innovative and revolutionary graphic design solutions during the course of the twentieth century.

Since environmental graphic design has only recently been recognized as a key discipline within the design professions, little if any documentation of importance, substance, or critical evaluation exists that deals with the history of typography, image, symbol, and visual storytelling in the context of our modern man-made world. The built environment that we experience in our everyday lives continually relies upon graphic design to communicate information and identity, shape our overall perception and memory of a sense of place, and ultimately enliven, enrich, and humanize our lives.

Graphic Design and Architecture: A 20th-Century History is the first historical overview of twentieth-century graphic design in the built environment. It provides the reader with an invaluable and comprehensive reference of visual and narrative material that illustrates and evaluates this unique and important history. This volume examines the relationship between typography, image, symbol, and visual storytelling in the modern world by exploring principal themes, major technical developments, important manufacturers, and pioneering designers over the last one hundred years. Unlike many recently published titles that focus primarily on isolated contemporary projects, *Graphic Design and Architecture* places the unique marriage of graphic design and architecture in the context of artistic, social, and cultural movements and influences of the twentieth century. This writer hopes that the reader, in looking back, can derive inspiration and insight into looking forward.

CONGRESS SHALL MAKE

RESPECTING AN ESTABLISH

OF RELIGION, OR PROHIBI

THE FREE EXERCISE THEREOF

OR ABRIDGING THE FREEDOM

OF SPEECH, OR OF THE PRESS;

OR THE RIGHT OF THE PEOPLE

PEACEABLY TO ASSEMBLE, AND

PETITION THE GOVERNMEN

GRIEVANCE

FOREWORD

JAMES STEWART POLSHEK, FAIA

James Stewart Polshek, FAIA—designer, public advocate, and educator—is in the fifth decade of his architectural career. In all three of these areas, he has provided an inspirational template for generations of architects. In 1962, he founded James Stewart Polshek, Architects, which ultimately became Polshek Partnership Architects. The legacy firm, Ennead Architects, is recognized internationally.

Mr. Polshek's reputation was initially established in 1963–1964 by his design of two research laboratory complexes in Japan. Over the past fifty years, he and his firm have completed many significant projects, including Santa Fe Opera, Santa Fe, New Mexico; The New York Times Printing Plant, New York City; the restoration and expansion of Carnegie Hall, New York; Rose Center for Earth and Space at the American Museum of Natural History, New York; and the William Jefferson Clinton Presidential Center and Park in Little Rock, Arkansas.

Mr. Polshek has received numerous awards for excellence, and he's received honorary degrees from Pratt Institute, the New School University Parsons School of Design, and New Jersey Institute of Technology. Since 2006, Mr. Polshek has been a member of the New York City Public Design Commission, appointed by Mayor Michael Bloomberg. He continues to serve as design counsel to Ennead Architects.

Newseum Building Facade (detail), 2008
Washington, D.C., USA
Poulin + Morris Inc. (est. 1989), Designers
New York, New York, USA
Ennead Architects (formerly Polshek Partnership;
est. 1963), Architects
New York, New York, USA

Buildings can tell stories. They do this by signifying an event, expressing the mission of an institution, and conveying the nature of a process. Fully achieving any of these intentions requires a synthesis of graphic design and architecture. Richard Poulin has, in his professional work and teaching, dramatically demonstrated how architecture can be enriched by symbols and typography. This book contains many examples—some as exaggerated as Venturi Scott Brown's Institute for Scientific Information in Philadelphia, others as subtle as Maya Lin's Vietnam Veterans Memorial.

Graphic Design and Architecture: A 20th-Century History will be mandatory reading for every graphic designer and architect, as well as all those that aspire to these two professions, and most importantly for all who are concerned with the humanizing possibilities inherent in the visual arts. This beautiful book deals with language, meaning, and their indivisibility with two- and three-dimensional design. It is enriched by a brief, but intense, history of the twentieth century (including a cameo appearance of the prehistoric cave paintings at Lascaux)—a virtual Jules Verne design voyage around the world!

Richard Poulin's sketches of each of the dozens of graphic designers and architects who populate this history are unfailingly generous. His selections are also stylistically catholic and cosmopolitan—as different as Hector Guimard and his timeless Paris metro stations and Barbara Stauffacher Solomon's innovative work with Charles Moore at Sea Ranch on the California coast—art nouveau at the end of the nineteenth century to supergraphics in the turbulent sixties. Also included are historic international events such as Robert Moses's 1964 New York World's Fair and the tragic Munich Olympics; monumental urban objects from the Eiffel Tower to Luis Barragán's colorful totems in Mexico City, legendary artists that include El Lissitzky, Gyorgy Kepes, Alvar Aalto, Lester Beall, and Herb Lubalin.

I came to first know Richard when we worked together on an addition to the Columbia University Law School in 1993. Our first meeting was memorable. He presented his preferred typographic font for the project in a way that can only be compared to a proud father holding up a day-old infant in front of his friends. He lovingly caressed every curve, solid, and void and comprehensively described his rationale for the fonts' appropriateness. Since then, we have collaborated on over 200 projects, all nonprofit institutions that include the Clinton Presidential Library in Little Rock, the National Museum of American Jewish History in Philadelphia, WGBH's headquarters in Boston, and Zankel Hall within Carnegie Hall in New York City. Richard and his partner, Douglas Morris, created, for each, singular graphic expressions that reinforce their identities and aspirations.

Richard Poulin's lifelong teaching career and professional practice provided him with the tools required to undertake the encyclopedic challenge he set for himself. But this never could have been completed so brilliantly without his intellectual curiosity and extraordinary visual judgment.

James Stewart Polshek

FOREWORD

DEBORAH SUSSMAN, HAIA, FSEGD

Deborah Sussman is recognized as a pioneer of environmental graphic design for creating arresting visual imagery and designing its highly imaginative applications for architectural and public spaces. Deborah's passion for the marriage of graphics and the built environment, fueled by her early career at the Eames Office, has led to extensive collaborations with planners, architects, other designers, and clients.

Her work, informed by perceptive observation and rigorous documentation of communities and cultures, has found its place in projects for cities, arts and entertainment venues, commercial developments, and the private sector around the world. She began to work with architects in the late 1960s and 1970s, then incorporated as Sussman/Prejza & Co. with husband Paul Prejza. Deborah has led the firm in designing an array of notable projects: the "look" of the 1984 Olympics, which received *Time* magazine's award for "Best of the Decade"; the identity and branding applications for the Gas Company of Southern California; the identity, product exhibits, and corporate interiors for Hasbro Inc.; and award-winning wayfinding systems for Walt Disney Resorts and the cities of Philadelphia and Santa Monica. More recent projects include comprehensive interiors for the Seattle Opera, McCaw Hall, and exhibit design for the Museum of the African Diaspora (MoAD) in San Francisco.

Cincinnati Civic Center Interior (detail), 2008
Cincinnati, Ohio, USA
Sussman/Prejza & Co. (est. 1968), Designers
Los Angeles, California, USA

This book is a gift to all current and future practitioners of, users of, and participants in, environmental graphic design. It demonstrates how this particular field of endeavor has deep roots. It explores and uncovers a history that was not examined or compiled until Richard Poulin delved into it. It organizes and points out major global contributions that have not been linked before. It is a massive collection of material, of benefit and illumination to everyone in the design disciplines. It has stimulated my memory and inspires me to continue.

When did I discover the power of words and symbols in the built environment we live in? Perhaps it was as a child, traveling the subway from my Brooklyn home to the great hub of Manhattan. Coming up for air as the train approached the bridge, the Squibb toothpaste tower sign convinced me that all was well.

However, it was another sign that really made me think—and worry. Close-by there was a large-scale message in red—probably handpainted: "Believe in the Lord Jesus Christ and Thou shalt be Saved." But we were Jewish. I did want to be saved but couldn't accept the risk. Yet those words called out to me every time I looked through the window. Finally, I decided that, as long as I read that message every time it appeared, life would be okay.

Those two icons demonstrate the lasting power of communication when messages and symbols participate in the urban fabric of the built environment.

The famous "trylon and perisphere" of the 1939 New York World's Fair became another lasting icon for me. In this case, it was the form and its whiteness, its newness, its bigness, and its simplicity that lives in memory. It wasn't architecture; it wasn't really sculpture, and certainly not graphic design. So what was it?

It did not fit into a category neatly. Could it have been "environmental graphic design"?

Walt Disney World Exterior Sign Program
(detail), 1989
Orlando, Florida, USA
Sussman/Prejza & Co. (est. 1968), Designers
Los Angeles, California, USA

That term, and even that profession as a discipline, did not exist until decades later. It was mainly in the 1960s that people began to practice EGD as a specialized, focused discipline. But it still really had no name. During those early years—and even into the 1980s—there were not so many of us. We were hard to label—not exactly graphic designers, not architects, not interior designers, and so on. Besides, it was (and in some ways still is) difficult to input into a powerful, established "modern" architecture that resisted change. But our numbers increased. A design discipline was born; schools began to support the discipline.

Also, as this book reveals, women emerged and continue to be leaders in this field—an interesting phenomenon, especially since women have long been considered minor players in the field of architecture. During the 1960s, the work of Barbara Stauffacher exploded on the buildings at Sea Ranch. In Los Angeles, Corita Kent took graphics off the page and into the street. Suddenly, words were floating in three dimensions—independent of, yet deliberately cognizant of, architecture. These pioneers were challenging the polite obeisance to rules that traditional graphic design was supposed to obey: to "fit" comfortably and "politely" into classically designated spaces. As the line between disciplines has finally become blurry, so too has the line between sacred and profane.

Just as I cannot forget my childhood memory of messages viewed from the window of a train going from Brooklyn to Manhattan and the emergence from dark to light, and then the mighty bridge—I cannot separate graphics from architecture, urban design, landscape, lighting, paving, utilities, performance, sound, and ultimately, the experiences of the people who use and need all of it.

Deborah Sussman

PRE-20TH-CENTURY INFLUENCES

IMP · CAES · DIV
ANTONINI · PII · GERM
SARMATICI · FILIVS · DIV
OMMODI · FRAT
IVI · ANTONINI · PII · NEPOS · DIVI · HA
O · NEPOS · DIVI · TRAIANI · PARTHIC
B · NEPOS · DIVI · NERVAE · ADNEP
SEPTIMIVS · SEVE
PIVS · PERTINAX · AV
RABICVS · ADIABENICVS · P
R · POT · IIII · IMP · VIII · Co · S · II ·
OLVMNAM · VII · TEMPEST
CONFRACTAM · RESTITVIT

PRE-20TH-CENTURY INFLUENCES

While many consider Rome the birthplace of Western typography, image, symbol, and visual storytelling in the built environment, as well as the early beginnings of their interaction with the man-made world, this unique design dialogue started much earlier in the history of mankind.

In the prehistoric era (30,000 BCE–5000 BCE), rock paintings or pictographs were mankind's first elemental drawings representing a concept, object, activity, place, or event and inevitably evolved into different forms of graphic communication systems, as well as visual symbols for the written and spoken word.

With the development of the world's earliest system of writing—cuneiform (from the Latin *cuneus*, meaning "wedge")—by the Sumerians in 3100 BCE, mankind began to communicate over long distances and record information for posterity. This innovative and radical new system of visual communication was based on abstract wedge-shaped signs made on clay tablets with a blunt reed or stylus, as opposed to naïve line drawings. From this point forward, writing systems evolved in different cultures throughout the civilized world.

In Western Europe, monuments and manmade structures communicated stories and symbolized rituals through their forms, compositions, and locations. The most distinctive archaeological remains from this period (3000–1000 BCE) were stone-built burial chambers that incorporated megaliths (large stones, from the Greek *megas*, "big," and *lithos*, "stone"), some engraved with decorative patterns.

For more than 1,500 years, capital square letters or *capitalis monumentalis* were the ideal Roman letterforms used primarily in inscriptions throughout the vast Roman Empire. Based on the pure geometric shapes of the square, triangle, and circle, these monumental inscriptions celebrated the achievements and victories of Roman leaders. With Roman triumphal arches, the written narrative was an integral part of the architecture and its letterforms had the same architectural integrity as any other architectural detail. The composition of the arch was a cohesive whole that provided focus to the narrative, as well as a functional and memorable threshold for ceremony.

The Middle or Medieval Ages (500–1300) began with the fall of the Roman Empire in 476, marking the end of the ancient world and the beginning of a modern one. During this time period, town seals, monograms, emblems, and coats of arms among the chivalry appeared throughout the built environment and were used as marks of identification, as well as protective shields in battle. In 1188, the monarchs of England, France, and Flanders (present-day Belgium and the Netherlands) unilaterally agreed to represent their military forces with specific graphic symbols and colors.

Medieval city dwellers formed guilds to regulate not only economic activities, but political and military affairs as well. Distinctive banners and flags were used by these guilds to identify their industries, such as blacksmiths, wine merchants, and tavern owners. Tradesmen, publicans, apothecaries, and merchants used signboards displayed outside their establishments to promote their offerings and wares.

The Renaissance (1300–1600), meaning "to be reborn," grew out of the Italian Middle Ages and marked the reevaluation and renewed understanding of classical European literature, music, science, art, and architecture that ultimately sparked a cultural revolution throughout Western Europe for the next 200 years. With the invention of printing and moveable type by Johannes Gutenberg (c. 1398–1468) in 1450, new and innovative ideas spread rapidly throughout Italy and then the rest of the European continent by the foremost minds of the time—Leonardo da Vinci (1452–1519), Michelangelo Buonarroti (1475–1564), Leon Battista Alberti (1404–1472), Sandro Botticelli (c. 1445–1510), and Filippo Brunelleschi (1377–1446).

The fifteenth and sixteenth centuries were an era of monarchs, divine right, and absolute rule with the undercurrents of unrest and inevitable revolt. Western Europe turned toward exploration, expansion, and colonization of new worlds. By the 1700s, the printing press had become commonplace throughout Europe and America. In the 1800s, posters and broadsides were primary advertising vehicles, appearing on building walls and signboards throughout Europe and the United States. New developments in typography and printing processes ultimately influenced graphic design in the built environment during this era.

The Industrial Revolution transformed the economy of the civilized world during the late 1700s and early 1800s from one based on agriculture in rural communities to one based on manufacturing in urban centers. This transformation began in Great Britain and spread throughout Europe and the Americas due to new inventions and technologies. Machine tools, steam engines, and measuring instruments facilitated and enhanced the growth of industries, transportation systems, and new forms of building construction that started to appear throughout the modern world.

Each of these influences left an indelible graphic signature on the built environments of the past. Historical developments in typography, materials, surface treatments, and architectural context have been an essential and invaluable series of references for the evolution of graphic design in the modern man-made world.

PETROGRAMS AND PETROGLYPHS

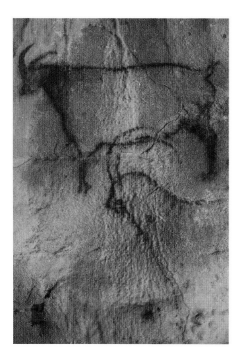

c. 13000 BCE

CAVE PAINTING
Cougnac, France

The realistic representations of hand stencils, drawings, and polychrome paintings of animals, human beings, and crude objects found on the walls of subterranean caves such as the ones in Lascaux and Niaux in southern France are considered to be the first and oldest known examples of graphic symbols created by mankind. These primitive images also communicated and commemorated the social and economic occurrences of the people who created them.

Crude pigments were created from charcoal and red and yellow oxides, mixed with fat, to create a medium that was then possibly smear-ed onto the walls of these caves with fingers or brushes made of bristles, reeds, or animal hair. Most historians agree that these actions do not mark the beginning of art, but they do signify the dawn of visual communications and one of mankind's first examples of graphic design in the built environment.

Petrograms (painted) or petroglyphs (engraved) were found in most parts of the world, from Europe to Africa, America, Asia, Australia, and the Polynesian Islands.

STONEHENGE

c. 1500 BCE

STONEHENGE
Wiltshire, United Kingdom

Stonehenge, a megalithic monument structure composed of 30-foot- (9.1 m) tall stones, was the ceremonial site of Celtic sun worship located in Wiltshire, United Kingdom, erected around 1500 BCE. Henge monuments were enclosures that functioned as local ritual centers surrounded by an earth berm and a ditch. Huge, monolithic stones were carefully placed to create a circular enclosed form and interior space that was either open to the heavens above or enclosed by a wooden or thatched roof.

Ritual stone circles and rows were prevalent throughout England and northwestern

Europe during the third millennium BCE. In many ways, these monumental structures were as impressive as their cultural and geographic counterparts—the colossal pyramids and temples in Egypt, Mesopotamia, Central America, and South America.

HIEROGLYPHICS

c. 2500 BCE

EGYPTIAN HIEROGLYPHICS
Abydos, Upper Egypt

Beginning in approximately 2500 BCE, the walls, surfaces, and passages of Egyptian pyramids were covered with hieroglyphic (in Greek, "sacred carving") writings of myths, hymns, and prayers supporting the Pharaoh's life in the afterworld. Hieroglyphics, a picture-writing system used in ancient Egyptian culture, consisted of three types of glyphs—phonetic or single-consonant characters that functioned similar to an alphabet; logographic; and ideographic. Hieroglyphics was a remarkably efficient writing system used by the Egyptians for over three and a half centuries that contained seven hundred hieroglyphs, with over one hundred that were strictly pictographic.

This expansive graphic language was used for decorative and inscriptional purposes everywhere in the Egyptian built environment. It was chiseled into stone or cut into wood as bas-relief or incised relief images, covering the exteriors and interiors of monumental stone temples and tombs and used on furniture, coffins, and clothing. Most hieroglyphics were organized vertically in a columnar composition, read from top to bottom and right to left. Their graphic characteristics were stylized, symbolic, and implicit—men had darker skin color than women; important people were shown in larger scale than less important ones; and the human body was always represented as a two-dimensional frontal figure or form with arms, legs, and head in profile.

THE GREEK
IONIC ALPHABET

403 BCE

**AN ICONIC VERSION OF THE GREEK
ALPHABET USED BY THE ATHENIANS**
Wiltshire, United Kingdom

designer/location unknown

The great civilizations of Greece, Etruria, and Rome represented the beginning of the Western European world. The Greeks adapted the Phoenician alphabet and modified it into a system of twenty-five characters. The Greek Ionic alphabet included five vowels (A, E, I, O, U), and written language read from left to right; however, there were still no visual separations between words and sentences, nor was there any punctuation.

The Greek Ionic alphabet was the sole source of all modern European scripts and is considered the world's first true alphabet. Concurrent with this graphic development, Greek architecture started to be built in either the Doric or Ionic style, named after the Greek dialects. A third style, Corinthian, came into use at the end of the century.

Each of these distinctive styles can be best described by their architectural columns that symbolize and characterize their stylistic conventions. The Doric column has an undecorated rounded capital with a tapered column of carefully joined stone drums carved with decorative fluting. The Ionic column is also fluted like its Doric counterpart, yet taller and slender, and its capital characterized by scroll-like appendages. The Corinthian column is capped with a ornamental capital shaped like an upturned bell decorated with carved acanthus leaves and became the leading architectural style of the Roman Empire.

The Parthenon, temple of the goddess Athena, is one of the greatest remaining examples of classical Greek Doric architecture. Located on the Acropolis in Athens, Greece, and completed in 447 BCE, the Parthenon was built in stone with continuous columns, within which stood a sanctuary containing a statue of Athena.

The carved decorations located in the principal friezes and triangular pediment of the temple communicated themes of special significance for honoring the gods. The inscriptions at the temple of Athena were the inspiration for the twentieth-century glyphic sans-serif typeface Lithos (Carol Twombly, b. 1959) designed in 1989.

ROMAN MONUMENTAL INSCRIPTIONS

81

ARCH OF TITUS
Rome, Italy
designer unknown

One of the most important developments of this time period was Roman inscriptional lettering known as *capitalis monumentalis*. These classic letterforms, based on early Etruscan and Greek alphabets and the basis for modern capital letterforms, were refined by the Romans so that they would retain their visual characteristics when engraved or cut in stone. Serifs originated with the carving of inscriptions into stone by Roman masons who added small hooks to the tips of letters to prevent their chisel from slipping. These carved inscriptions would then be infilled with cast bronze letters attached with "tangs" or wooden pegs.

Roman lettering appeared on buildings and public spaces in each and every town and added to the visual branding of the Roman Empire.

Monumental inscriptions on the Roman Forum's three triumphal arches—Titus (81; at right), Septimius Severus (203), and Constantine (315), and at the base of the Trajan Column (113; see page 30), illustrate the critical visual relationships that occurred between letterform, material, surface, and composition in the Roman built environment.

The Arch of Titus, completed in 81, was erected by Domitian (81–96) to commemorate Vespasian's victory over the Egyptians and Titus's capture of Jerusalem 230 years earlier.

The arch's composition has a single portal opening flanked on each side by bas-relief columns with early examples of Corinthian capitals (at right). The soffit and flanking facades of the arch are adorned with figurative reliefs of the emperor and his campaign in Jerusalem. Serif-like monumental capital letterforms, carved into its marble fascia, are composed symme-

continued on page 30

113

207

**INSCRIPTION FROM BASE OF COLUMN
ERECTED FOR THE EMPEROR TRAJAN**
Rome, Italy
Apollodorus of Damascus (c. 65–110), Architect
Damascus, Syria

AN INSCRIPTION OF SEPTIMIUS SEVERUS
Rome, Italy
designer unknown

trically within the arch's attic story and are even-stroked and architecturally proportioned. They are also closely spaced and clearly reflect the simplicity and restrained organization of the arch itself.

These commemorative monuments were constructed to celebrate and bear witness to the episodes and victories of Roman emperors and generals. They were architectural and graphic compositions of great detail and provided designers and architects with a design vocabulary that would be relied upon for centuries to come.

Erected in 113, the Trajan Column was designed by Greek sculptor and architect Apollodorus (c. 65–110) of Damascus to commemorate Trajan's military victories in the Dacian (present-day Romania) wars (98–117).

Located in the Roman Forum, this 131-foot (40 m) victory column, which was originally topped with a bronze statue of Trajan, consists of 18 blocks of pristine white Carrara marble, each 4 feet (1.2 m) high and 11.5 feet (3.5 m) in diameter and adorned with a continuous spiraling, bas-relief sculpture depicting the epic wars between the Romans and Dacians and carved

capitalis monumentalis inscriptions considered to be the finest surviving examples of Roman capital lettering. The twentieth-century old style, all-capital typeface Trajan (Carol Twombly, b. 1959) is based on the letterforms found in these Roman square capital inscriptions.

The design of the Trajan Column has inspired numerous commemorative monuments and victory columns throughout ancient and modern history.

THE PANTHEON

125

THE PANTHEON
Rome, Italy

Apollodorus of Damascus (c. 65–110), Architect
Damascus, Syria

Built by Trajan's son Hadrian (76–138), one of the greatest architectural patrons of all time, the Pantheon is one of the most celebrated architectural masterpieces of Western civilization. It also has one of the finest examples of early Roman inscriptions ever to be integrated to an architectural structure.

The simplicity and perfect proportions of the building's design is world renowned as an architectural benchmark and engineering achievement due to its huge dome hidden behind the building's classical portico. The typographic inscriptions on its exterior entablature and portico facade are also impressive examples of early Roman graphic design in the built environment. The letterforms are logically centered with comfortable spacing, creating a very legible and well-proportioned bronze typographic inscription that reads: M - AGRIPPA L F COS TERTIUM FECIT (translated: Marcus Agrippa the son of Lucius, three times consul built this).

CHURCH OF SANT' APOLLINARE NUOVO

549

CHURCH OF SANT' APOLLINARE NUOVO
Ravenna, Italy

Theodoric the Great (454–526), Architect
Pannonia, province of the Roman Empire

Ravenna, Italy, was the last capital of the Roman Empire after the fall of Rome in 476 and renowned for some of the world's most remarkable Byzantine mosaics in the Church of Sant' Apollinare Nuovo (549). Entire walls and ceilings of the church are covered on an epic scale with minuscule fragments of glass, colored marble, and semiprecious stones cut to fit drawn or painted figurative scenes and set in an oblique manner to catch daylight. Mosaic panels depicting scenes from the Old Testament and the childhood of Jesus Christ adorn the apse and surrounding entablature of the building's interior. Biblical quotations and prayers are inscribed in archaic Latin lettering, sometimes set against the luminescent gold of the mosaics enveloping the interior.

The mosaic techniques used during this time period were made of minute "cards" or quadrangular fragments of a pebble or vitreous (glasslike) paste mixture. The latter offered an almost infinite range of colors, including bright hues of vermilion, emerald green, and cerulean blue. Transparent glass fragments were covered on their back surfaces with sheets of gold leaf that provided a visual depth to the background on which the figures stand out.

The church's mosaics illustrate the fusion between Eastern and Western art influences during this time period. Their organization and architectural integration are also reminiscent of the sculptural figurative friezes found on earlier monuments of the Roman Empire.

CHARTRES CATHEDRAL

1220

CHARTRES CATHEDRAL
STAINED GLASS WINDOWS
Chartres, France
designer unknown

The great Gothic cathedrals of the medieval era, such as Notre Dame (1350) in Paris, France, and the Cathedral of Our Lady of Chartres (1220) in Chartres, France, marked the beginning of a period of wealth and prosperity for the Roman Catholic church in northwestern Europe. This new French High Gothic style of architecture was characteristic of soaring ribbed vaults, flying buttresses, pointed arches, ornamental gargoyles, carved turrets and canopies, and stained glass windows.

Stained glass, as an early form of graphic design in the built environment, reached its pinnacle during the Middle Ages in France and England when it became a primary means of visually communicating symbolic narratives from either the Bible, history, or literature through the use of universal imagery to largely illiterate congregations.

Chartres was one of the first architectural structures of the era to accommodate the extensive use of stained glass. Its magnificent stained glass windows, totaling 176, function as illuminated wall decorations inspired by medieval illuminated manuscripts that transform the interiors of this religious monument with a blaze of light and color.

BASILICA OF SANTA MARIA NOVELLA

1470

BASILICA OF
SANTA MARIA NOVELLA BUILDING FACADE
Florence, Italy
Leon Battista Alberti (1404–1472), Architect
Genoa, Italy

The Basilica of Santa Maria Novella in Florence, Italy, is considered to be one of the first great monuments of the Renaissance. It is also one of the first primary examples of how letterform, as well as its visual characteristics, proportions, and material, played an important and active role in the design of an architectural facade.

Leon Battista Alberti (1404–1472), the first great architect and theoretician of the Renaissance era, was the first to consider classical letterforms as an integral and consistent visual element in all of his work.

With Santa Maria Novella, Alberti relied upon many of the proportional principles and pure geometric design elements found in the Pantheon (125; see page 31).

Alberti considered ornament, including Roman square capital letterforms, as a decorative surface treatment, and this is reflected in the building facade's broad frieze, pilasters, entablature, and oculus, all crowned by a pediment depicting the Dominican order's solar emblem. The entablature directly below this pediment carries the name of the church's patron: IOHAN(N)ES ORICELLARIUS PAU(LI) F(ILIUS) AN(NO) SAL(UTIS) MCCCCLXX (Giovanni Rucellai son of Paolo in the blessed year 1470). Here, letterform and architecture are one and the same with the inscription running the full length and height of the surface of the entablature.

PIAZZA CAMPIDOGLIO

1538

PIAZZA CAMPIDOGLIO
(Completed in 1940)
Rome, Italy

Michelangelo Buonarroti (1475–1564), Architect
Caprese, Italy

Michelangelo di Lodovico Buonarroti Simoni, also known simply as Michelangelo (1475–1564), an Italian sculptor, painter, poet, engineer, and architect, was one of the defining creative minds of the Renaissance.

In 1505, he was invited to Rome by Pope Julius II (1443–1513) to design his tomb, a tumultuous association that would last for more than 40 years. In 1508, Michelangelo began work on a monumental fresco depicting scenes from the Old Testament for the Sistine Chapel ceiling, which he completed four years later.

Following the completion of the Sistine frescoes, he became the chief architect of St. Peter's Basilica in Rome in 1546.

Michelangelo also designed the Capitoline, the site of the capital of the Roman Empire in Rome, in 1538. The site's urban plaza is a powerful spatial and visual demonstration of what graphic design and architecture can achieve.

The pavement pattern of the Capitoline's Piazza Campidoglio, an early form of optical illusion used in a public space, comes alive with the perception that a dome composed of an interwoven twelve-pointed star is rising into the void of the space framed by the surrounding buildings. While the pavement design was never executed in Michelangelo's lifetime, Italy's Fascist dictator Benito Mussolini (1883–1945) ordered the pavement completed in 1940.

TAJ MAHAL

1653

TAJ MAHAL
Agra, India
Ustàd Ahmad Lahauri (1580–1649), Architect
Lahore, Persia

The Taj Mahal or "crown of palaces" in Agra, India, marks the culmination of Shah Jahan's (1592–1666) architectural activities and was erected in memory of his beloved consort, Mumtaz-i-Mahal (1593–1631).

Built in the Mughai architectural style, a style that combines elements of Persian, Turkish, and Indian architectural influences, the Taj Mahal is one of the most admired and widely recognized buildings in the world and has been described as "the jewel of Muslim art in India."

Its construction began in 1632 and was completed in 1653, employing thousands of artisans and craftsmen. The Taj Mahal's decorative and commemorative elements were created by applying paint, stucco, semiprecious stone inlays, and carvings to the building's white marble facades and interior wall surfaces. Islamic inscriptions taken from the Koran are either calligraphic, abstract, or plant-based in motif since Islamic law forbids the use of any anthropomorphic or human-based forms.

THE SHAKER AESTHETIC

1842

MEETINGHOUSE SIGN
New Lebanon, New York, USA
Hancock Shaker Village, Pittsfield, Massachusetts, USA
designer unknown

The Shaker aesthetic has been an inspirational influence on graphic design in the built environments of the modern world. The Shakers anticipated the future principles of functionalism and American architect Louis Sullivan's (1856–1924) famous dictum "form follows function" when they affirmed "hands to work, hearts to God" and "the best is that which functions best."

The first Shaker community was founded by Ann Lee (1736–1784) in Manchester, England. At the age of twenty-two, she joined the Quakers, who at the time were being persecuted in England. In 1774, she escaped oppression by fleeing to America, where she established a community in Watervliet, New York.

The household tools, furniture, objects, and various wares designed by the Shaker communities were truly remarkable, both on a creative and aesthetic level. Rocking chairs, stoves, their famous boxes, and meetinghouse signs were all imbued with a purity and simplicity of form, whether made from wood or metal.

CORN PALACE

1892

CORN PALACE BUILDING FACADE
Mitchell, South Dakota, USA
Rapp & Rapp (est. c. 1900), Architects
Chicago, Illinois, USA

Originally built in 1892, the Corn Palace (also known as the Corn Belt Exposition) showcased the rich agricultural opportunities available in South Dakota and encouraged people to settle in the state.

The building is also a graphic and architectural celebration of corn, farming, and agriculture in South Dakota. Rebuilt in 1921, this Moorish Revival building is decorated throughout with crop art, its murals and decorative details made of corn and other harvested grains from the region. This "living" building facade is redecorated every year by local artists and designers with only natural-colored corn and two tons of grains and grasses.

This popular tourist attraction serves as a local arena and civic auditorium for numerous community and regional events and is visited by more than 500,000 people every year.

THE ARTS AND CRAFTS MOVEMENT

1893

GREEN DRAGON HOTEL BUILDING FACADE
Hereford, United Kingdom
Craven Dunhill & Co. Ltd. (est. 1872), Designers
Shropshire, United Kingdom

The Arts and Crafts movement, led by British textile designer, artist, writer, theorist, and socialist William Morris (1834–1896), celebrated traditional craftsmanship, simple forms, and a reliance on the decorative arts. One of the movement's fundamental goals was to elevate the applied arts to the same level as fine arts in the public's perception. These tenets became the basis for the birth of modernism, as well as for the genesis of the Bauhaus in Germany in the early 1900s.

During the late 1800s, elaborate architectural facades were enhanced with typographic and ornamental motifs communicating the wares and offerings of commercial establishments and often constructed from standard and repetitive units of glazed ceramic tiles.

The exterior facade of the Green Dragon Hotel is a prime example of this construction technique used during the Arts and Crafts era. The building's tiled facade reflects the most durable and permanent of all forms of advertising and is composed of glazed machine-pressed relief tiles containing stylistic letterforms of the era, designed and manufactured by Craven Dunhill & Co. Ltd. (est. 1872), one of the United Kingdom's leading producers of ceramic tiles.

II

THE MODERN AGE 1900–1950

THE IMPACT OF INVENTION 1879–1933

At the beginning of the twentieth century, change appeared everywhere. In civilized cultures throughout the world, traditional beliefs were starting to be overshadowed by emerging new ideas. A flood of groundbreaking innovations and inventions redefined the architecture and built environment and forever transformed the now-industrialized modern world.

In the 1870s, the invention of electricity and the incandescent lightbulb by Thomas Alva Edison (1847–1931) ultimately enhanced the way in which people interacted with one another and with the built environments they lived in. Communication was also dramatically altered in the late nineteenth century by the introduction of the telephone by Alexander Graham Bell (1847–1922) and his assistant, Thomas Watson (1854–1934).

The development of the first commercially successful internal combustion engine in 1858 by Belgian engineer Étienne Lenoir (1822–1900) and improvements to the assembly line technique of mass production by American industrialist Henry Ford (1863–1947) in the early 1900s, revolutionized the manner in which people traveled from destination to destination, ultimately allowing them to explore every corner of the world.

At the beginning of the century, there were approximately 8,000 automobiles in the United States. In 1906, President Theodore "Teddy" Roosevelt (1858–1919) initiated American domestic tourism by encouraging Americans public to take to the road and "See America First." Americans' love affair with the new automobile and their desire to be mobile and explore the open road grew, and with it came the development of the country's city, state, and federal road systems; service stations, motor courts, and motels.

New and revolutionary explorations in art and architecture around the world also inevitably influenced graphic design in the built environment during this time period. While the art nouveau movement reached its peak of popularity at the end of the nineteenth century, the birth of modern art, which set the stage for modernism, was considered by many to have begun with Pablo Picasso's (1881–1973) groundbreaking painting *Les Demoiselles d'Avignon (The Young Ladies of Avignon)*, completed in 1907.

Innovative building materials and construction technologies created towering skyscrapers that began to appear in the built landscape that literally altered the urban experience. Improved transportation systems redefined urban metropolises like Paris, Moscow, New York, and London.

These and many more twentieth-century innovations and inventions transformed the potential for graphic design in the built environment in the modern world more rapidly and widely than in any previous century.

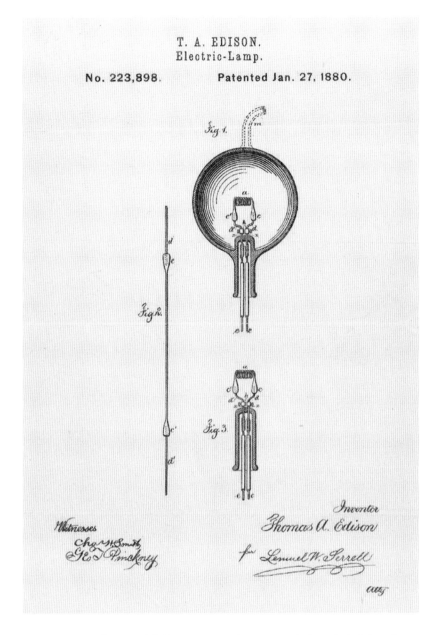

T. A. EDISON.
Electric-Lamp.

No. 223,898.   Patented Jan. 27, 1880.

THE INCANDESCENT LIGHTBULB

1879

**CARBON-FILAMENT ELECTRIC LIGHTBULB
PATENT DRAWING**
Menlo Park, New Jersey, USA
Thomas Edison (1847–1931), Inventor
Milan, Ohio, USA

Thomas Alva Edison (1847–1931) was an American inventor, scientist, and businessman who greatly influenced modern life throughout the twentieth century. He was one of the most prolific inventors in history, with over 1,000 U.S. patents, as well as many held in the United Kingdom, France, and Germany. Edison is credited with numerous inventions that contributed to the rapid development of the modern, industrialized world including the stock ticker, electric power, the phonograph, the motion picture camera, and the incandescent lightbulb.

He was born in Milan, Ohio, and grew up in Port Huron, Michigan. His initial interest in mass communications was an outgrowth of his early career as a telegraph operator. Edison began his career as an inventor in Newark, New Jersey, in 1877 with an entrepreneurial spirit and business acumen that led him to found fourteen companies over the course of his career, including General Electric in 1892, one of the world's largest publicly traded companies.

In 1878, Edison created the Edison Electric Light Company in New York City with several investors, including American financier J. P. Morgan (1837–1913) and members of the Vanderbilt family. On December 31, 1879, he made the first public demonstration of his incandescent lightbulb in Menlo Park, New Jersey.

While Edison did not invent the first electric lightbulb, he did invent the first commercially practical incandescent lightbulb. By 1879, he had produced a high-heat-resistance lamp with a carbon filament that burned for hundreds of hours and glowed a warm light comparable to that of a candle's flame. He then developed the lightbulb's extensive commercial applications and was able to market it to homes and businesses by mass-producing relatively long-lasting lightbulbs, as well as creating a complete system for the generation and distribution of electrical power.

The incandescent lightbulb had a tremendous impact on the evolution of graphic design in the built environment and revolutionized the way in which we experience the nuances of type, image, symbol, and visual storytelling in the modern architectural world.

EIFFEL TOWER

1889

EIFFEL TOWER
Paris, France

Alexandre Gustave Eiffel (1832–1923), Architect
Dijon, France

The Exposition Universelle of 1889, marking the centennial of the storming of the Bastille and the beginning of the French Revolution, was located on the banks of the river Seine in Paris running along the Champs de Mars and the Trocadero. The world's fair covered 237 acres (95.9 ha), had 7,000 foreign exhibitors, and was attended by 32.2 million visitors by the time of its closing.

The main symbol and focal point of the Exposition Universelle was the Eiffel Tower, which served as the main-entrance archway to the fair. It was constructed of puddle iron, a form of wrought iron, and was named after its designer, Gustave Eiffel (1832–1923).

Alexandre Gustave Eiffel was a French structural engineer, as well as an architect, entrepreneur, and specialist in metal structures. In addition to the acclaim he received for designing and building the Eiffel Tower for the 1889 Exposition Universelle, he was also notable for designing the inner supporting armature for the Statue of Liberty (1886) in New York Harbor.

He attended the École Centrale des Arts et Manufactures in Paris, where he studied chemistry, receiving the equivalent of a master of science degree in 1855. The École Centrale was a liberal private school that is now known as one of the top engineering schools in Europe.

At the time of its completion, the Eiffel Tower was the world's tallest structure at 985 feet (305 m), illuminated by gaslights from top to bottom and painted five shades of red, from a dark bronze at the base to a golden yellow at its apex. The tower quickly became Paris's top tourist attraction, drawing millions of people to the city and large amounts of money into France's economy. At the time, few disagreed with an American news correspondent who wrote that it deserved to be included with "the wonders of the world."

While it was initially considered an unsightly folly to many Parisians, this iconic spire has reigned over Paris for more than a century. After the closing of the exposition, it was set to be demolished but was left intact because of its added function as a radio transmission tower. The Eiffel Tower has become a universal symbol for France, as well as for the creative pioneering spirit that marked the beginning of the industrialized modern era.

THE MODERN BILLBOARD

1891

OCEAN BREEZES ELECTRIC BILLBOARD
New York, New York, USA

Oscar J. Gude (1862–1925), Designer
New York, New York, USA

A billboard (also known as a "hoarding" in the United Kingdom and in many other areas of the world) is a large outdoor advertising structure, typically located alongside busy roads and in high-traffic urban areas, that displays large-scale commercial advertisements to passing pedestrians and motorists.

In the late 1800s and early 1900s, the billboard took on many evolving forms in the built environment. American showman P. T. Barnum (1810–1891) relied upon huge banners and woodcuts to advertise his P. T. Barnum American Museum (est. 1841) at Broadway and Ann Street in New York City. "Walking billboards" or sandwich men paraded up and down Broadway and other busy commercial thoroughfares in New York City advertising the latest entertainments and offerings.

In 1889 at the Exposition Universelle in Paris and four years later at the 1893 World's Columbian Exposition in Chicago, the world's first twenty-four-sheet billboard was introduced and quickly became the standard format for various types of large-scale advertising throughout Europe and the United States.

Prior to the automobile, large-scale outdoor advertisements were limited to being painted on building walls of cities and towns throughout the world. In the early 1900s, billboards were painted in large production studios throughout the United States. To create a typical billboard advertisement, an image was first projected on a series of individual panels that made up the entire billboard, then "pounced" on the panels, which marked in outline all of the visual elements of the advertisement, such as figures, products, and letterforms. Production artists would then use large brushes and oil paints to complete the billboard image. Once the individual panels were installed, art-

continued on page 44

1900

H. J. HEINZ ELECTRIC BILLBOARD
New York, New York, USA
Oscar J. Gude (1862–1925), Designer
New York, New York, USA

ists would then touch up the edges between each panel.

With the introduction of electricity to New York City in 1882 by Thomas Edison (1847–1931; see page 41), billboard advertisements in cities around the world started to rely upon this new lighting technology in new ways.

Oscar J. Gude (1862–1925), one of New York City's first sign impresarios, designed the first electric billboard in 1891. Located on the facade of the Cumberland Hotel at the intersection of 23rd Street, Broadway, and Fifth Avenue, this 80-foot- (24.4 m) high by 60-foot- (18.3 m) wide typographic billboard was composed of 1,457 incandescent lightbulbs, built and

installed by the Edison Electrical Company, and advertised the Long Island Railroad's new Coney Island resort—Ocean Breezes.

Nine years later, Gude's electric billboard for the H. J. Heinz Company in 1900 covered the same building facade of the Cumberland Hotel and was the first to use a pictorial image, in this case a giant 40-foot (12.2 m) wide pickle, flashing on and off against a contrasting and complementary colored blue and orange background. Directly below were some of Heinz's fifty-seven varieties also displayed in electric typographic lights. This new and innovative method of advertising marked the beginning of the "sign spectacular" (see page 100) that was

to become a common sight along New York City's future Great White Way (see page 48).

In 1908, the Model T automobile was introduced in the United States by industrialist Henry Ford (1863–1947). With the advent of new printing technologies and an increase in the number of automobiles worldwide, advertising billboards grew larger and more colorful. By the next decade, many more motorists were taking to the roads, and therefore the billboard advertisement became an ever-present element in the modern built landscape.

HECTOR GUIMARD AND THE PARIS METRO

1898

PARIS METRO ENTRANCES
Paris, France

Hector Guimard (1867–1942), Architect
Lyon, France

Architect Hector Guimard's (1867–1942) art nouveau–styled station entrances for the Paris underground railway system have become timeless symbols for the city of Paris, known throughout the world. Introduced in 1889 at the Paris Exposition Universelle, the initial controversial design ultimately inspired a visual style known as Metro.

Guimard was born in Lyon, France, and studied at the École Nationals des Arts Décoratifs and École des Beaux-Arts in Paris. While his early design influences came from the English Arts and Crafts movement, he became one of the primary representatives of the art nouveau movement during the late eighteenth and early nineteenth centuries. In addition to his famous entrances for the Paris metro, he was known for other renowned projects throughout Paris, such as Villa Bérthe (1896), Le Castel Béranger (1897), and Maison Coilliot (1898).

His metro station entrances, constructed solely of curvilinear cast iron and glass and culled from natural forms, are seminal examples of visual harmony and continuity in the art nouveau style. Guimard's innovative and pragmatic use of standardized formed-metal elements allowed the entrances to be assembled in varied sizes and configurations. Their distinctively sinuous and organic lines, also evident in their decorative patterns, figurative ironwork, mosaics, stained glass, and hand-drawn art nouveau–style letterforms inspired by the work of French type designer George Auriol (1863–1938), provided a graphic vitality and identity that is still an integral part of the Paris metro's visual brand.

COMMERCE AND THE URBAN STREETSCAPE

ca. 1900

NEW YORK CITY STREETSCAPE
New York, New York, USA
designers/architects unknown

In the later part of the nineteenth century, the urban streetscape started to transform itself due to the effects and outcome of the industrialized world. The heights of buildings grew taller and taller; telegraph and telephone wires crisscrossed thoroughfares, creating weblike patterns overhead; and commerce expanded at an accelerated rate, thereby increasing the number of advertising and promotional signs evident on any given city street. All of these modern developments added to the visual chaos of the new urban streetscape.

During this same time period, the general store began to disappear in most cities and was replaced by the modern department store. Large-scale retailers such as Macy's, Benjamin Altman, and Lord & Taylor in New York City; Whiteleys in London; La Samaritaine (1906; see page 55) in Paris; Marshall Field and Co. in Chicago; and Wanamaker's in Philadelphia became an integral part of the urban streetscape. While these retailers became the universal providers for the general public, there was also a new need for discounted merchandise.

The F. W. Woolworth Co. was among the first "five-and-dime" retail stores to sell discounted general wares and merchandise at fixed prices, usually five or ten cents, to the American public while simultaneously undercutting the price of other local merchants.

1902

F. W. WOOLWORTH STORE SIGN
Wilkes-Barre, Pennsylvania, USA
designer unknown

Woolworth's, as it came to be popularly known, was also one of the first retailers to locate merchandise out in the open or "on the floor" for the shopping public to view, handle, and select without the assistance of sales staff. The pervasive and popular general store up until this time period had kept all merchandise behind a sales counter, and customers presented a list of items they wanted to purchase to the sales clerk for processing.

The first Woolworth store was opened in Wilkes-Barre, Pennsylvania, in 1902 by the company's founder, Frank Winfield Woolworth (1852–1919) and was an immediate success.

Its storefront also stood apart from any other establishment on the commercial street. Its distinctive bright-red sign band spanned the entire length of the storefront and displayed large-scale, cast-serif, all-capital letterforms painted in metallic gold—a graphic treatment used for decades on all its storefronts that reinforced their brand, which came to be known for ease of shopping and reasonable prices.

THE GREAT WHITE WAY

1903

1905

1929

NEW AMSTERDAM THEATER FACADE
New York, New York, USA

Herts & Tallant (est. 1900), Architects
New York, New York, USA

THE HIPPODROME BUILDING FACADE
New York, New York, USA

Thomas Lamb (1871–1942), J. H. Morgan
(dates unknown), Architects
Dundee, Scotland; birthplace unknown

HOLLYWOOD REVUE MARQUEE
New York, New York, USA

Mortimer Norden (1873–1962), Designer
New York, New York, USA

During the late nineteenth century, New York City's Theater District, originally located in lower Manhattan, moved steadily north due to the expansion of the city's transit system (see page 52), which brought a growing population to theaters in Union Square, Madison Square, Herald Square, and finally, in the late 1890s, to Longacre Square or what is now known as Times Square.

In 1880, a section of Broadway between Union Square and Madison Square was illumi-

nated by Edison's new invention—the incandescent lightbulb (1879; see page 41), making it among the first electrically illuminated streets in the United States. By the late 1890s, Broadway from 23rd Street to 34th Street was so brightly illuminated by marquees and billboard advertising signs, people began calling the area "the Great White Way." When the Theater District relocated uptown, between 42nd and 53rd Streets, and encompassed Times Square, the name was transferred to this relocated area.

The New Amsterdam Theater was, for many years, the most prestigious theater along the Great White Way and home to legendary Broadway impresario Florenz Ziegfeld's (1867–1932) world-renowned follies. Designed by theatrical architects Herts & Tallant (est. 1900) and completed in 1903, the theater's interior is one of the few remaining examples of art nouveau architecture in New York City. The original theater's entrance spanned three stories and was the most lavish feature of the

building's ornamental exterior with a triumphal arch portal flanked by rusticated piers that supported paired marble columns at the second floor. Elaborate stone carvings, floral scrolls, and five figurative sculptures—a knight, a maiden, and three statues representing comedy, drama, and music, designed by American sculptor George Grey Barnard (1863–1938)—prominently rested on the facade's cornice with art nouveau–styled bronze flower motifs framing the windows located directly above.

The restored interior is a seamless visual extension of the theater's facade and among the most richly detailed and ornamented buildings from the turn of the century. It is distinguished by art nouveau–styled botanical motifs framing bas-relief frieze paneling depicting scenes from Shakespeare, Wagner, and Faust.

In 1982, the theater was designated a New York City Landmark and was placed on the National Register of Historic Places.

The Hippodrome was known as the largest theatrical structure in the world at the time of its completion in 1905. Located on Sixth Avenue (now known as Avenue of the Americas) be-

tween 43rd and 44th Streets in New York City, it was designed by American architects Thomas Lamb (1871–1942) and J. H. Morgan (dates unknown) and built by show promoters Frederic Thompson (1872–1919) and Elmer S. Dundy (1862–1907), who also created Luna Park (see page 51) on Coney Island the same year.

This eclectic Beaux-Arts– and Moorish-styled building included a 5,300-seat auditorium with 5,000 incandescent lightbulbs that formed a glowing sunburst pattern in its ceiling. The Hippodrome's vast projecting stage was large enough to hold 600 performers, two circus rings, and a large elliptical water tank and was well known at the time for its theatrical extravaganzas, performances by dancing elephants, boxing matches, and operas.

The building's block-long exterior was conceived as one of the first electrically illuminated billboards and was said to "throw a fire and glare of electric illumination for miles." Framed by its two corner towers, each supporting a sparkling illuminated sphere outlined in white incandescent lightbulbs, the entrance facade was composed of varied-scaled illuminated

typographic statements identifying the auditorium, as well as advertising current attractions and performances.

Mortimer Norden (1873–1962) was one of the earliest commercial sign designers responsible for conceiving many of the illuminated sign displays in Times Square during the 1920s and 1930s. He was born in New York City in 1873, studied at City College and Cooper Union, and worked as an electrician for years before becoming a sign maker.

In 1929, then general manager of the commercial sales division of General Outdoor Advertising Company (est. 1925), Norden designed the one-of-a-kind and never-seen-before "living" Hollywood Revue sign. The sign, or faux facade, was located at the corner of Broadway and West 45th Street in New York City and positioned directly above the marquee of the Astor Theater (George Keister, 1906), where the revue was performing.

The sign was notorious because at timed intervals throughout the evening, live chorus

continued on page 50

The Great White Way, continued

1931

1933

TRANS-LUX THEATER MARQUEE
New York, New York, USA

Thomas Lamb (1871–1942), Architect
Dundee, Scotland

BILL MINSKY'S BURLESQUE
BUILDING FACADE
New York, New York, USA

designer unknown

girls would step out onto a series of catwalks and perform for the passing crowds in Times Square. No other advertisement or promotional gimmick has ever surpassed Norden's concept. It was memorable, eye-catching, and provided the most immediate means, visual and experiential, for promoting a live revue in the theater.

The Trans-Lux Theater, deemed as "the modern theater" in 1931, was on the corner of 58th Street and Madison Avenue in New York City. It was the first movie theater to use a rear-projection system and featured modern amenities such as larger seats, larger screen, more legroom, and wider aisles than the average theater of its day. Its rear-projection technology allowed the house lights to remain low so patrons could read their programs and easily locate their seats, eliminating the need for ushers, and also eliminated the distraction of a

beam of light slicing down through the crowd from an overhead projection booth.

The building interior, as well as its distinctive art deco–style Moderne facade, was designed by renowned theater architect Thomas Lamb (1871–1942).

Minsky's Burlesque was one of the most popular entertainment venues in New York City's Times Square during the 1930s. It also refers to a brand of American burlesque presented by the infamous Minsky Brothers during the early 1900s, which was declared obscene, immoral, and outlawed in most cities throughout the country.

Following the Great Depression (1929–1940), legitimate theaters were finding it more and more difficult to draw the American public to their productions and still stay profitable. During this same time period, Michael Wil-

liam "Billy" Minsky (1887–1932) realized that burlesque could be presented in a refined and sophisticated manner and proposed bringing the Minsky brand of tawdry entertainment to Broadway in the midst of the district's respectable theatrical shows. In 1931, the Republic Theater (Albert Westover, 1900) just west of Broadway on 42nd Street was acquired by the owners of the burlesque circuit, the Minsky Brothers.

The Republic became Minsky's flagship theater and, soon after, the burlesque capital of the United States. The theater's facade became well known for its bold, whimsical typography and checkerboard photographic pattern, juxtaposed with large-scale reproductions of the faces of his leading ladies, including the famous stripper Gypsy Rose Lee (1914–1970).

The Republic theater is now known as the New Victory Theater.

LUNA PARK

1903

LUNA PARK
Coney Island, New York, USA
Frederic Thompson (1872–1919), Elmer Dundy
(1862–1907), Designers
Irontown, Ohio, USA; Omaha, Nebraska, USA

Luna Park was one of the world's first amusement parks that operated in Coney Island in New York City from 1903 to 1944. This 4.15-acre (1.68 ha) fantasyland of exotic spires, towers, minarets, and domes with colorful half-moons adorning its facades and entrances looked like no other city in the world.

At night, it was transformed with more than one million incandescent lightbulbs that outlined the façade of every structure. It amazed the public and drew international attention at a time when electrification was still a novelty, and there was nothing else like it in America. At its peak of popularity in 1904, Luna Park attracted 90,000 visitors a day.

The park's innovative creators, Frederic Thompson (1872–1919) and Elmer "Skip" Dundy (1862–1907), were showmen who entertained the American public at the turn of the century. Both men had made a name for themselves at the Pan-American Exposition held in Buffalo, New York, in 1901. It was there that they had created a highly popular attraction or cyclo-rama show called "A Trip to the Moon," where the public was transported by an enormous ship with huge, flapping wings on an imaginary journey to the Moon. The name of this winged ship was Luna—the Latin word for Moon.

The park became an instant success and featured attractions such as "War of the Worlds"—a monster battleship with turrets, spontoons, and protruding guns; "Twenty Thousand Leagues under the Sea"—a submarine ride to the polar regions; the Electric Tower; the Dragon's Gorge; a wild animal show and circus; and hundreds of other rides and attractions. The premier attraction at Luna Park was Thompson and Dundy's "A Trip to the Moon."

It was a visual spectacle and pleasure garden where anyone who visited could be immediately transported to a picturesque wonderland—a unique and memorable experience that would not be replicated or redefined until some fifty years later with Walt Disney's Disneyland (1955; see page 130).

NEW YORK CITY SUBWAY

1904

FULTON STREET SUBWAY STATION
New York, New York, USA

Heins & LaFarge (est. 1886), Architects
New York, New York, USA

New York City's first subway system, the Interborough Rapid Transit Company (IRT), opened in 1904 and immediately provided the inhabitants of the largest city in the world with a new means of transportation like they had never experienced before. The initial subway line, acclaimed for its high speeds of 40 miles per hour, connected City Hall in Lower Manhattan with the city's northern borough of the Bronx.

The first IRT stations were public monuments to the classical Beaux-Arts style of the era and designed by the architectural firm Heins & LaFarge (est. 1886). Philadelphia-born architect George Lewis Heins (1860–1907) and Christopher Grant LaFarge (1862–1938) first met at the Massachusetts Institute of Technology (MIT) in Cambridge and subsequently worked together at the Boston offices of prominent American architect Henry Hobson (H. H.) Richardson (1838–1886) before opening their own firm. They were also well known for winning the design competition for the Cathedral of St. John the Divine in New York City.

The IRT stations were graphic and architectural showplaces for mosaics and polychrome terra-cotta panels set within Guastavino*-tiled arches and vaults. Each station was based on a common organizational grid of supporting columns spaced every 15 feet (4.58 m) that created a series of spaces or bays that became the surface area for unique visual motifs designed for each station. Each rectangular bay was clad with 3 X 6-inch (.9 X 1.83 m) white glass tiles that served as a common field or visual ground for distinctive graphics and identification tablet signs that collectively distinguished one station from another. As a counterpoint to the repetitive pattern of bays and columns, a continuous wainscot of yellow Norman brick was also incorporated on all wall surfaces to visually unify all stations.

Identification tablet signs were composed of small mosaic tiles in both serif and sans-serif capital letterforms and framed within a decorative graphic border. Directional signs incorporating arrows indicated exits from each station and were also made of mosaic tiles in both styles of letterforms. Faience polychrome panels depicting various New York iconography such as Robert Fulton's steamship the *Clermont* and

initial letters such as S for Spring Street were also incorporated into the walls of the IRT's twenty-eight subway stations for identification and enhancement purposes.

As the transit system grew and incorporated the Brooklyn-Manhattan Transit (BMT) and the Independent (IND) lines in 1940, station identification evolved into other graphic styles that were derived from the time period when that station was built.

Guastavino refers to the Guastavino Tile Arch System that was created in 1885 by Spanish architect Rafael Guastavino (1842–1908). The system allows for the construction of self-supporting arches and architectural vaults using interlocking tiles that follow the profile of a curve.

ONE TIMES SQUARE AND THE FIRST ZIPPER

1904

ONE TIMES SQUARE
New York, New York, USA
Eidlitz & McKenzie (est. 1900), Architects
New York, New York, USA

One Times Square, also known as 1475
Broadway, the New York Times Building, and
the New York Times Tower, was a 25-story,
395-foot-high (110.6 m) skyscraper located at
the "Crossroads of the World"—the intersection
of 42nd Street, Broadway, and Seventh Avenue
in New York City's Times Square. The building,
designed by the architectural and engineering
firm Eidlitz & McKenzie (est. 1900), became the
second tallest building in Manhattan when it
was completed in 1904.

It was originally built as the headquarters
of the *New York Times*, which even before the
building's opening utilized electrically powered
incandescent lighting displays on its facade,
including a searchlight on its roof that could be
seen for more than 30 miles, to announce the
election of Theodore Roosevelt (1858–1919) as
president in November 1904. When the publisher held its opening celebration with a display
of fireworks on January 1, 1905, at midnight, it
became an annual tradition in Times Square to
this day. The famous New Year's Eve ball drop
tradition began in 1907.

The iconic electric news ticker or "zipper"
display was introduced in 1928 and was first
used to announce the results of the U.S. presidential election that year. Encircling the entire
base of the building, the zipper display was
composed of 14,800 incandescent lightbulbs
and was active twenty-four hours a day, seven
days a week.

To this day, the data-driven ticker or zipper is universally known as one of the most
effective and universally identifiable vehicles
to communicate real-time news and financial
information to the worldwide public.

Times Square, New York City.

FRANK LLOYD WRIGHT AND
THE LARKIN BUILDING ATRIUM

1904

LARKIN BUILDING ATRIUM
Buffalo, New York, USA
Frank Lloyd Wright (1867–1959), Architect
Richland Center, Wisconsin, USA

Frank Lloyd Wright (1867–1959), recognized by many as the greatest architect of all time, was an American architect, interior designer, author, and educator. He promoted "organic architecture," was a leader of the Prairie School style of architecture, and developed the concept of the Usonian home. His pioneering work includes original and innovative examples of many different building types, including office buildings, churches, schools, skyscrapers, hotels, and museums such as Robie House (1910), Fallingwater (1935), Johnson Wax Building (1939), Taliesin West (1937), Price Tower (1956), and the Solomon R. Guggenheim Museum (1959). He also designed many of the interiors of his buildings, including their furniture, lighting, textiles, and stained glass.

In 1904, Wright designed the Larkin Administration Building for the Larkin Soap Company of Buffalo, New York. This five-story, dark-red sandstone brick building was one of the first buildings in the United States to utilize steel construction, as well as incorporate innovations such as air-conditioning, built-in furniture, and a rooftop garden and recreation area for the needs of the new, modern-day office worker.

One of the building's most distinctive elements was its 76-foot- (23 m) tall light court or top-lit atrium in the center of the building, which provided natural daylight to all of its floors, as well as a large central work space for employees, located at the atrium's base.

Between the light court's supporting piers, Wright incorporated a series of typographic inscriptions displayed in the spandrel panels of the galleries. Forty-two inspirational words set in all-caps, serif-styled letterforms, articulated in gold leaf, and framed in sets of three typographic lines with decorative geometric motifs

communicated moral and virtuous messages ranging from "intelligence, enthusiasm, control" to "cooperation, economy, and industry."

At the time of its opening, The Larkin Administration Building drew international acclaim and was described as "the most advanced office of its time, with perhaps the most perfect relationship between architectural invention and organizational innovation that has ever been achieved."

LA SAMARITAINE DEPARTMENT STORE

1906

LA SAMARITAINE DEPARTMENT STORE
Paris, France
Frantz Jourdain (1847–1935), Architect
Antwerp, Belgium

La Samaritaine Department Store, designed by architect Frantz Jourdain (1847–1935) in 1906, is located in Paris, France, and is one of the most notable buildings in the city for its art nouveau–styled design.

Jourdain studied architecture at the École des Beaux-Arts in Paris from 1867 to 1870.

The building's facade employs a multitude of traditional art nouveau motifs that are integrated in a purely decorative manner, thereby softening the rigorous lines of its steel and glass facade with a forest of metal scrollwork, foliage, and ornamental embellishments. Spandrels are inlaid with colored enamel and ceramic tiles identifying "Samaritaine," as well as displaying a variety of merchandise and wares available at the store graphically articulated in lushly ornate, hand-drawn letterforms of the time period.

Delicate decorative ironwork on staircases and balustrades, floors made of glass tiles, and breathtaking floral-motif frescoes of colored faience and glazed ceramic tiles are also prominent graphic features within the building.

This brilliantly enhanced building is one of the primary visual examples in the early-twentieth-century built environment that used lavish decorative ornament that was simultaneously rational and functional.

MICHELIN BUILDING

1911

MICHELIN BUILDING
London, United Kingdom
Françoise Espinasse (1880–1925), Architect
Clermont-Ferrand, France

Located at Fulham Road in the Chelsea section of London, the Michelin Building was designed by Françoise Espinasse (1880–1925), who was employed as an engineer in the construction department at Michelin's headquarters in Clermont-Ferrand, France. It is an eclectic mix of art nouveau and art deco styles and graphic motifs evident in several prominent elements on its facade, as well as in its interior.

The building's tiled exterior is a colorful, three-dimensional advertisement for the company with images containing hand-painted pictorial panels and depicting scenes of early-twentieth-century motoring. Typographic and numeric panels identify Michelin and related advertising slogans in letterform styles of the time period. Etched glass street maps of Paris appear in windows along the first floor, and decorative metalwork carries stylized typographic monograms of the company. Two glass cupolas, which appear as if they are a pile of tires, frame either side of the building's entrance.

Three large stained glass windows feature the Michelin Man or "Bibendum," designed by the French artist and cartoonist Marius Roussillon (aka O'Galop; 1867–1966), and is one of the world's oldest trademarks, first introduced at the Lyon Exhibition of 1894.

The building is one of the few primary examples built at the beginning of the twentieth century that illustrates the potential of graphic design in the built environment fully realized as one integrated, holistic point of view.

HORN & HARDART AUTOMAT

1912

HORN & HARDART AUTOMAT
New York, New York, USA

designer unknown

Inspired by the successful Quisiana Automat in Berlin, Germany, Joseph Horn (1861–1941) and Frank Hardart (1850–1918) opened their first Horn & Hardart Automat restaurant in 1902 in Philadelphia, with the first New York City–based Automats opening in Times Square and Union Square in 1912. As one of the first fast-food restaurant chains in the United States, Horn & Hardart Automats quickly became popular in northern industrial cities during the Great Depression due to their offering of simple food, quick turnaround, and low prices. These self-service, coin-operated restaurants featured prepared foods displayed in individual-serving compartments behind glass doors. Initially they offered only buns, beans, fish cakes, and coffee, with each item costing five cents and available for purchase by dropping a nickel into a slot. Eventually, they served lunch and dinner entrées, such as beef stew and Salisbury steak with mashed potatoes.

Each wall of vending machine windows was capped with a series of white translucent glass panels displaying highly stylized, black in-line, all-capital Moderne letterforms identifying each food category, such as soup, vegetables, entrées, pies, cakes, and hot coffee. Horn & Hardart was one of the first venues in the United States to mass market art deco–like graphic styling during the austere times of the Depression to promote and advertise their offerings to the general public. Their graphic branding raised simple food at low prices to a higher level in the public's perception.

Originally, the vending machines took only nickels. A diner would insert the required number of coins in a slot then lift a window, which was hinged at the top, to remove a meal. The machines were filled from the kitchen behind.

Horn & Hardart Automats were particularly popular during the Depression when their macaroni and cheese, baked beans, and creamed spinach were staple offerings. By the early 1940s, Horn & Hardart had 157 restaurants in the Philadelphia and New York region, serving more than 500,000 customers per day.

GRAND CENTRAL TERMINAL

1913

GRAND CENTRAL TERMINAL
New York, New York, USA

Warren & Wetmore (est. 1887), Architects
New York, New York, USA

At the heart of New York City stands one of the greatest public spaces ever to be built in the twentieth century—Grand Central Terminal. It is also one of the few interior public spaces in the modern world that has been designed to convey clarity and an intuitive ease to circulation, no matter where one enters the space.

Grand Central Terminal is located at 42nd Street and Park Avenue in midtown Manhattan in New York City. Built in 1913 and named for

the New York Central Railroad at the prime of long-distance passenger train travel in America, it is the largest train station in the world, covering an area of 48 acres (19 ha) with forty-four platforms and sixty-seven railroad tracks.

This Beaux-Arts–style masterpiece was designed by architects Warren & Wetmore, established by Whitney Warren (1864–1943) and Charles Wetmore (1866–1941) that had one of the most successful practices of its time.

The building's exterior focal point, a 13-foot-diameter (4 m) clock on its south facade, displays the world's largest example of Tiffany glass by American artist and designer Louis Comfort Tiffany (1848–1933) and is surrounded by a symmetrical massing of figurative sculptures titled "The Glory of Commerce." This colossal 48-foot- (14.6 m) high sculptural trio

continued on page 58

Grand Central Terminal, continued

1913

1913

THE GLORY OF COMMERCE
New York, New York, USA

Jules-Alexis Coutan (1848–1949), Designer
birthplace unknown

depicts Mercury (the personification of travel
and speed) flanked by Hercules and Minerva
and was designed by French sculptor and École
des Beaux-Arts professor Jules-Alexis Coutan
(1848–1949).

   At its base is an ornamental cornice that
frames a typographic frieze of all-capital serif
letters identifying the edifice in a ceremonial
and formal manner reminiscent of early Roman
triumphal arches (see page 29).

   One of the most notable features of the
building's majestic interior main concourse is a

GRAND CENTRAL TERMINAL CEILING
New York, New York, USA

Paul Helleu (1859–1927), Designer
Vannes, France

vast, elaborately decorated astronomical mural
on its cerulean blue, barrel-vaulted ceiling directly above. Designed by Paul Helleu (1859–
1927), a renowned French portrait artist and
one of the most celebrated Edwardian artists of
the era, this celestial mural depicts a Mediterranean winter sky dotted with approximately
2,500 luminescent stars lined in gold leaf. The
sixty largest stars, which identify the constel-
lations, were illuminated from behind with an
adjustable, incandescent lighting system that
gave them the correct celestial prominence.

   Located on the main concourse's south
wall were the original information displays that
identified times and track numbers for all arriving and departing trains. This electromechanical
display system was composed of rows of black
flip panels displaying white typographic and numerical information and was a standard system
used by most train stations of the modern era.

   A small prototype of this display system,
designed and manufactured by Solari Udine
(est. 1725) of Italy, is in New York City's Museum
of Modern Art's design collection.

ON THE ROAD

1914

FIRST MODERN TRAFFIC LIGHT
Salt Lake City, Utah, USA

Lester Wire (1887–1958), Designer
Salt Lake City, Utah, USA

Traffic lights, also known throughout the world as stoplights, traffic lamps, traffic signals, or semaphores, are visual signaling devices at road intersections, pedestrian crossings, and other road locations to control competing flows of vehicular and pedestrian traffic. These visual devices use a universal color code—green for traffic to proceed in the appropriate direction, yellow/amber for traffic to caution and prepare to stop short of the intersection, and red to prohibit traffic from proceeding forward. These three colors are always displayed in a precise sequence that enables people who are color-blind to comprehend the same information.

The first modern red–green electric traffic light was invented by Lester Wire (1887–1958), a Salt Lake City policeman, in 1912. This new system relied upon two complementary colors, red and green; a buzzer that provided an audible warning to drivers and pedestrians when each color changed; and a default control that allowed police and fire stations to control signals in case of an emergency.

In 1923, the first three-way traffic signal was invented by Garrett Morgan (1877–1963) that used a three-armed signal mounted to a T-shaped pole indicating "stop" and "go" for traffic in two directions and a third signal for stopping traffic in all directions before the stop and go signals changed. This third signal was the forerunner to the modern yellow or amber traffic light.

The earliest road signs in the built environment were milestones or stone obelisks that appeared along the Roman Empire's Appian Way (312 BCE). In the Middle Ages, multidirectional signs at road intersections became commonplace, giving directions to nearby towns and cities.

1923

FIRST THREE-WAY TRAFFIC SIGNAL
Cleveland, Ohio, USA

Garrett Morgan (1877–1963), Designer
Cleveland, Ohio, USA

By the early 1900s, modern-day road sign systems were being developed throughout the world. Their standardization based on shape, color, and universal graphic symbols, was set at the 1908 International Road Congress in Rome, Italy. Subsequently, the United Kingdom and the United States further developed their own road sign systems, which were adopted or modified by many other nations worldwide by the 1920s.

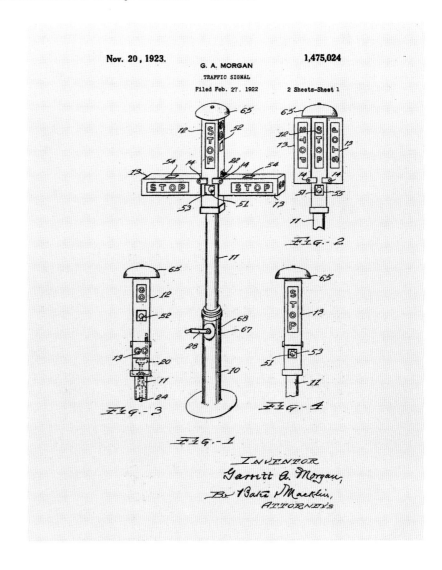

GEORGES CLAUDE AND LIQUID FIRE

1915

NEON LIGHTING TUBE PATENT DRAWING
Paris, France
Georges Claude (1870–1960), Inventor
Paris, France

Georges Claude (1870–1960) was a French engineer known for the invention and commercialization of neon tube lighting. Neon tube lighting is created by a chemical reaction or electrical glow discharge that occurs between an electrode and neon or other gases contained within brightly glowing glass tubing or bulbs. For example, neon gas produces an intense red, while argon gas produces a grayish blue. By coating the interior surface of the glass tube, an expanded range of colors can be achieved.

Considered by some as "the Edison of France," Claude gave his first public demonstration of this new technology that was composed of two 39-foot (12 m) bright-red neon glass tubes at the Salon de l'Automobile et du Cycle (Paris Motor Show) in 1910. The City of Light's first neon sign, 3 ½-foot- (1 m) high glowing white letters, was for the vermouth Cinzano that illuminated the night skies of Paris in 1913.

In 1915, a U.S. patent (No. 1,125,476) was issued to Claude for the design of electrodes for neon gas–discharge lighting. This patent became the basis for a monopoly in the United States held by him and his company, Claude Neon Lights, for neon tube lighting that became an extremely popular technology for outdoor advertising signs and displays from the 1920s through the 1940s.

The first commercial sign application of neon in the United States was for a Los Angeles–based Packard dealership in 1922. The sign read "Packard" in luminescent orange script letters framed within a complementary illuminated bright-blue border. Visible even during the day, people would stop and stare at the sign for hours and quickly dubbed it "liquid fire."

By midcentury, neon lighting became an important cultural phenomenon in the modern

1923

PACKARD NEON SIGN
Los Angeles, California, USA
Georges Claude (1870–1960), Designer
Paris, France

built environment. In the United States, Times Square in New York City and Glitter Gulch in Las Vegas (see page 120) were transformed by designers such as Douglas Leigh (1907–1999; see page 100) and Young Electric Sign Company (est. 1920) and became world renowned for their nighttime neon extravaganzas or "spectaculars" (see page 100).

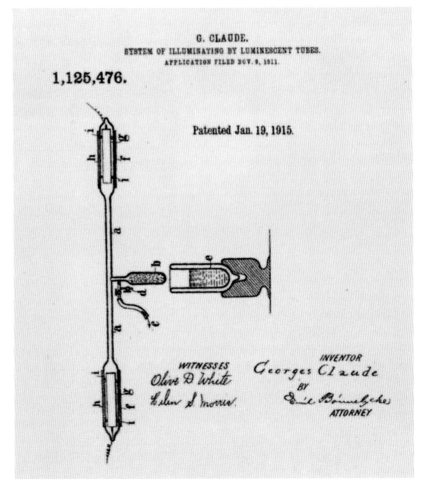

HOLLYWOODLAND

1923

HOLLYWOODLAND SIGN
Los Angeles, California, USA

Thomas Fisk Goff (1890–1984), Designer
Los Angeles, California, USA

The Hollywood sign was erected in 1923 and originally read "HOLLYWOODLAND" with each of its white, monolithic sans-serif letterforms measuring 45 feet (14 m) high and totaling 350 linear feet (110 m). When first erected, the letters were fabricated of unprotected wood and sheet metal and were illuminated with 4,000 20-watt incandescent lightbulbs, spaced 8 inches apart. At night, the sign blinked marquee-style with a flashing, alternating sequence of "Holly," then "wood," and finally "land."

During World War II, this popular landmark sign fell into disrepair and was left in a dilapidated state for decades. In 1949, it was restored by the City of Los Angeles with the decision to not replace its lighting, to remake each of its monumental letterforms in white corrugated sheet metal, and to remove the last four letters spelling "land."

Initially built as a temporary promotional billboard and identifier for an upscale real estate development located in the Hollywood Hills of Los Angeles, the Hollywood sign has lasted for more than 90 years and has become a visual symbol and memorable icon for the movie-making industry as well as a universally known locale.

THE MODERN AGE 1900–1950

BURMA-SHAVE

1925

BURMA-SHAVE ROADSIDE SIGNS

designer unknown

In 1925, the Burma-Shave Company initiated an innovative and memorable roadside promotional program that literally changed the manner in which the American motorist was introduced to product advertising.

Burma-Shave was a brushless shaving cream that was initially introduced to the American consumer by the Burma-Vita Company. Unfortunately, the public's response was tepid, and the company decided to start over by developing a new product with a wider appeal.

The result was the Burma-Shave advertising sign program that presented humorous and rhyming promotional messages displayed on small-scaled, sequential billboards alongside the nation's highways. Each promotional message was organized in five or six consecutive sign panels, always keeping the reader engaged with the promise of a punchline by the end sign panel. These messages were posted along a roadside edge and spaced for sequential reading by passing motorists. The last panel in the sequence always identified the product name—Burma-Shave.

The panels were produced in two-color combinations—red and white and orange and black. The brand's logotype was displayed on one side and "travel poetry" set in a bold, sans-serif typeface appeared on the other side with memorable phrases such as "He had the ring/he had the flat/but she felt his chin/and that was that/Burma-Shave." Public safety messages were also featured in some of the sequenced messages, usually reminding drivers about alertness and speeding.

The program was an immediate success, making Burma-Shave the second-highest-selling brushless shaving cream in the United States during the 1930s and 1940s.

AaBbCcDdEe
FfGgHhIiJjKk
LlMmNnOoPp
QqRrSsTtUu
VvWwXxYy
Zz fi fl Qu

EDWARD JOHNSTON, HENRY BECK, AND THE LONDON UNDERGROUND

1916

UNDERGROUND TYPEFACE
London, United Kingdom

Edward Johnston (1872–1944), Designer
San José, Uruguay

In 1908, Frank Pick (1878–1941) was appointed publicity officer for the London Underground and in the following two decades drastically improved its overall visual appearance, advertising, and public information system. During his tenure, he commissioned some of the most influential artists and designers of the modern era, including renowned British typographer Edward Johnston (1872–1944), who designed the system's famous roundel symbol (1918) and its unifying typeface. This typeface, used extensively throughout the railway system, became

an integral part of London's built environment and is still evident today.

Edward Johnston was a man of letters—master calligrapher, letterer, educator, author, and typeface designer. He was born in San José, Uruguay, in 1872, and as a young man, abandoned his early studies in medicine at Edinburgh University to pursue his passion for lettering and calligraphy. In 1898, he began teaching at the Central School of Arts and Crafts and then at the Royal College of Art in London, where he influenced and inspired many early-twentieth-

century calligraphers and type designers, including his student—sculptor, stonecutter, and type designer Eric Gill (1882–1940).

He is most famous for his epoch-making sans-serif typeface that he designed for the London Underground, as well as for creating its famous roundel symbol, used throughout the railway system. His influential Johnston typeface, also known as Underground (1916), changed the direction and perception of modern typography in the twentieth century and provided inspiration for a number of subsequent

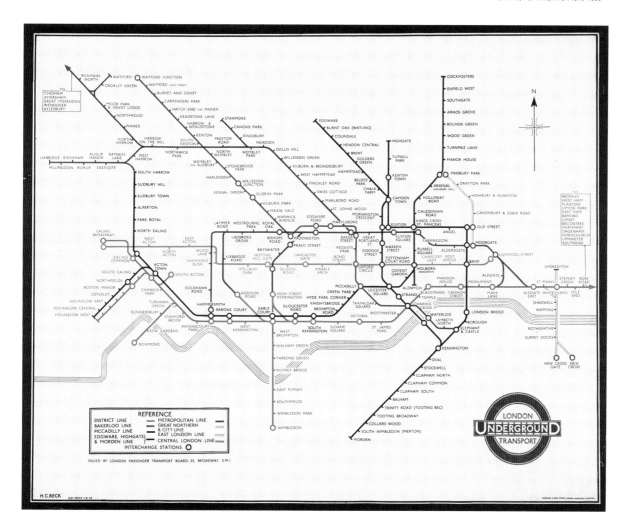

1933

LONDON UNDERGROUND MAP
London, United Kingdom

Henry C. Beck (1902–1974), Designer
London, United Kingdom

humanist-based sans-serif typefaces including Gill Sans (Eric Gill, 1927). Its dual simplicity has the basic proportions and profiles of classical Roman letterforms, yet has consistent letter strokes and weights.

By the 1930s, the London Underground had expanded into an increasingly complex underground railway system and Pick was appointed its new managing director. In 1933, he commissioned Henry C. Beck (1902–1974), an engineering draftsman employed by the railway system, to design a wayfinding map to assist

system users in understanding, navigating, and accessing its various lines, destinations, and services.

The map's success is based on a diagrammatic, multicolored representation of the system, as opposed to a literal, geographic image laden with surface detail that provided the user with a simplified version of a complex transportation system. Organized solely on a rigorous octagonal grid of vertical, horizontal, and 45-degree diagonal lines, the map identifies each coded route with a bright color with each

station clearly marked by a graphic "nib" visually interrupting the colored route line.

Beck's innovative, groundbreaking, and rational graphic design solution masterpiece has become the prototype for the modern-day transit map and is still in use today.

ART AND TECHNOLOGY: A NEW UNITY 1901–1928

Café de Unie Facade, 1925
Rotterdam, Netherlands
J. J. P. Oud (1890–1963), Architect
Rotterdam, Netherlands

In 1908, influential Austrian architect Adolf Loos (1870–1933) stated that "architecture ornament is a crime" in his design manifesto titled *Ornament and Crime*. This groundbreaking essay, combined with the newly established art movements of Dutch de Stijl (1917) and Russian constructivism (1919), paved the way for defining a new and fundamental approach to graphic design in the built environment during the modern era and directly inspired graphic designers and architects such as Peter Behrens (1868–1940), El Lissitszky (1890–1941), Herbert Bayer (1900–1985), Gerrit Rietveld (1888–1965), Paul Renner (1878–1956), Otto Wagner (1841–1918), Aleksandr Rodchenko (1891–1956), J. J. Oud (1890–1963), Piet Zwart (1885–1977), Theo van Doesburg (1883–1931), and Walter Gropius (1883–1969).

Avant-garde visual thinking was a significant and long-lasting influence on graphic design in the built environment in Western Europe throughout the early twentieth century. These new developments, fueled by the social and political revolutions occurring in Europe and Russia at the time, also grew out of the modernist art movements of cubism and fauvism and emphasized pure form, abstraction, and geometry as their primary visual principles.

During this same time period, a radical experiment conceived by Gropius single-handedly altered the course of graphic design and archiecture in the modern world. He defined his experiment as "the building of the future . . . combine architecture, sculpture, and painting in a single form . . . to one day rise toward the heavens from the hands of a million workers as the crystalline symbol of a new and coming faith."

Gropius's Bauhaus (est. 1919), originally located in Weimar, Germany, was based on the belief that hands-on learning was an essential element of education and that ultimately good design should serve the needs of ordinary people. He also based it in part on William Morris's (1834–1896) utopian socialist theories; the English Arts and Crafts movement; and the de Stijl art movement, which was formulated on the basis that all visual arts, whether fine or applied, had their genesis in craft, thereby eliminating any clear distinction between them. Students were taught the intrinsic value of an interdisciplinary approach to all visual arts, which in the 1920s was a radical idea but now is the basis for most education in the applied arts throughout the world.

In 1924, the Bauhaus relocated to Dessau due to the Weimar government withdrawing their financial support from the school and revised its mission to encompass technology as reflected in its new motto: "art and technology—a new unity." From this moment forward, the school's philosophy of "form following function" defined the Bauhaus as the most influential force of art, design, and architecture in the twentieth century that the modern world has ever known.

The outcome of this radical, new philosophy paved the way for a unified visual language that would eventually resonate throughout the design disciplines, including modern graphic design and architecture for the remaining decades of the twentieth century.

OTTO WAGNER AND DIE ZEIT

1901

DIE ZEIT DISPATCH BUREAU FACADE
Vienna, Austria

Otto Wagner (1841–1918), Architect
Penzing, Austria

Otto Wagner (1841–1918) was an Austrian architect and urban planner who played a significant role in changing the appearance of Vienna in the late 1800s and early 1900s, as well as shaping the future of twentieth-century design and architecture.

He was born in the Penzing district of Vienna, Austria, in 1841, and as a young man studied architecture at the Polytechnikum and the Viennese Academy of Visual Arts in Vienna and at the Royal Building Academy in Berlin, Germany. In 1864, he designed his first buildings based on the historicist Jugendstil (New Art) or art nouveau style of the time.

In 1897, he joined the founders of the Vienna Secession—painter Gustav Klimt (1862–1918), architect Joseph Maria Olbrich (1867–1908), designer Josef Hoffmann (1870–1956), and graphic artist Koloman Moser (1868–1918)—and started to develop his own unique design philosophy that had references to both classicism and modernism.

One of Wagner's most acclaimed buildings that reflects an early example of graphic design in the built environment is his Majolika Haus (1898) with its decorative six-story facade completely covered with hand-painted tiles of swirling linear graphic patterns with colorful, floral art nouveau motifs.

In the late 1890s, he began to oppose the prevailing trends of historicist architecture and started to incorporate new materials and new forms to reflect the changes the modern world was undergoing. In his lectures and teachings, he stated, "new human tasks and views called for a change or reconstitution of existing forms."

In pursuit of his new forward-thinking theories on design and architecture, Wagner produced the first modernist building in Vienna that reflected its intended function—the telegram dispatch office for the newspaper *Die Zeit*. Its facade was clad entirely in aluminum and glass, articulated with protruding mechanical rivets, no-nonsense bare-bulb incandescent light fixtures, and stylized Jugendstil (New Art) or art nouveau letterforms identifying "Die Zeit" and "Telegram." These graphic and architectural elements collectively communicated not only a new attitude for Viennese architectural modernism but also an unconventional and appropriate message for an enterprise immersed in daily news events.

The Die Zeit office was destroyed during the early 1900s. A model of its facade was reconstructed for a 1985 exhibition titled "Dream and Reality," Museum fuer Angewandte Kunst, Vienna, Austria.

PETER BEHRENS AND AEG

1909

AEG TURBINE HALL
Berlin, Germany
Peter Behrens (1868–1940), Architect
Hamburg, Germany

Peter Behrens (1868–1940) was a true visionary and the first Renaissance designer of the modern age, moving with ease from one discipline to another—painting, architecture, product design, furniture design, and graphic design. His creative interests were boundless. Behrens was the first to pursue a seamless integration of graphic design and the built environment and was an inspiration to the founders of the modernist movement.

As a young man, he worked as a fine artist, illustrator, and bookbinder in his native Hamburg. While the organic and curvilinear forms of the Jugendstil (New Art) or art nouveau were a strong influence on him in his early career, he quickly realized that he was more interested in simplified geometric forms. In the early 1900s, he became one of the leaders of architectural reform in Germany and one of the first architects of factories and office buildings utilizing a modernist palette of brick, steel, and glass.

His ideas and teachings on design for industry, as well as everyday objects and products, influenced a group of young designers that would ultimately alter the direction of twentieth-century graphic design and architecture worldwide, including Ludwig Mies van der Rohe (1886–1969), Le Corbusier (1887–1965), Adolf Meyer (1881–1929), and Walter Gropius (1883–1969), founder of the Bauhaus (1919; see page 75) in Weimar, Germany.

In 1907, Allegemein Elektricitats-Gesell-schaft (AEG), Germany's largest electrical utility, appointed Behrens as their new artistic advisor and design consultant. It was at AEG that he created a unified and comprehensive visual brand for every aspect of the company—office buildings, factories, products, retail outlets, and print communications material.

In defining his approach, Behrens stated, "Design is not about decorating functional forms—it is about creating forms that accord with the character of the object and that show new technologies to advantage." His visionary approach with AEG not only influenced their entire corporate culture, it became the first seminal example of corporate identity and branding that would inevitably become the primary focus within the graphic design and architecture professions in the later part of the twentieth century.

EL LISSITZKY AND PROUN

1923

PROUN ROOM INSTALLATION
(Reconstructed in 1971)
Berlin, Germany

El Lissitzky (1890–1941), Designer
Pochinok, Russia

Lazar Markovich Lissitzky (1890–1941), better known as El Lissitzky, was a Russian artist, graphic designer, photographer, typographer, educator, and architect involved in the Russian avant-garde movement of the 1920s. His work greatly influenced the Bauhaus (1919; see page 75) and constructivist movements, as well as the development of twentieth-century architecture and graphic design.

Lissitzky was born in Pochinok, Russia, in 1890 and spent his early childhood developing a keen interest and talent in art and drawing. In 1909, he left Russia to study architecture and engineering at the Technische Hochschule in Darmstadt, Germany. Upon his return to Moscow in 1914, he furthered his studies in both fields by attending the Polytechnic Institute of Riga. In 1918, he received his diploma with a degree in engineering and architecture and immediately started working as an assistant at various architectural offices.

In 1919, Lissitzky was invited to teach at the Vitebsk Art School in Belarus, where he met avant-garde artist and theorist Kazimir Malevich (1879–1935).

Inspired by Malevich and his Suprematist movement of nonobjective, geometric forms, Lissitzky worked at developing a new style of his own, which he defined as Proun (Project for the Affirmation of the New Art)—a series of abstract, geometric shapes he used to define the spatial relationships in his compositions. While his initial development of Proun concerned itself with the two-dimensional surface of painting, Lissitzky ultimately evolved this new style into a three-dimensional scale, or as he described it, "a half-way station between architecture and painting," which was realized in his *Proun Room* of 1923.

The *Proun Room* was an interior space articulated with the basic elements of graphic design and architecture—volume, mass, color, space, and rhythm. These two- and three-dimensional graphic motifs, abstract and simultaneously symbolic, communicated these new ideals as well as created what Lissitzky called the "total environment art experience."

The original installation was created by Lissitzky for an exhibition in Berlin. A reconstruction of the *Proun Room* is located in the Stedelijk-Van-Abbemuseum in the Netherlands.

ALEKSANDR RODCHENKO AND MOSSELPROM

1924

**MOSSELPROM DEPARTMENT STORE
BUILDING FACADE**
Moscow, USSR
Aleksandr Rodchenko (1891–1956), Designer
St. Petersburg, Russia

Aleksandr Rodchenko (1891–1956), one of the most prolific Russian avant-garde artists of the twentieth century, was born in St. Petersburg, Russia, and educated in Kazan, where he attended its School of Art from 1910 until 1914. Following his graduation, he moved to Moscow to study sculpture and architecture at the Stroganov Institute of Applied Arts, where he developed a keen interest in nonobjective art, the pioneering work of Kazimir Malevich (1879–1935), and the constructivist movement.

Constructivism, an art and architectural movement that originated in Russia in 1919 during the Bolshevik Revolution, rejected the idea of "art for art's sake" in favor of art as a means for social change. It combined advanced practices in engineering and technology with its central aim of instilling the avant-garde into every aspect of life, including architecture, theater, film, dance, fashion, industrial design, and graphic design. This was clearly evident in the Mosselprom building.

Mosselprom (the Moscow Association of Enterprises Processing Agro-Industrial Products) was built between 1923 and 1924. This constructivist-styled, modernist, ten-story building was one of the tallest buildings in Moscow when it was completed. It was also one of the largest state-run department stores in the USSR, famous for its unusual advertisements.

At the time of its opening, Mosselprom had commissioned Rodchenko and poet Vladimir Mayakovsky (1893–1930) for its advertising slogans that were emblazoned on the facades of the building—"Nowhere else but Mosselprom" and "Everything for everyone at Mosselprom." The artist and poet collaborated on numerous projects and called themselves "advertising constructors." Together, they designed graphically bold, eye-catching images and typographic statements that featured bright colors, geometric shapes, and avant-garde letterforms.

GERRIT RIETVELD AND SCHRÖDER HOUSE

1924

SCHRÖDER HOUSE
Utrecht, Netherlands
Gerrit Rietveld (1888–1964), Architect
Utrecht, Netherlands

Gerrit Rietveld (1888–1964) was one of the first architects and designers to break with the past design traditions of the English Arts and Crafts style and late-nineteenth-century rationalism. He was a pioneer of the avant-garde de Stijl movement and introduced the world to a new form of architecture composed of colored spatial planes in space.

In his youth, he worked in his father's furniture workshop and subsequently as a draftsman before pursuing his studies in drawing, ornamentation, and the applied arts. In 1911, he established a furniture workshop in Utrecht and soon after designed an unpainted armchair. This armchair remained unpainted until 1918 when he produced a colored version in red, blue, yellow, and black—known as the *Red and Blue Chair*, which brought him international acclaim. It was composed of horizontal and vertical planes overlapping at their intersection points, which cradled thin, angled planes for the chair's seat and back, thereby minimizing its volume and mass.

Throughout his career, Rietveld continued to experiment with primary colors in combination with monochromatic white, black, and gray in his architecture and furniture. He believed that color must respect form and ultimately emphasize it.

In 1924, Rietveld received his first major architectural commission that would provide him with the opportunity to fully realize his unorthodox ideas for the first time—Schröder House. Located on the outskirts of Utrecht, the house was designed for Mrs. Truus (G. A.) Schröder-Schräder (1889–1985). Its exterior is composed of varying-size gray and white planar surfaces intersecting one another combined with horizontal and vertical accents in primary

colors and black, minimizing the distinction between exteriors and interior spaces.

Rietveld's Schröder House is the only building to have been created completely according to de Stijl design principles.

HERBERT BAYER

1924

NEWSPAPER KIOSK, UNBUILT
Herbert Bayer (1900–1985), Designer
Haag, Austria

Herbert Bayer (1900–1985), a pioneering
graphic designer, typographer, architect, painter,
photographer, and educator, was born in the
mountainous region of Haag, near Salzburg.
After completing his military service, he began
his career as an architect's apprentice on a
wide variety of commissions, including interiors,
furniture, and packaging.

In 1921, Bayer enrolled as a student at the
Bauhaus (1919; see page 75) in Weimar, where
he studied under artist and theorist Wassily
Kandinsky (1866–1944) and later under legendary photographer Laszlo Moholy-Nagy (1895–
1946). Following the closing of the Bauhaus in
Weimar, arrangements were made to transfer
the school to Dessau, Germany, and in 1925
Bayer and five other former students, including
modernist architect Marcel Breuer (1902–1081),
typographer Joost Schmidt (1893–1948), and
artist Josef Albers (1888–1976) were appointed
teachers or "masters."

As an educator, he transformed the Bauhaus by eliminating the use of lithography and
woodcuts and introducing movable type and
mechanical presses to the Dessau workshops.
The use of serif black letter and capital letterform ended; the use of sans-serif lowercase
letterforms began. Typographic form was now
asymmetric, simple, and direct.

His experimental grotesque sans-serif
typeface, Universal (1925), eliminated all
capital letters and reduced the alphabet set to a
series of geometrically constructed characters.
Universal became the sole typeface for the Bauhaus and was used on all of its exterior signs in
Dessau.

During his years at Dessau, Bayer also
conceptualized a series of inventive and experimental three-dimensional prototypes that
included kiosks, advertising displays, exhibition

1925

UNIVERSAL ALPHABET

Herbert Bayer (1900–1985), Designer

Haag, Austria

pavilions, and most notably a streetcar station and newspaper stand. These small-scale structures, composed of strong horizontal and vertical planes that cut through one another forming open-sided spaces, were articulated and accentuated with red, yellow, blue, black, and white-painted walls. He also incorporated large-scale, sans-serif letterforms and newspaper enlargements to reinforce the function and identity of each kiosk. In some situations, Bayer used bold arrows that transitioned and changed direction from one planar surface to another, directing the viewer's attention toward the

opening of the kiosk where one could purchase newspapers or streetcar tickets. The walls of the kiosks were constructed from prefabricated materials to enable mass production in keeping with Bauhausian tenets.

Bayer left the Bauhaus in 1928 and relocated to Berlin. In 1938, like many artists and designers in Germany at the time, he fled the Nazis and emigrated to the United States, where he became a design consultant to the Container Corporation of America and the Aspen Design Conference as well as a self-appointed spokesperson for the Bauhaus movement.

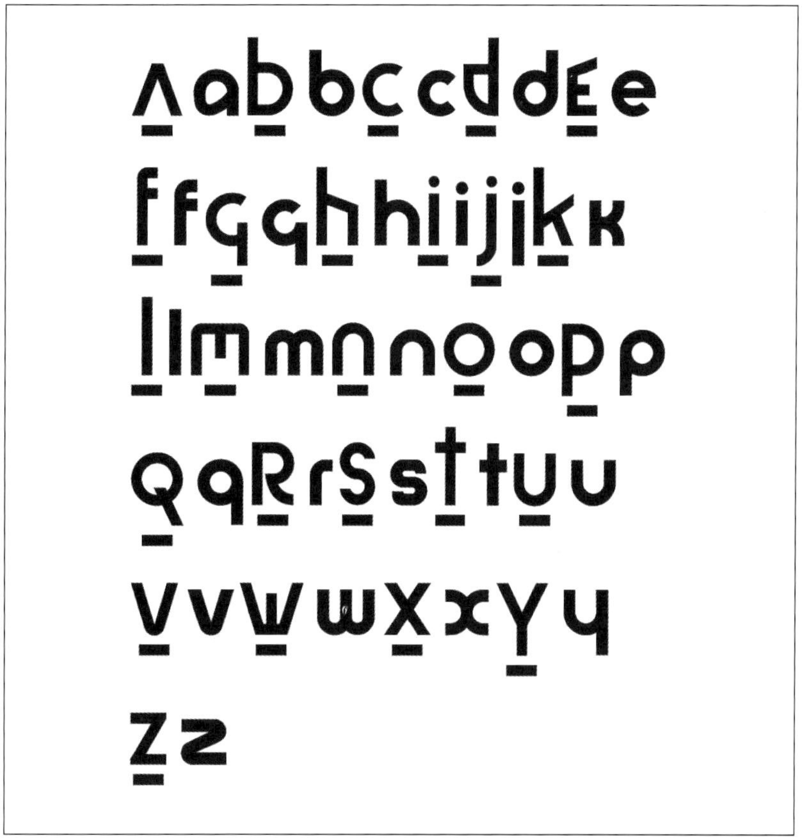

J. J. P. OUD AND CAFÉ DE UNIE

1925

CAFÉ DE UNIE BUILDING FACADE
Rotterdam, Netherlands

J. J. P. Oud (1890–1963), Architect
Rotterdam, Netherlands

Café de Unie, designed by J. J. P. Oud in 1925, is a seminal example of the de Stijl art movement and a twentieth-century visual benchmark for graphic design in the built environment.

Jacobus Johannes Pieter (J. J. P.) Oud (1890–1963) was a Dutch master of contemporary architecture. He studied architecture at the Quellinus School of Applied Art and at the Rijksnormaalschool voor Tekenonderwijzers, both in Amsterdam, from 1904 to 1910, and at the Technische Universiteit in Delft, before joining the offices of several architects in the Netherlands. Together with artist and architect Theo van Doesburg (1883–1931; see page 79), Oud cofounded the famous artists group and magazine *de Stijl* with painter Piet Mondrian (1872–1944), designer Vilmos Huszar (1884–1960), and writer and poet Antony Kok (1882–1969) in 1917.

Oud designed the famous Café de Unie facade in 1925. Located in Rotterdam, Netherlands, the building's facade illustrates his attempt at applying de Stijl principles to graphic design and architecture, treating it as a pure, singular graphic composition, articulated with bold geometric Deco-style sans-serif typography, also designed by Oud, and in bright primary colors of red, yellow, and blue, with black and white. The facade clearly illustrates Oud's vision of visual order, harmony, and balance on a monumental scale.

Here, graphic design and architecture become one structure, one sign, one message, and, ultimately, one integrated identity.

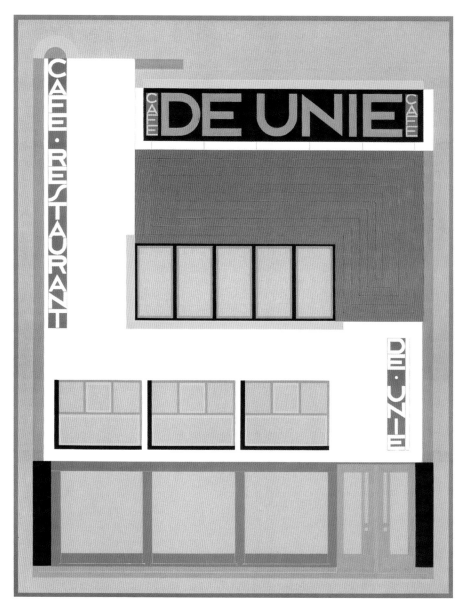

DESSAU BAUHAUS

1926

DESSAU BAUHAUS
Dessau, Germany

Walter Gropius (1883–1969), Architect
Berlin, Germany

The Bauhaus was one of the most important design institutions of the twentieth century and a major influence on the development of modern graphic design and architecture.

Established by architect Walter Gropius (1883–1969) in Weimar, Germany, in 1919, this unified school of art—which he named Bauhaus (Building House)—was based on the belief that hands-on learning was an essential element of education and that ultimately good design should serve the needs of ordinary people. Its system of teaching was culled from the early teaching methods of William Morris (1834–1896), the father of the English Arts and Crafts movement, in which different craft skills, such as metalwork, pottery, glass, ceramics, cabinet-making, and textiles were taught in a workshop environment in combination with the teaching of fine arts—primarily painting and sculpture.

Students were called apprentices and teachers were called masters. The school's initial faculty included painters Lyonel Feininger (1871–1956) and Johannes Itten (1888–1967) followed by painters Paul Klee (1879–1940), Wassily Kandinsky (1866–1944), and Josef Albers (1888–1976); photographer Laszlo Moholy-Nagy (1896–1946); and architects Marcel Breuer (1902–1981) and Ludwig Mies van der Rohe (1886–1969).

In 1923, Gropius modified the curriculum so that its emphasis was less on individual expression and more focused on the applied disciplines of design. He also changed the slogan of the Bauhaus from "A Unity of Art and Handicraft" to "Art and Technology, a New Unity."

In 1926, and with continued political pressure from the Weimar government, the Bauhaus moved to a new building in Dessau, which was designed by Gropius and reflected his theory of architectural form. Considered a twentieth-century landmark in the history of architecture, the building is composed of a series of functional parts—workshops, classrooms, dormitories, and administrative offices, all unified under one roof.

continued on page 76

Dessau Bauhaus, continued

It symbolizes the Bauhausian ideal—a union of art and science fully realized by modern technology and materials.

Walter Gropius (1883–1969) was a German architect who, along with Mies van der Rohe and Le Corbusier (1887–1965), is widely regarded as one of the pioneering masters of modern architecture. He studied architecture at the Technical Colleges of Berlin and Munich in Germany from 1903 to 1907. His early professional training occurred at the architectural offices of Peter Behrens (1868–1940, see page 68). In 1910, he left that position and together with architect Adolf Meyer (1881–1929) established their first office in Berlin.

In 1928, Gropius resigned as director of the Bauhaus. That same year, Mies van der Rohe took over as director of the school. It was closed five years later in 1933 by Hitler's National Socialist government.

While growing Nazi persecution led many faculty members to flee to the United States, their emigration also had a dramatic influence on the evolution of American design in the post–world war era. Gropius and Breuer taught architecture at Harvard University in Cambridge, Massachusetts. Moholy-Nagy established the New Bauhaus (now the Institute of Design) in Chicago, and Bayer became a prominent designer in the United States.

While its life was brief, the global influence of the Bauhaus was and still remains astounding. Its revolutionary principles of teaching changed the way art and design is taught today. Its influence on our everyday lives by way of design has also improved the way we live and interact with one another in the modern world.

IZVESTIA

1926

IZVESTIA BUILDING FACADE
Moscow, Russia

Grigori Barkhin (1880–1969), Architect
birthplace unknown

Izvestia (meaning "delivered messages"), a long-running, high-circulation Russian daily newspaper, was the official newspaper of the Soviet government (in contrast to *Pravda*, which was the Communist Party's newspaper).

Its headquarters building, an example of early-twentieth-century constructivist architecture, is located in Moscow's Pushkin Square and was built ten years after the Russian Revolution to house both the newspaper's office and printing presses. Constructivist architecture was a form of modernist architecture prevalent in the Soviet Union during the 1920s and 1930s that combined advanced building technology and engineering with the social imperatives of the new Communist political regime.

This modernist architectural movement produced several prominent structures and buildings, including El Lissitzky's (1890–1941) Lenin Tribune (1920), Mosselprom Department Store (1924; see page 70), Konstantin Melnikov's (1890–1974) Soviet Pavilion (1925), and Grigori Barkhin's (1880–1969) Izvestia Headquarters (1926), a modern office building for mass media.

Izvestia's building facade is heavily glazed and asymmetrical in the constructivist style, based on a square grid of reinforced concrete. It is accentuated with horizontal spandrels that were originally used as a visually emphatic backdrop for propaganda messages accentuated in the color red. An asymmetrically located vertical inset running the full height of the facade reinforced the location of the building's entrance as well as provided a large planar surface for larger-scale propaganda images and messages of the era.

As in its name, Izvestia, the building as well as its facade were the primary graphic and architectural vehicles for delivering the messages of the times to the Russian people.

PIET ZWART AND
FIRST CHURCH OF CHRIST SCIENTIST

1926

FIRST CHURCH OF CHRIST SCIENTIST
GRAPHIC TILE PANELS
The Hague, Netherlands

Piet Zwart (1885–1977), Designer
The Hague, Netherlands

Piet Zwart (1885–1977), a Dutch craftsman, draftsman, architect, photographer, and pioneer of modern typography, was born in Zaandijk, north of Amsterdam. From 1902 to 1907, he attended Amsterdam's School of Arts and Crafts, where he became interested in architecture. His early work involved designing textiles, furniture, and interiors in a style that showed his affinity for the de Stijl art movement.

Zwart was influenced by many of the modern, avant-garde movements, as well as Jan Tschichold's (1902–1974) *Die Neue Typographie* (The New Typography, 1928). He was also one of the first modernist designers in Holland to apply the principles of de Stijl and constructivism to graphic design in the built environment during the 1920s.

From 1921 to 1927, Zwart worked for H. P. Berlage, the most influential Dutch architect of the era. Hendrik Pieter (H. P.) Berlage (1856–1934) was the architect for the First Church of Christ Scientist complex in The Hague. This modernist complex is composed of a church, assembly hall, residence, and school with its interiors designed by Berlage, in collaboration with Zwart.

One primary example of this collaboration is located above the entrance to the complex in a series of metallic gold-on-blue ceramic tiles containing bold, square, sans-serif "fat-face" letterforms designed by Zwart to visually integrate with the rectangular architectural form of the church. Throughout the auditorium, typographic inspirational quotations are located

on walls and ceilings articulated in a similar graphic manner by Zwart, reinforcing a strong visual integrity to the graphic and architectural identities of the buildings.

Zwart synthesized two distinct and contradictory points of view—the constructivist movement's visual playfulness and de Stijl's formal functionality. With the First Church of Christ Scientist, as well as with his entire body of work, this typotekt, as he called himself, created a unified language that has prevailed for the last eighty years and to this day strongly influences contemporary graphic designers.

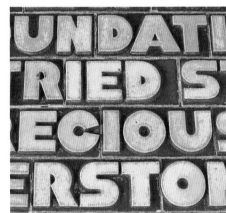

THEO VAN DOESBURG AND CAFÉ L'AUBETTE

1926

CAFÉ L'AUBETTE INTERIOR
Strasbourg, France

Theo van Doesburg (1883–1931), Designer
Utrecht, Netherlands

Theo van Doesburg (1883–1931) is best known as one of the founders and leaders of the de Stijl art movement. Born Christian Emil Marie Küpper in Utrecht, Netherlands, in 1883, he was a self-educated Dutch artist and architect, practicing painting, writing, poetry, and architecture.

In the early 1910s, he became increasingly influenced by the work of architects, artists, and designers such as J. J. P. Oud (1890–1963; see page 74), Gerrit Rietveld (1888–1964; see page 71), and Piet Mondrian (1872–1944), all who became actively engaged in the de Stijl movement. This movement advocated the rejection of

traditional art forms and the adoption of a new vocabulary of pure, abstract form.

In 1926, he received a commission with abstract painter and sculptor Hans (Jean) Arp (1886–1966) and his wife and artist Sophie Taeuber-Arp (1889–1943) to refurbish the interiors of a large restaurant, cinema, and dance hall in Strasbourg, France—Café l'Aubette.

This commission gave Doesburg an opportunity to apply his theories of Elementarism in creating a revolutionary, new type of modern interior. His theory maintained the use of right angles based on strict horizontal and vertical

axes but also relied on angled lines and forms to create a dynamic visual tension that could not be achieved with de Stijl's rigid principles.

The design of the café's interior walls, based on a rigorous grid, was composed of colored gray planar surfaces juxtaposed with panels in vibrant primary colors. Doesburg also employed inclined planes and plaster contours between these panels in high and low relief to further activate these flat planar surfaces and rectilinear compositions. Here, he succeeded in eliminating the boundaries of space with diagonal and orthogonal fields reduced to pure simplicity, harmony, and abstraction.

While these revolutionary interiors were unpopular with café patrons, it was a crowning achievement for de Stijl as a total and integrated representation of graphic design in the built environment, similar to Rietveld's Schröder House (1924; see page 71).

PAUL RENNER AND FUTURA

FUTURA TYPEFACE
Germany
Paul Renner (1878–1956), Designer
Wernigerode, Prussia

1927

Paul Renner (1878–1956) was a German typographer, graphic designer, author, and teacher best known as the designer of the sans-serif typeface Futura (1927), a groundbreaking landmark of modernist typographic design still popular today.

During the 1920s and 1930s, he was a prominent member of the Deutscher Werkbund (German Work Federation) while creating his first book designs for various Munich-based publishers. As an author, he fashioned a new set of guidelines for balanced book design in his books *Typografie als Kunst* (*Typography as Art*, 1922) and *Die Kunst der Typographie* (*The Art of Typography*, 1939).

Renner established the Meisterschule fur Deutchlands Buchdrucher (Advanced School of German Bookprinting) in Munich and recruited fellow type designers George Trump (1896–1985) and Jan Tschichold (1902–1974) to teach there. In 1933, Tschichold was removed from his post and interned by the Nazis for "subversive typography," and four years later, in 1937, Renner himself was forced to resign.

Based on pure geometric forms, the typeface Futura became a symbol of the new typography and Bauhaus (1919; see page 75) thinking and ideals, even though Renner was not directly associated with the school. The original typeface design had a set of lowercase experimental characters, Old Style figures, and two display styles that were abandoned by the Bauer Type Foundry (est. 1837) before its initial commercial release in 1927. Following its release, Futura quickly became one of the most influential typefaces of the twentieth century, inspiring the creation of similar geometric sans-serif typefaces such as Erbar (Jakob Erbar, 1926), Kabel (Rudolf Koch, 1927), and Avenir (Adrian Frutiger, 1988).

Renner's Futura is a seminal geometric sans serif typeface that is symbolic of a time period and an era of modernist design that still resonates today.

DE VOLHARDING COOPERATIVE

1928

**DE VOLHARDING
COOPERATIVE BUILDING FACADE
(Reconstructed in 1996)
The Hague, Netherlands**
Jan Buijs (1889–1961), Architect
Surakarta, Indonesia

The De Volharding (Persistence) Cooperative Building, designed by Jan Willem Eduard Buijs (1889–1961) and completed in The Hague, Netherlands, in 1928, was constructed for a workers' cooperative by that name and designed to house its offices, shops, product storage, and dental clinic.

Buijs, a Dutch architect, was raised in Surakarta, Indonesia, and returned to the Netherlands with his family in 1908. In 1909, he entered the Technical College at Delft (now the Delft University of Technology) to study architectural engineering. After graduating in 1919, he worked as an assistant architect on public works projects before forming his architectural practice in 1924.

The building design, influenced by the de Stijl movement and Russian constructivism design aesthetics, is clad entirely in glass. Its primary light tower rises above a large, transluscent, illuminated architectural surface that simultaneously functions as a billboard sign composed of white, yellow, and blue glass identifying the cooperative. Framed by glass block, the majority of the building facade consists of ribbon windows separated by opal glass spandrels and multiple gangways with lettering mounted behind the glass, advertising the benefits of membership to the cooperative. Both glass areas displayed monumentally proportioned sans-serif, block-like, all-capital letterforms that appeared black during the day and silhouetted at night.

The building has been described as a large-scale advertisement, a city-scale luminescent sculpture, and one of the most famous luminous buildings in the world.

Author's Note: This photograph is of the restored Buijs' building for the Volharding Cooperative involving the Dutch graphic design firm Lust (est. 1996) where they have set typographic texts for the building facade's transluscent glass panels with bit-mapped screen fonts as a counterpoint to the de Stijl typography of the earlier part of the twentieth century that was last used on the building.

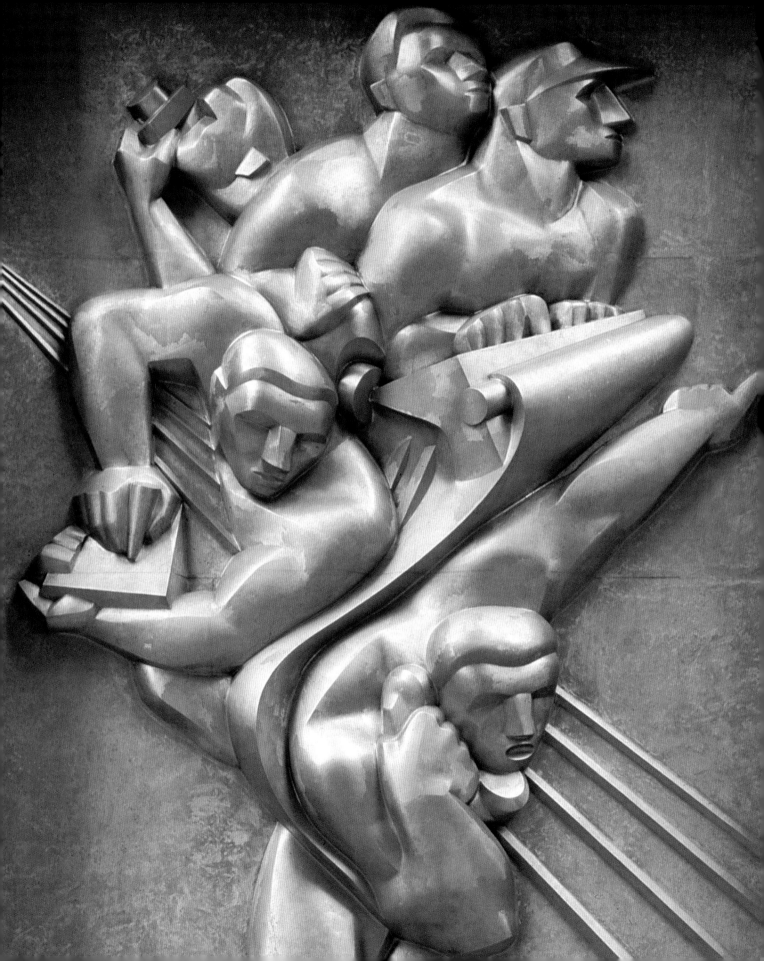

STYLE AND THE MASS MARKET
1924–1947

News, 1937
New York, New York, USA
Isamu Noguchi (1904–1988), Designer
Los Angeles, California, USA

During the 1920s and 1930s, freedom of expression and a preference for aesthetic appearance over functional performance became prevalent throughout most of the modern world. Two of the most predominant and popular styles in graphic design in the built environment to emerge during this time period were art deco and streamline moderne.

Art deco, a direct counterpoint to its decorative and organic predecessor Art Nouveau, was represented in practically every facet of the applied arts, especially graphic design in the built environment, and was characterized by linear symmetry, geometry, sleek forms, and design motifs derived from Machine Age aesthetics—French decorative cubism, German Bauhaus, Italian futurism, and Russian constructivism. While this lavish, ornamental style was first introduced at the *Exposition Internationale des Arts Decoratifs et Industriels Modernes* (International Exposition of Modern Industrial and Decorative Arts) in Paris in 1925, it remained extremely popular throughout the modern world for the next two decades.

In New York City, art deco styling redefined the city's urban skyline, as well as the modern skyscraper, with the iconic Chrysler Building (1930), the Empire State Building (1931), and Rockefeller Center (1937). In San Francisco, it became the predominant motif for the Golden Gate Bridge (1937) and in Miami Beach, Tropical Deco ultimately inspired an entire city.

Streamline Moderne emerged as a later development of art deco during the late 1920s and 1930s in reaction to austere economic times caused by the onset of the Great Depression in 1929. To increase sales and profit margins, more and more businesses were placing an unprecedented emphasis on "form over function" with their products. As a result, designers quickly streamlined everyday objects—from soft-drink bottles and household appliances to locomotive trains and automobiles. It was devoid of unnecessary ornament and emphasized motion and speed through aerodynamic forms and profiles and exaggerated horizontal lines. Exotic materials such as inlaid wood, stainless steel, and stone were now replaced with utilitarian materials of glass, aluminum, and concrete. By the 1940s, the streamline style had become commonplace in the American built environment.

The work of twnetieth century graphic designers and architects, such as Robert Mallet-Stevens (1886–1945), Victor Horta (1861–1947), Josef Hoffmann (1870–1956), Eileen Gray (1878–1976), Jacques-Émile Ruhlmann (1879–1933), William Van Alen (1883–1954), Raymond Hood (1881–1934), S. Charles Lee (1899–1990), Donald Deskey (1894–1989), and Walter Dorwin Teague (1883–1960) was highly influenced by these autere and decorative art movements.

Both of these quintessential styles were unequivocal models of modernity, were extremely popular with the public, and ultimately had a profound influence on the emergence of new graphic design and architectural styles in the later part of the twentieth century.

MIAMI ART DECO DISTRICT

1924

MIAMI BEACH ART DECO BUILDINGS
Miami, Florida, USA
various designers and architects

Miami Beach, Florida, is home to one of the world's largest collections of art deco–styled buildings dating from the 1920s to the 1940s. This enclave of eclectic art deco, Streamline Moderne (see page 97), and Nautical Moderne architectural landmarks, known as the Miami Art Deco District, is located along thirty blocks of South Beach; it is composed of more than 900 apartment buildings, residences, and hotels and is traditionally known as tropical deco.

The term *art deco* was first used for the 1966 Paris exhibition—"Les Années 25," subtitled "Art Deco." It celebrated the 1925 *Exposition Internationale des Arts Decoratifs et Industriels Modernes* (International Exposition of Modern Industrial and Decorative Arts; see page 86) that marked the culmination of Art Moderne at that time.

These pastel-colored buildings of light blue, sea green, warm pink, and sunburst yellow represent an era when Miami Beach was being developed as a seaside "tropical playground"; therefore, its buildings were designed to reflect the current wave of modernity, functionality, flair, glamour, and elegance that was so prevalent throughout this time period. They were graphically and architecturally characterized by the use of stepped profiles, chevron patterns, ziggurat shapes, and radiating sunburst motifs coupled with a repertoire of local floral and fauna in their facades and details. Entrances and doorways were made more prominent by the incorporation of marquees with streamlined letterforms sculpted in aluminum or neon that unified the total design of each building. Modern sans-serif typefaces such as Futura (1927), designed by Paul Renner (1878–1956; see page 80), and Broadway (1927), designed by American type designer Morris Fuller Benton (1872–1948), were used on many of the building facades and entrances due to their precise, angular, and geometric appearance.

In 1979, the Miami Beach Art Deco Architectural District was listed on the U.S. National Register of Historic Places.

EXPOSITION INTERNATIONALE DES ARTS DECORATIFS ET INDUSTRIELS MODERNES

1925

EXPOSITION INTERNATIONALE DES ARTS DECORATIFS ET INDUSTRIELS MODERNES
Paris, France

various designers and architects

The *Exposition Internationale des Arts Decoratifs et Industriels Modernes* (International Exposition of Modern Industrial and Decorative Arts) opened in Paris, France, in 1925 and remains one of the most notable and influential world fairs of the twentieth century, since it signaled the introduction of a new avant-garde style that was flourishing internationally in the fields of graphic design, architecture, and the applied arts—Art Moderne.

It was located on 57 acres (23 ha) between the Esplanade des Invalides, Avenue Alexandre III, and the entrances of the Grand Palais and the Petit Palais and was attended by approximately five million visitors during its short six-month run.

The exposition exemplified Art Moderne or what was to become known later as art deco, a widely popular modernist movement characterized by sleek, machine-age forms and design motifs derived from many different styles of the early twentieth century, including French decorative cubism, German Bauhaus, Italian futurism, and Russian constructivism. This new visual style relied solely on the graphic design principles of linear symmetry and geometry, which was a distinct departure from the flowing asymmetrical, organic lines of its predecessor movement—art nouveau. It also drew inspiration from ancient Egyptian, Babylonian, Mayan, and Aztec graphic forms.

Highlights of the *Exposition Internationale des Arts Decoratifs et Industriels Modernes* included displays of work in glass, bookbinding, ceramics, textiles, furniture, and decorative arts ranging from complete interiors to children's toys. This groundbreaking work was created by modernist artists, architects, and designers from around the world, including Sonia Delau-

nay (1885–1979), René Lalique (1860–1945), Robert Mallet-Stevens (1886–1945), Victor Horta (1861–1947), Josef Hoffmann (1870–1956), Eileen Gray (1878–1976), and Jacques-Émile Ruhlmann (1879–1933).

GRAUMAN'S CHINESE THEATRE

1927

GRAUMAN'S CHINESE THEATRE FORECOURT
Hollywood, California, USA

Meyer & Holler (est. 1911), Architects
Los Angeles, California, USA

Grauman's Chinese Theatre, also known as Mann's Chinese Theatre, is located along the historic Hollywood Walk of Fame (1958; see page 131) on Hollywood Boulevard in Hollywood, California. Since its opening, it has been the site of more gala movie premieres than any other theater in the world. Millions of visitors flock to Grauman's on an annual basis to see its forecourt with the famous hands and footprints of Hollywood legends set in cement.

The opulent, palace-like building, designed by architect Raymond Kennedy (1891–1976) of

Meyer & Holler (est. 1911), resembles an over-scaled, red Chinese pagoda and showcases his exuberant use of color, texture, pattern, scale, and combination of eclectic art deco styles. The building exterior features a huge dragon across its front, two stone lion–dogs guarding the main entrance, and graphic silhouettes of tiny dragons running up and down the sides of the theater's copper roof.

Among the theater's most distinctive features are its concrete pavement blocks set in the forecourt, which bear the signatures,

footprints, and handprints of popular motion picture personalities from the 1920s to the present. Intricate Chinese art deco patterns and 10-foot- (3 m) high lotus-shaped fountains flank the markings of some of Hollywood's most elite and welcome its visitors into the magical world of fantasy and whim also known as Tinseltown.

More than 200 Hollywood celebrities are immortalized in the theater's Forecourt of the Stars concrete pavers. Variations of this honored tradition include imprints of Harold Lloyd's eyeglasses, Groucho Marx's and George Burns's cigars, Betty Grable's legs, John Wayne's fist, Al Jolson's knees, and Jimmy Durante's and Bob Hope's noses.

These simple, humanistic graphic gestures, each unique in its own right, have turned a generic concrete public space into one of the most iconic and memorable storytelling venues in the history of American cinema.

THE NEW YORK CITY SKYSCRAPER

1927

THE FRENCH BUILDING
New York, New York, USA

H. Douglas Ives (b. 1888) and Sloan & Robertson
(est. 1924), Architects
Toronto, Ontario, Canada; New York, New York, USA

The term *skyscraper* was first coined in the late nineteenth century to describe the public's reaction of amazement to buildings of steel frame construction that were ten stories or higher. By the turn of the century, skyscrapers started to dominate the skylines of American cities such as Chicago and New York City.

During the 1920s and 1930s, the New York City skyscraper became world renowned as a graphic and architectural symbol of that time and included the French Building, the Fuller

Building, the Chrysler Building, the Empire State Building, and the Daily News Building.

The French Building, located on the northeast corner of Fifth Avenue and East 45th Street, was a namesake commercial office building built by the New York City real estate developer Fred Fillmore French (1883–1936). It was completed in 1927 with a striking and gleaming art deco facade that contributed significantly to the international reputation and renown of Fifth Avenue.

The building's arched gateway entrance is richly decorated with bas-relief bronze figurative motifs of flying horses, reclining figures, and botanical forms. Its marble lobby has gold trimmings and ceiling decor based on an eclectic combination of decorative graphic patterning from Egyptian, ancient Greek, Near Eastern, and early art deco influences.

The 38-story, 429-foot- (130.8 m) high building, designed by H. Douglas Ives (b. 1888) and Sloan & Robertson (est. 1924), rises from

1929

FULLER BUILDING
New York, New York, USA
Walker & Gillette (est. 1906), Architects
New York, New York, USA

a three-story base clad in limestone and decorated bronze paneling. The austere, vertically accentuated facade of orange brick is enhanced by terra-cotta decor on its stepped, pyramid-like setbacks. The tower rises uninterrupted for seventeen floors all the way to the triplex penthouse, topped by a water tank that is masked with large, rectangular bas-relief panels depicting allegorical themes.

The French Building was first listed on the National Register of Historic Places in 2004.

The 40-story, 492-foot- (150 m) high Fuller Building, on the northeast corner of Madison Avenue and East 57th Street, has been called "a jazz-age testament" by the *New York Times* for its many distinctive art deco features evident on its dramatic black-and-white-skinned facade, as well as in the interior public spaces of this iconic New York City building.

Designed by American architects Walker & Gillette (est. 1906) in 1929 for one of the largest construction companies in America at the time, the building facade and crown are richly clad in art deco iconography—zigzags, stars, chevrons, and patterns of radiating arcs.

The building's three-story, monumental entrance portal is framed by white stone pilasters and capped with a lintel containing the building's name set in art deco–styled monolithic letterforms. Directly behind these sans-serif letterforms is a distinctive sculpted bas-relief depicting two stylized construction workers holding a clock backed by the city's skyline, both designed by American modernist sculptor Elie Nadelman (1885–1946).

The building's six-story base is clad in black granite and the tower above in limestone, topped with a stepped, pyramidal ziggurat crown faced with bold, alternating black-and-

white stone triangular graphic patterns. In the building lobby, similar geometric graphic patterning, realized in marble and bronze, appears in floor medallions, representing major buildings built by Fuller Company, and in the figurative bronze-paneled elevator doors, representing different building tradesmen.

The Chrysler Building is a seminal example of the decorative geometric style of art deco and considered by many to be a twentieth-century architectural masterpiece.

Located on the northeast corner of Lexington Avenue and East 42nd Street in New York City, the building was designed by American architect William Van Alen (1883–1954) in 1930 for Walter P. Chrysler (1875–1940), founder and chairman of Chrysler Corporation. Standing at

77 stories and 1,048 feet (319 m) high, it was the world's tallest building for eleven months, surpassed by the Empire State Building (see page 92) in 1931.

William Van Alen was born in Brooklyn, New York, in 1883 and studied architecture at Pratt Institute. In 1908, he was awarded the Paris Prize scholarship that led to his studying in Paris at the École des Beaux-Arts.

The distinctive ornamentation of the building is a seminal example of graphic design and architecture celebrating, as well as communicating, a singular story—the automobile. The building's exterior ornamentation was modeled on features that were being used at the time on

continued on page 90

1930

THE CHRYSLER BUILDING
New York, New York, USA

William Van Alen (1883–1954), Architect
Brooklyn, New York, USA

Chrysler automobiles. For example, American bald eagle gargoyles on the building corners of the sixty-first floor are replicas of Plymouth hood ornaments; corner ornamentations on the thirty-first floor are replicas of radiator caps; and all are in stainless steel. Simplified graphic abstractions of hubcaps and fenders are realized in the glazed-enamel, white-and-gray brick cladding of the building's facade—all symbolizing the machine age of the 1920s.

The building also stands visually apart from other skyscrapers in the New York skyline due to its well-recognized, terraced crown and spire. Composed of seven concentric radiating arcs, its polished stainless steel cladding is ribbed and riveted in a stylized sunburst motif.

Its three-story-high entrance lobby is also lavishly adorned with art deco graphic compositions realized in a rich palette of materials—marble, granite, onyx, amber, wood, and stainless steel. The lobby's 97- X 110-foot (29.6 X 33.5 m) ceiling mural, titled "Transport and Human Endeavor" and designed by American artist Edward Trumbull (1884–1968), depicts the building, as well as celebrates technical progress and innovation with buildings, airplanes, and scenes from the Chrysler assembly line.

To this day, the Chrysler Building remains a beloved New York City landmark and a beacon to American industry. The building was declared a National Historic Landmark in 1976.

The Daily News had the largest circulation of any daily newspaper in the United States when it moved into its new headquarters building in 1930. Designed by Raymond Hood (1881–1934), the new thirty-seven-story, 476-foot (145 m) art deco skyscraper, located on East 42nd Street in midtown Manhattan, was one of the first skyscrapers to be built without a

1930

DAILY NEWS BUILDING
New York, New York, USA

Raymond Hood (1881–1934), Architect
Pawtucket, Rhode Island, USA

traditional base, shaft, and capital, or an ornamental crown. The building was organized in a
sequence of varied height and monolithic slabs
and contained the newspaper's offices, printing
presses, and speculative office space.

Hood was an American architect who
worked in the art deco style, evident in his 1922
winning submission for the famed Chicago
Tribune Tower building competition. He was
educated at Brown University, Massachusetts
Institute of Technology (MIT), and the École des
Beaux-Arts in Paris.

The building's exterior facade features a
three-story-high limestone bas-relief panel
adorned with stylized figurative images of office
workers underneath a sunburst motif illuminating the News Building rising above. Terra-cotta
and black spandrels are located between the
windows, and polychrome white brickwork
creates articulated vertical ribbons that were
rumored to suggest rolls of newsprint. The
tower's bold verticality, its repetitive windows,
and its monolithic, flat facade were all early
characteristics of the International Style that
would gain increasing popularity in the United
States after World War II.

The building is also well known for its
towering lobby, which houses a dramatically
lit, giant revolving globe set in a recessed well
of rear-illuminated glass and surrounded by
an inlaid terrazzo floor of articulated bronze
directional lines radiating from the points of a

compass identifying distances to cities around
the world. Large-scale displays of thermom-
eters, wind speed indicators, and international
time clocks displaying data are located in the
surrounding black glass walls of this public
entry space. These displays, which were once
one of the city's prime tourist attractions, were
meant to symbolize the global scope of the
newspaper when the building first opened.

The building was designated a New York
City Landmark in 1981 and a National Historic
Landmark in 1989.

The Empire State Building is a 102-story,
1,250-foot- (381 m) tall architectural landmark
and American cultural icon in New York City at
the intersection of Fifth Avenue and West 34th
Street. Its name is derived from the nickname
for New York—the Empire State.

continued on page 92

1931

THE EMPIRE STATE BUILDING
New York, New York, USA

Shreve, Lamb & Harmon (est. 1925), Architects
New York, New York, USA

It was designed by the architectural firm Shreve, Lamb & Harmon (est. 1925) and stood as the world's tallest building for forty years, from its completion in 1931.

William Frederick Lamb (1883–1952) was the principal designer of the building. He was born in Brooklyn, New York, and studied at Williams College, Columbia University's School of Architecture, and the École des Beaux-Arts in Paris.

This quintessential limestone and nickel-chromium steel-clad skyscraper features a restrained art deco architectural style, typical of pre–World War II buildings from this era. This is evident in the stylized carved and aluminum-leafed letterforms appearing above the entrances to its three-story lobby, which prominently features a symmetrically composed wall mural of a map of metropolitan New York realized in bright aluminum strips inlaid in marble with an aluminum bas-relief elevation of the building (without its antenna, which was added to the building's spire in 1952) and the sun's rays emanating from its spire. Stylized metallic ceiling murals inspired by both the skyward heavens and machine age graphic motifs were originally designed by artist Leif Neandross (*dates unknown*).

The building and its street-level interiors are designated landmarks of the New York City Landmarks Preservation Commission. The building was designated a National Historic Landmark in 1986.

ROCKEFELLER CENTER AND RADIO CITY MUSIC HALL

1932

RADIO CITY MUSIC HALL
New York, New York, USA

Edward Durrell Stone (1902–1978); Donald Deskey
(1894–1989), Architects
Fayetteville, Arkansas, USA; Blue Earth, Minnesota, USA

Rockefeller Center is a 12-acre (4.8 ha) building complex in midtown Manhattan developed by American philanthropist John D. Rockefeller, Jr. (1874–1960) between 1929 and 1940. The original master plan, designed by American architect Raymond Hood (1881–1934), was composed of fourteen limestone-clad, aluminum-trimmed, monolithic massed buildings designed in the art deco style and was the largest private construction project in the world when it began in 1929.

The centerpiece of Rockefeller Center is the 70-story, 872-foot (266 m) GE Building (formerly known as the RCA Building) at 30 Rockefeller Plaza.

The center's scope, visionary plan, and groundbreaking integration of architecture and graphic art and sculpture created by some of the world's most renowned artists and designers was unprecedented at the time of its completion and became a showcase of art deco design principles.

This is clearly evident in American sculptor Paul Manship's (1885–1966) monumental, 18-foot high, bronze gilded statue of the Greek mythological legend Prometheus recumbent in pose, while bringing fire to mankind, located prominently in the sunken plaza at the base of 30 Rockefeller Plaza.

American sculptor Lee Lawrie (1877–1963) contributed the largest number of individual works, twelve in all, including the statue of Atlas facing Fifth Avenue and "Wisdom"—the ornamental recessed figurative bas-relief frieze above the main entrance to the GE Building. This 37-foot high, monumental panel is made of

continued on page 94

Rockefeller Center and Radio City Musical Hall, continued

1937

ROCKEFELLER CENTER
New York, New York, USA
Raymond Hood (1881–1934), Architect
Pawtucket, Rhode Island, USA

a single slab of carved, polychrome-painted and gilded limestone and 240 cast glass bricks. Its typographic quote (from *Isaiah 33:6*), imagery, symbolism, and narrative communicate the power and vision of mankind's accomplishments throughout history.

Japanese-American artist Isamu Noguchi's (1904–1988) gleaming stainless steel bas-relief *News* depicts typewriters, cameras, telephones, and newsmen at work. This dramatic relief is located above the main entrance of 50 Rockefeller Plaza (the Associated Press Building) and at the time was the largest metal bas relief (measuring 23 feet high by 17 feet wide) in the world, and branded the building with a very specific and appropriate symbolic message.

These sculptural and graphically communicative forms animated the building exteriors

and simultaneously functioned as essential storytelling devices for an otherwise austere architectural experience.

A large number of graphic artists also contributed work to the interiors of the center, including sculptor Carl Milles (1875–1955), muralist Hildreth Meiere (1893–1961), photographer Margaret Bourke-White (1904–1971), and sculptor Leo Friedlander (1890–1966).

José María Sert's (1876–1945) 41-foot long mural on the west wall of the GE Building's grand lobby is titled *American Progress* and depicts a vast allegorical scene of men constructing modern America and contains figures of Abraham Lincoln, Mahatma Gandhi, and Ralph Waldo Emerson, among others.

At street level, the plaza is framed on three sides and transformed on a regular basis with

an ever-changing display of flags—of the United Nations member countries, of the United States and its territories, and various decorative and seasonal flags throughout the year.

All of these visual elements create one of the truly memorable, accessible, intimately scaled, and easily navigable public spaces ever designed and built in the United States.

Radio City Music Hall is one of the world's most famous entertainment venues and is located in New York City's Rockefeller Center. At the time of its opening in 1932, it was promoted as the largest and most opulent theater in the world. Its original intended name was the International Music Hall, but this was changed to reflect the name of its neighbor—Radio City, as the new NBC Studios in the RCA Building was known at the time.

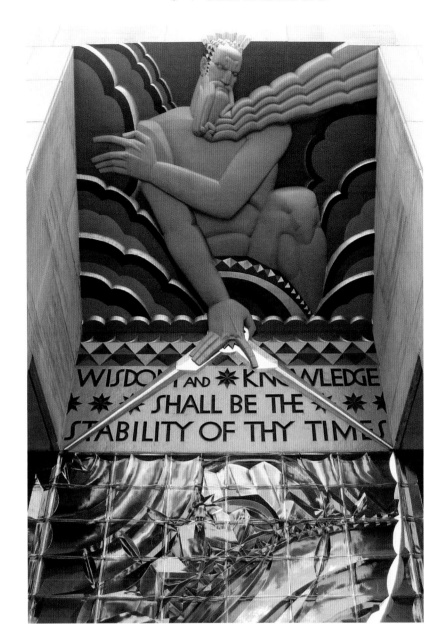

1937

WISDOM
30 Rockefeller Plaza (GE Building)
New York, New York, USA
Lee Lawrie (1877–1963), Designer
Rixdorf, Germany

Designed by architect Edward Durrell Stone (1902–1978) and interior designer Donald Deskey (1894–1989), the building and its interiors were groundbreaking when completed because they represented an obvious departure from the traditional rococo ornamentation associated with most grand theaters and movie palaces built at the time.

Stone was born in Fayetteville, Arkansas, in 1902 and attended the University of Arkansas, where he became interested in architecture. Following his relocation to Boston to work with his brother, James, who was also an architect, he studied at the Boston Architectural Club, Harvard University, and Massachusetts Institute of Technology (MIT), but never received a degree from any of those institutions. While in Boston, he apprenticed at Henry Hobson

(H. H.) Richardson's (1838–1886) successor firm Coolidge, Shepley, Bulfinch and Abbott (est. 1924) before moving to New York City in 1929. There, he began working at the offices of Reinhardt Hoffmeister Hood & Fouilhoux (est. c. 1930), who were among the team of architects responsible for the design of Rockefeller Center. Stone became the principal designer on Radio City Music Hall, working in collaboration with Donald Deskey.

Deskey studied architecture at the University of California but did not enter that profession upon graduation. Instead, he worked as an artist and ultimately became a pioneer in

the field of industrial design. Following his attendance of the 1925 *Exposition Internationale des Arts Decoratifs et Industriels Modernes* (see page 86) in Paris, which he found highly influential, Deskey returned to New York City, where he established his own firm that specialized in furniture and textile design.

In 1930, he won a competition to design the interiors for Radio City Music Hall, which gained him international recognition following its opening in 1932. During the 1940s and 1950s, he designed some of the most recog-

continued on page 96

1937

**NEWS
50 Rockefeller Plaza
(Associated Press Building)
New York, New York, USA**
*Isamu Noguchi (1904–1988), Designer
Los Angeles, California, USA*

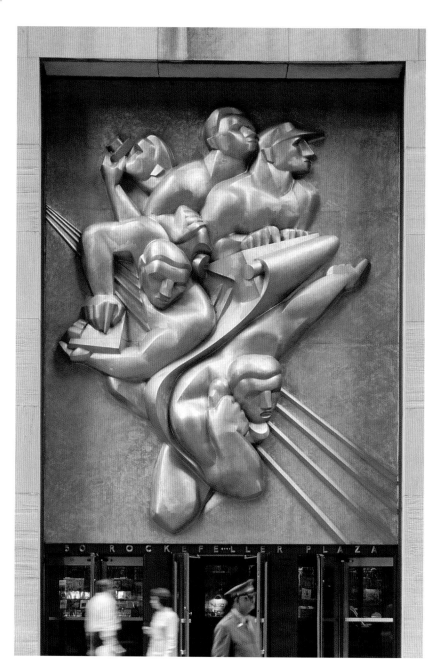

nizable product icons of America's modern era, including packaging for Crest toothpaste (1955) and the Tide detergent bull's-eye (1946). Deskey's bold, geometric motifs were realized in glass, aluminum, stainless steel, chrome, and leather throughout the hall's wall coverings, carpet, light fixtures, and furniture.

From its colorfully banded and neon-illuminated red, yellow, and blue marquee wrapping its corner entrance to its breathtaking entrance lobby, Radio City Music Hall is a showcase of art deco magnificence realized in architectural and graphic form.

The music hall's breathtaking public lobby spaces and lounges feature the graphic and sculptural work of many Depression-era American artists—a large 60-foot long mural by Ezra Winter (1886–1949) titled *Fountain of Youth* in the grand foyer; a set of murals by Louis Bouche (1896–1969) collectively known as *The Phantasmagoria of the Theater* in the grand lounge; and three cast-aluminum figurative sculptures titled *Goose Girl* by Robert Laurent (1890–1970), *Eve* by Gwen Lux (1910–1988), and *Spirit of the Dance* by William Zorach (1887–1966).

The hall's auditorium gilded, semicircular, radiating arches representing an abstract sunrise are located above the proscenium stage with a visual impact that is unmatched in any other modern interior.

Radio City Music Hall became the largest movie theater in the world and single biggest tourist attraction in the history of New York City when it opened in 1932. Its interior architecture, one of the world's greatest examples of art deco design, was declared a New York City Landmark in 1978.

STREAMLINE STYLING IN AMERICA

1935

PAN-PACIFIC AUDITORIUM FACADE
Los Angeles, California, USA

Wurdeman & Becket (est. 1933), Architects
Los Angeles, California, USA

Streamline styling, also referred to as Style Moderne, or simply Moderne, was extremely popular in the United States from the 1920s through the 1940s and was expressed in styles traditionally classified as art deco, WPA Moderne, and Streamline Moderne.

This styling concept was a direct reaction to art deco, as well as a reflection of austere economic times. Unnecessary ornament was gone, sharp angles were replaced with pure, aerodynamic forms visually communicating a smooth, frictionless, and machine-driven pro-

gress, with exotic and expensive materials replaced by concrete and glass.

As a result of its popularity, American architects and designers such as Raymond Loewy (1893–1986), Walter Dorwin Teague (1883–1960; see page 111), Gilbert Rohde (1894–1944), and Norman Bel Geddes (1893–1958), quickly modernized and streamlined everything from the design of buildings to everyday utilitarian objects.

The Pan-Pacific Auditorium was a landmark building in Los Angeles that was the pre-

mier location for indoor public events in the city from 1935 until its closing in 1972.

Designed by architects Wurdeman & Becket (est. 1933), the auditorium was one of the prime examples of Streamline Moderne architecture in the United States. Its green and white facade was framed by four stylized entrance towers and flagpoles that echoed a reverence for speed and technology. At the time of the building's opening, it was widely reported that Norman Bel Geddes (1893–1958), the renowned American industrial designer, consulted with the architects on the building design.

The Academy Theater is one of the largest theaters ever built in the Los Angeles area, with a seating capacity of 1,200. It is located in Inglewood, California, and was built to host the annual Academy Awards, although it was never

continued on page 98

1939

ACADEMY THEATER FACADE
Inglewood, California, USA

S. Charles Lee (1899–1990), Architect
Chicago, Illinois, USA

used for that purpose and it continued to show movies until its closing in 1976.

This streamlined building was one of the first buildings in Southern California to use glass blocks and aluminum sections. A distinctive 125-foot- (38.1 m) high tower featured spiral fins that appeared to be winding up the shaft to its apex pinnacle. The asymmetrically located tower, as well as the theater's marquee, was illuminated at night with luminous and dramatic colors that literally altered the overall appearance of the building's facade.

One of the most memorable Streamline Moderne buildings to be built during this time period was the Tower Bowl in San Diego, California. When it opened in 1941, Tower Bowl was billed as a complete entertainment complex, offering two cocktail lounges, a billiard room, restaurant, dance floor, seating for 400 spectators, and twenty-eight bowling lanes.

Its facade was marked by a dramatic 80-foot- (24.4 m) high curved steel tower, displaying rotating bowling balls 5 feet (1.5 m) in diameter, spelling out in individual bold, all-capital sans-serif letterforms "Tower Bowl" on one side

and "Bowling" on the other. This monumental sign, as well as the entire building façade, was enhanced with more than 1,000 feet (305 m) of brilliant colored neon tubing.

The Academy Theater and Tower Bowl were both designed by one of the most prolific and distinguished architects of the Streamline Moderne style—S. (Simeon) Charles Lee (1899–1990), who was an early proponent of opulent show palaces and theaters throughout Southern California. He attended Chicago Technical College, where he graduated in 1918. After completing his first commission for the City of Chicago, he enrolled at the Armour Institute of Technology to study architecture. At that time, the course followed the principles of the École des Beaux-Arts, which can be clearly seen in his

early drawings. In 1922, Lee relocated to Los Angeles, where his work became more playful and exciting.

As Lee began to design more and more motion picture houses, he took into consideration the increasing importance of motorcar traffic by incorporating prominent, streamlined shapes and forms to attract the attention of passing motorists.

THE DRIVE-IN SERVICE STATION

1936

TEXACO TYPE C STATION
Alexandria, Virginia, USA

Walter Dorwin Teague (1883–1960), Designer
New York, New York, USA

In the early 1900s with the advent of the auto-mobile, drive-in service stations started to become more of a necessity and more apparent on the American road.

Initially, drivers purchased gasoline at a variety of venues—liveries, repair shops, or general stores. They would pour the purchased gasoline into a bucket and then funnel it into their gas tank. This primitive and dangerous method became obsolete in 1905 when a common water pump was used for pumping gas and became known as the "service station."

By the 1920s, curbside gasoline pumps could be found outside general stores and pharmacies in most small towns throughout the United States. With the increasing number of automobiles on the road coupled with the construction of new roads throughout the nation, oil companies began to develop new and innovative means to identify, promote, and distribute their product to the American consumer.

Shell and Standard Oil companies of California were the first to paint their company logotype on their stations and trucks. By the

1930s, Phillips Petroleum and Texaco standardized the design of their service stations.

In 1936, Texaco commissioned American industrial designer Walter Dorwin Teague (1883–1960) to design a basic "drive-in" service station structure. Adopting the 1930s Streamline Moderne functionalist style, this prototype design was implemented throughout the continental United States and was built with materials available to each region—porcelain-enameled steel, brick, concrete block, or frame and stucco. This groundbreaking, universal design became an immediate and recognizable visual identity for the new oil company that became quickly known for their efficient service and quality products, and attracted the attention of motorists all along the nation's highways and roadways, making it possible for them to now travel faster and farther.

Texaco's new prototype building program expressed America's obsession with automobiles, speed, and new technologies; established a benchmark model for its competitors to copy; and generated an archetypal service station design that lasted well into the early 1960s.

DOUGLAS LEIGH AND
THE SIGN SPECTACULAR

1936

WRIGLEY'S SPEARMINT GUM SPECTACULAR
New York, New York, USA

Dorothy Shepard (1906–2000), Designer
birthplace unknown

Douglas Leigh (1907–1999) was an American advertising executive, lighting designer, and a pioneer in sign design and outdoor advertising. From the early 1940s to the 1960s, he literally changed the face of Times Square on a regular basis with new and exciting sign technologies.

After financing his own education at the University of Florida by purchasing the exclusive right to sell advertising for the university's yearbook, he became a top salesman for a local sign company in Birmingham, Alabama. In 1929, he relocated to New York City, working as a

salesman for the General Outdoor Advertising Company (est. 1925) before starting his own business in 1933.

His first major commission was for the St. Moritz Hotel on Central Park South in New York, in which he designed the rooftop sign for the hotel in exchange for the exclusive right to live there and to use the hotel's address for his new business.

Later that same year, he came up with a groundbreaking idea for a steaming coffee cup for A&P, advertising their popular Eight O'Clock

Coffee brands. The 25-foot- (7.6 m) high sign, located at the southeast corner of West 47th Street and Seventh Avenue in New York City, discharged clouds of steam from a large cup of coffee and became the first of the many memorable signs that he would create over the next forty years.

He gave New York City's Great White Way, as well as the world, the sign "spectacular," a term he coined. These spectaculars were nothing less than well-planned, highly synchronized, high-tech visual attractions.

1941

THE SMOKING CAMEL SPECTACULAR
New York, New York, USA

Douglas Leigh (1907–1999), Designer
Anniston, Alabama, USA

One of his most memorable spectaculars was his legendary billboard for Camel cigarettes. First introduced in 1941, the billboard featured smoke rings generated from a hidden steam generator that grew wider and wider as they floated above Broadway. Leigh ingeniously used an existing Con Edison Company steam duct for the smoke, which was blown out in rings every four seconds. This innovative and memorable sign lasted for twenty-six years and was duplicated in twenty-two other cities throughout the world.

Leigh created other memorable spectaculars in Times Square for Kool cigarettes, featuring a blinking penguin; Ballantine Beer had circus clowns tossing rings in the shape of the Ballantine ale logotype; Super Suds detergent generated three 3,000 large, floating bubbles per minute; and Bromo-Seltzer discharged actual effervescent action.

His most ambitious and most popular project was a sign spectacular above the Bond Clothing Store building in Times Square, completed in 1948.

In 1936, the City Bank Farmers Trust Company built a modernist, two-story building in Times Square with a large-scale sign on its roof that more than doubled the height of the building. The building also contained a theater, retail stores, and the International Casino nightclub. The sign itself appeared virtually skeletal during the day but spectacular at night. It became a huge electric light display of fish blowing bubbles that advertised Wrigley's Spearmint Gum.

continued on page 102

1948

1959

BOND CLOTHING STORE SPECTACULAR
New York, New York, USA
Douglas Leigh (1907–1999), Designer
Anniston, Alabama, USA

Designed by artist Dorothy Shepard (1906–2000) and built by General Outdoor Advertising Company, it was the largest advertising sign yet to be erected in Times Square.

In 1948, Bond Clothes took over ownership of the building as well as the rooftop sign and commissioned Leigh to erect the most astounding display the Broadway district had ever seen.

The new 50-foot- (15.2 m) high spectacular ran 200 feet (61 m) from West 44th to West 45th Streets with two 50-foot- (15.2 m) tall figures, one male and one female, flanking a central 50,000-gallon waterfall that was 27 feet (8.2 m) high and 120 feet (36.6 m) long. At night, strands of incandescent white lights clothed the modernist-styled classical figures, but by day, they appeared nude. Above was a digital clock with a message—"Every Hour 3,490 People Buy at Bond."

At the base of the sign was an electronic news zipper display composed of 23,250 incandescent lightbulbs running the entire length of the building.

The combination of three-dimensional figurative sculptures, falling water, and moving lights and messages made this sign spectacular one of Leigh's most memorable creations in New York City history.

Much of the visual excitement of Times Square that was realized during the 1930s through the 1960s was a result of Leigh's genius as a kinetic and luminal designer.

PEPSI-COLA WATERFALL SPECTACULAR
New York, New York, USA
Douglas Leigh (1907–1999), Designer
Anniston, Alabama, USA

THE MODERN RETAILER

1937

1947

FORSYTHE SHOES
New York, New York, USA
Morris Lapidus (1902–2001), Architect
Odessa, Ukraine

HOFFRITZ FOR CUTLERY
New York, New York, USA
Morris Lapidus (1902–2001), Architect
Odessa, Ukraine

In the 1930s and 1940s, a new approach to the design of the modern retail built environment took hold in major urban cities around the world. At the forefront of this new movement was architect Morris Lapidus (1902–2001). Lapidus made a significant impact on the design of the modern commercial retail store, since he was one of the first designers to utilize expansive glass storefronts, focused interior lighting, unorthodox floor configurations, exaggerated typographic letterforms, and theatrical staging techniques for the display of merchandise.

Lapidus was born in Odessa, Russia, in 1902, but his orthodox Jewish family fled to New York City with him when he was an infant. As a young man, he initially studied theater set design and then architecture at Columbia University. He worked as a staff architect for Warren & Wetmore (the Beaux-Arts architects

of Grand Central Terminal; see page 57) before working independently as a retail showroom architect for the next twenty years.

Lapidus's commercial retail stores and showrooms not only relied upon attention-getting elements such as sweeping curves, backlit ceilings, irregular-shaped forms, and perforated walls but also on several graphic design elements to reinforce and enhance the overall retail experience.

He was one of the first designers to open up the retailer's storefront to prominently display merchandise and the store interior itself. Bright color palettes, large-scale neon-lit letterforms, and dramatic lighting were also used to attract customers. He introduced curvilinear, serpentine walls to his store interiors, intentionally creating spatial suspense so that customers would move naturally through the space.

During his successful career as a store designer, Lapidus developed a palette of amorphous shapes and forms used in ceiling treatments, furniture, merchandise displays, and interior wall surfaces that he later called "beanpoles," "woggles," and "cheese holes." Beanpoles were purely decorative, painted steel poles running from floor to ceiling at an angle and sometimes extending directly though a table or display; woggles were free-form shapes used for ceiling, lighting, and carpet motifs; and cheese holes were walls perforated with imperfectly shaped circular openings.

While initially frowned upon by most of the modernist design community at the time, today these playful, theatrical, and visually impactful design concepts and techniques are instantly recognizable and have been adopted by major international retailers.

BETWEEN THE WARS
1932–1945

The years between the great world wars are remembered as a time of turmoil and recovery throughout the world. Following the end of World War I in 1918, the civilized world fell into an economic, political, and social downfall caused by the Great Depression.

Fascism, a radical authoritarian nationalist movement, grew out of post–World War I anxiety, accelerated and gained momentum in Italy, Germany, and Spain during the 1920s and 1930s. This time period was also marked by radical changes in the international order of world prominence and power. New countries and ideologies were formed; old ones were abolished, with every nation wanting to make its mark on the new world order.

The potential power, impact, and influence of political propaganda communicating messages of patriotism and military service, as well as economic and social devastation, was at its height during this era. One of the most persuasive images used to encourage recruitment of young men in the U.S. Army for both world wars was American artist and illustrator James Montgomery Flagg's (1877–1960) popular "I Want You for the U.S. Army" poster with a firm and determined Uncle Sam looking directly into the eyes of each and every young American man.

The American political theorist and philosopher Hannah Arendt (1906–1975) wrote extensively on the nature of power, politics, authority, and totalitarianism—"only the mob and the elite can be attracted by the momentum of totalitarianism itself; the masses have to be won by propaganda."

Whether it was the world powers of the United States, Britain, Russia, and the countries of Western Europe, everyone had a stake in exploiting their own ideals and ideologies in some manner, shape, or form. These powerful and persuasive messages took many visual forms, including graphic design in the built environment.

PSFS BUILDING

1932

PHILADELPHIA SAVINGS FUND SOCIETY (PSFS) BUILDING SIGN
Philadelphia, Pennsylvania, USA

Howe and Lescaze (est. 1929), Architects
Philadelphia, Pennsylvania, USA

Considered to be the first modernist skyscraper and one of the most important buildings built in the United States during the early part of the twentieth century, the Philadelphia Savings Fund Society Building, or PSFS Building, is located in Philadelphia. This landmark 36-story, 491-foot (150 m) tower is at the corner of 12th and Market Streets and was designed by architects William Lescaze (1896–1969) and George Howe (1886–1995) in 1932.

Both men were instrumental in introducing the International Style—a term that would be coined two years after the building was completed—to the United States, since the building design demonstrated for the first time the tenets of International Modernism, applied to both exterior and interior detailing of any American building. The main characteristics of

this new aesthetic were volume over mass, balance rather than a preconceived symmetry, and lack of ornamentation in the building design.

This landmark building is also a key benchmark icon in the history of graphic design in the built environment, since it was one of the first to express typography and corporate branding as a visual element intrinsic to its architectural form.

The skyscraper is topped by a distinctive series of large-scale, sans-serif letterforms announcing the bank's name—PSFS—in front of an enclosure that hides rooftop mechanical equipment. This building sign is 27 feet (8.2 m) high, appearing white by day and illuminated with red neon tubing by night. Visible for 20 miles (32 km), this typographic-based sign has become a Philadelphia icon. At the time of its construction, corporate symbols and acronyms

were rarely seen on buildings, but architects Lescaze and Howe supported their use, as the bank's full name would have been illegible from the ground.

The PSFS Building was listed as a National Historic Landmark in 1976.

CENTURY OF PROGRESS EXPOSITION

1933

AVENUE OF FLAGS
Century of Progress Exposition
Chicago, Illinois, USA
Joseph Urban (1872–1933), Architect
Vienna, Austria

Joseph Urban (1872–1933) was a prolific illustrator, architect, and one of the most innovative designers of the twentieth century, who initially gained international recognition for his production and theater set design in the early 1900s.

He was born in Vienna, Austria, in 1872 and studied architecture at the Akademie der Bildenden Kunste, also in Vienna, before immigrating to the United States in 1912 to become the art director for the Boston Opera Company. In 1914, he relocated to New York City, where he designed extravagant productions for both the Ziegfeld Follies and the Metropolitan Opera.

Unfortunately, most of his architectural work in the United States has been destroyed with the exception of Mar-A-Lago (1926) in Palm Beach, Florida, and the New School Auditorium (1929) and the Hearst International Magazine Building (1929), both in New York City.

In 1933, he was appointed design consultant for the Century of Progress Exposition, a world's fair on 427 acres (173 ha) off the shores of Lake Michigan in Chicago, celebrating the city's centennial. The exposition's theme was technological innovation with the motto "Science Finds, Industry Applies, Man Adapts" and was attended by approximately 40 million visitors during its 1933–1934 run.

One of the most memorable displays designed by Urban for the exposition was its Avenue of Flags—a visually striking pedestrian promenade that was framed with a towering colonnade of 90-foot- (27.4 m) high angled poles with brightly colored flags welcoming thousands of visitors daily to the fair.

Urban also oversaw the creation of the Fair's modern, multicolored "rainbow city," in contrast to the neoclassical "white city" of the 1896 World's Columbian Exposition that had occurred in the same location thirty-seven years prior. He used color extensively to create distinct and varied visual experiences throughout the fairgrounds. More than 10.5 million square feet (96,000 sq m) of building facades, architectural elements, and wall surfaces were covered in twenty-eight custom colors designed specifically for the fair. Urban's goal was to use color not just as a decorative element, but also as a unifying and harmonizing graphic force for the disparate, architecturally styled buildings at the fair.

Urban not only revolutionized the design of the 1933 Chicago World's Fair, and fairs to come, but also the future of America's design sensibilities with regard to graphic design and architecture in the modern world.

FASCIST AND NAZI PROPAGANDA

1934

"SI SI SI" (YES, YES, YES) BUILDING MURAL
Rome, Italy

designer unknown

During the 1930s and 1940s, the forces of Fascism and Nazism embraced the potential power of political propaganda, which ultimately took many visual forms, including graphic design in the built environment.

Benito Mussolini (1883–1945) was a politician who led Italy's National Fascist Party and was credited with being one of the key twentieth-century figures in the creation of Fascism. In 1922, he became the fortieth prime minister of Italy and soon after began using the title "Il Duce," meaning "the Leader." To further his authority and encourage his continued popular support by the public, Mussolini became an expert in using visually sophisticated propaganda to elevate his cause.

Throughout his reign as dictator of Fascist Italy, Mussolini used his own visage, as well as bold and provocative typographic statements to proclaim his new imperialism. These images and messages of propaganda were displayed in monumental scale and in bright, illuminated neon letterforms emblazoned on the facades of buildings in every large city throughout Italy.

While not proven, it seems that Mussolini culled this dictum from Albert Speer (1905–1981), chief architect for the Nazi party, who declared, "along the Grand Boulevards neon signs were to be employed profusely."

In 1933, Adolf Hitler (1889–1945) became chancellor of Germany and head of the Nazi party. During his twelve-year reign as a totalitarian dictator, all displays of Nazi propaganda, including the annual Nuremberg mass rallies, were designed and choreographed by Speer, who was deemed by Hitler as the party's Commissioner for the Artistic and Technical Presentation of Party Rallies and Demonstrations.

1938

NUREMBERG RALLIES
Nuremberg, Germany

Albert Speer (1905–1981), Architect
Mannheim, Germany

From 1933 to 1938, Speer masterminded huge organized rallies attended by more than 400,000 people and designed to show the world the power of Nazi Germany. He designed spectacular visual treatments for each annual rally, which always included an extensive exploitation of flags and banners used as a pure visual propaganda tool for each public event. Here, scale, color, light, movement, and symbol—all fundamental elements and principles of graphic design—functioned as key visual components of the built environment to engage the German public, as well as create a dramatic and memorable experience.

NEW YORK WORLD'S FAIR

1939

NEW YORK WORLD'S FAIR
Queens, New York, USA
various designers and architects

The 1939 New York World's Fair was in Flushing Meadows Corona Park in New York City and was the second-largest American world's fair of all time, exceeded only by St. Louis's Louisiana Purchase Exposition of 1904. It covered 1,216 acres (4.9 sq km) and was attended by more than 5 million visitors during its two-year period.

The fair, dubbed "Building the World of Tomorrow," symbolically marked the end of the Great Depression and was themed as a celebration of American industry and progress. It was divided into seven different "zones"—communications and business systems, community interests, food, medicine and public health, production and distribution, science and education, and transportation, with a 280-acre (113 ha) area for amusements.

Each thematic zone was arranged in a semicircular pattern centered on the fair's "Theme Center"—the modernistic and monumental Trylon and Perisphere. The triangular obelisk-shaped Trylon was 700 feet (210 m) in height and its adjacent companion, the spherical Perisphere, was 180 feet (54.9 m) in diameter and 18 stories high. These iconic forms, the only buildings at the fair painted white, were designed by architects Wallace K. Harrison (1895–1981) and J. Andre Foulihoux (1879–1945) and were the graphic and architectural symbols of the fair.

The fair's provocative, modernist, and futuristic pavilions were showplaces for introducing the public to the industrial design revolution taking hold in America and included the National Cash Register Pavilion designed by Walter Dorwin Teague (1883–1960; see page 111), the House of Jewels designed by Donald Deskey (1894–1989), Alvar Aalto's Finnish Pavilion (see page 110), and Norman Bel Geddes's (1893–1958) "Futurama" for General Motors.

While the Trylon and Perisphere were the only white structures at the fair, avenues and areas radiating from the center of the fair were designed with a palette of rich colors that evolved and changed the farther a visitor walked from the fairground's center. For example, one area would appear in a progression of blues, starting with pale tints and ending in deep, saturated ultramarines.

At night, the latest lighting technology was used to transform each area into a magical kaleidoscope of similar ranges from the color spectrum. This was also the first extensive demonstration of several new lighting technologies, including the introduction of the first fluorescent light fixture at the fair, that was ever seen by the public and would become commonplace in future decades.

ALVAR AALTO AND
THE FINNISH PAVILION

FINNISH PAVILION
New York World's Fair
Flushing, New York, USA
Alvar Aalto (1898–1976), Architect
Helsinki, Finland

Hugo Alvar Henrik Aalto (1898–1976) was one of the most influential modernist architects and designers of the twentieth century, especially for what has come to be identified as "Nordic modernism." During his career, he gained worldwide recognition for his modern yet humanistic buildings, his furniture that resulted from experiments with molded plywood bent into two-dimensional curves, his organic glass designs, and his textiles.

He was born in Kuortane, Finland, and completed his basic education in 1916. That same year, Aalto enrolled as an architectural major at the Helsinki University of Technology, graduating in 1921. Two years later, he opened his first architectural practice—Alvar Aalto Office for Architecture and Monumental Art.

In the early 1930s, he became strongly influenced by the new modernism that was developing at a fast pace throughout Europe, especially by the pioneering work of Laszlo Moholy-Nagy (1895–1946) and Le Corbusier (1887–1965).

His reputation grew considerably in the United States following the critical reception of his design for the Finnish Pavilion at the 1939 New York World's Fair. The landmark modernist building, as well as its exhibition, was described by renowned American architect Frank Lloyd Wright (1867–1959) as a "work of genius."

The 15-meter- (49.2 foot) high interior of the pavilion, still considered by many to be one of the few acknowledged architectural masterpieces of the fair, was meant to suggest "a flaming Aurora Borealis." It was composed of a series of four-story-high, oblique undulating birch plywood paneled walls that formed the backdrop for the exhibition of modern wood furnishings, as well as revealed large-scale, black-and-white photographic murals communicating the people, natural resources, commerce, and products of Finland.

Aalto's vanguard design for the Finnish Pavilion at the 1939 New York World's Fair reflects a fusion of Finnish naturalism and twentieth-century modernist ideals that still is relevant to architects, as well as graphic and exhibition designers today.

WALTER DORWIN TEAGUE AND
THE NATIONAL CASH REGISTER PAVILION

1939

NATIONAL CASH REGISTER PAVILION
New York World's Fair
Flushing, New York, USA

Walter Dorwin Teague (1883–1960), Designer
Pendleton, Indiana, USA

Walter Dorwin Teague (1883–1960) was an American architect and one of the most prolific industrial designers of the twentieth century.

He was born in Pendleton, Indiana, in 1883 and moved to New York City in 1902. As a young man, he painted signs and drew illustrations for mail-order catalogs while attending the Art Student League at night. In 1926, while traveling in Europe, he was introduced to the modernist work of renowned architect Le Corbusier (1887–1965) and decided that on his return

to New York he would pursue the design or restyling of products for American manufacturers, which ultimately led him and a group of his colleagues to establish industrial design as a separate profession in the United States.

For the next forty years, Teague created some of the most influential products and buildings for the American consumer—Kodak cameras, Texaco gas stations (1936; see page 99), Polaroid land cameras, Boeing aircraft, and numerous structures, visitor pavilions, and

exhibitions for international expositions and world's fairs.

This included the Texaco Exhibition Hall for the 1935 Texas Centennial Exposition in Dallas; the Ford Pavilion for the 1935 California Pacific International Exposition in San Francisco; and his memorable National Cash Register Pavilion for the 1939 New York World's Fair.

The pavilion was deemed the "world's largest cash register"—a 74-foot- (22.6 m) high model of National Cash Register's latest deluxe model for 1939. Designed by Teague, the giant cash register rang up both the daily public attendance figures of the fair and the total attendance figures to date, displayed in 2 ½-foot- (.8 m) high, bold sans serif numerals, as it continually revolved on its base so that it could be seen by fairgoers from any location in the surrounding environs.

The exhibition displays in the interior of the pavilion included the same cash register, also designed by Teague, and all of its 7,857 parts exhibited under glass.

WORKS PROGRESS ADMINISTRATION (WPA)

1941

FARM SECURITY ADMINISTRATION MURAL
Grand Central Terminal
New York, New York, USA

various designers

The Works Progress Administration or WPA (renamed the Works Projects Administration in 1939) was the largest and most ambitious New Deal–era agency that employed millions of unskilled American workers to implement public works projects during the country's Great Depression. Created by President Franklin Delano Roosevelt (1882–1945), the WPA was funded by the U.S. Congress with the passage of the Emergency Relief Appropriation Act of 1935. Between 1935 and 1943, the WPA provided approximately 8 million jobs for Americans throughout the country.

During Word War II, numerous large-scale murals communicating a variety of propaganda messages of patriotism and military service were funded and produced by the WPA that employed hundreds of graphic artists and photographers and adorned the walls of major public buildings throughout the United States.

On December 14, 1941, the "World's Greatest Photomural," measuring 96 X 118 feet (29.3 X 36 m), weighing more than 50 tons, and covering the entire east wall of Grand Central Terminal's Main Concourse (1913; see page 57), was dedicated in New York City. The mural, *What America Has to Defend and How*

1945

BUY DEFENSE BONDS MURAL
Pennsylvania Station
New York, New York, USA

Raymond Loewy (1893–1986), Designer
Paris, France

It Will Defend It, was composed of three main photographic collages depicting land, children, and industry, flanked and protected by towering soldiers representing the armed services. Crowning this triptych was a photographic collage of U.S. military might underscored with the statement "that government by the people shall not perish from the earth."

The mural was created and produced by the legendary documentary photography unit of the Farm Security Administration's Information Division to promote the sale of defense bonds and stamps. This federal agency supported artists by hiring documentary photographers to record American farm life throughout the Depression era—the most notable being Dorothea Lange (1895–1965) and Walker Evans (1903–1975).

Pennsylvania Station, designed by architects McKim, Mead & White (est. 1879) in 1910 and one of New York City's greatest Beaux-Arts public monuments ever to be built, was also used as a venue for the display of many WPA-funded murals during wartime. In 1945, a patriotic photographic mural featuring Pennsylvania Railroad staff that were helping with the war effort, enlisted or not, was installed on the station's General Waiting Room walls. This inventive mural, designed by renowned American designer Raymond Loewy (1893–1986), was composed of a series of large-scale, cut-out, black-and-white photographic portraits, each measuring approximately 20 feet (6.1 m) high. This allowed the towering ornamental walls of the station to be revealed, as well as function as a visual ground for the mural's figures, while simultaneously providing a restrained backdrop for bold typographic messages that called for the purchase of war defense bonds and stamps by the American public.

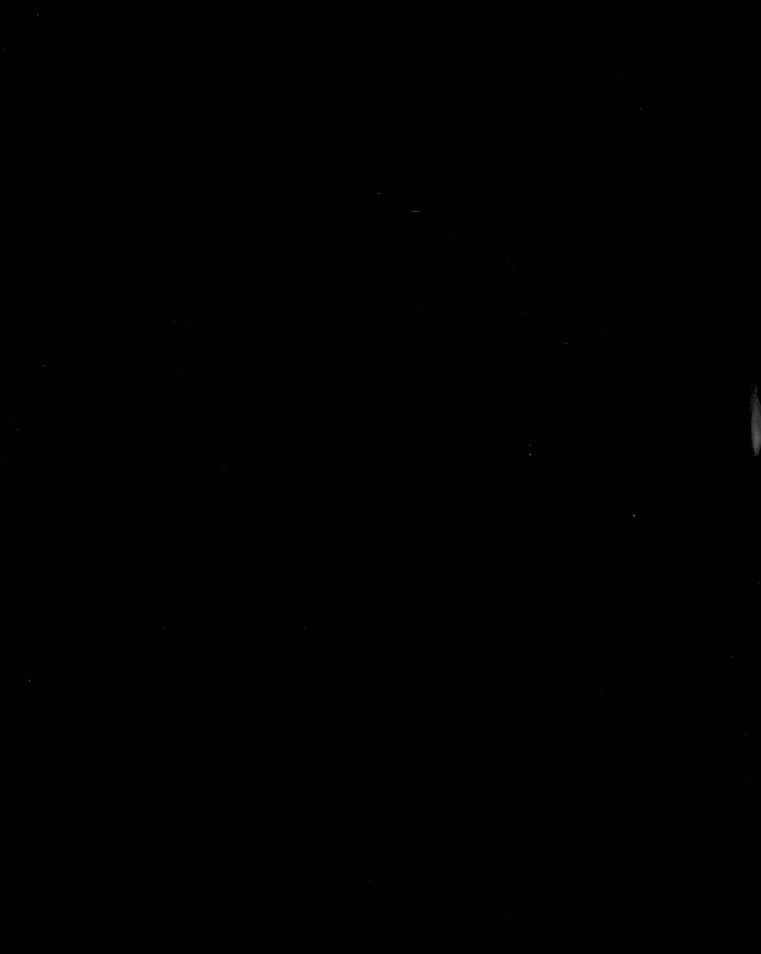

III

THE POSTWAR WORLD
1950–2000

POPULUXE: THE AMERICAN INFLUENCE 1946–1961

MODERNISM AND

THE INTERNATIONAL STYLE 1950–1979

POSTMODERNISM AND BEYOND 1966–1995

POPULUXE: THE AMERICAN INFLUENCE 1946–1961

Golden Nugget Casino Exterior Signs, 1946
Las Vegas, Nevada, USA
Young Electric Sign Company (est. 1920), Designers
Salt Lake City, Utah, USA

*The word *populuxe* was invented by American social critic Thomas Hine (b. 1936), who used it throughout his 1986 book of the same name.

For most of the modern world, the late 1940s to the early 1960s was a time of reconstruction and rebuilding due to the consequences of World War II. America was the exception.

The post–World War II era marked the beginning of a new world order and America's influence on the world at large. It was a time of growth, prosperity, and a collective vision of looking forward toward a bright and optimistic future that ultimately transformed the nation, as well as the world that it was now leading. At the end of World War II, British prime minister Winston Churchill (1874–1965) stated that "America at this moment stands at the summit of the world." It was not only perceived as the new leader of the free world, but also the leader of the world's potential economic and social growth and prosperity.

Starting in 1945, America's recovery began with the overwhelming influx of young servicemen returning home, who ultimately brought about profound and enduring changes to the American way of life. The nucleus of this way of life was the American family. During this era, American families lived together, played together, and vacationed together.

Due in great part to the economic boom, the country experienced rapid growth spurred by new families, new jobs, new homes, and new needs. Americans could now live the American dream by affording their own single-family homes. During the 1950s, William Levitt (1907–1994), an innovative New York–based real estate developer, created the new American suburban lifestyle by building modest, inexpensive single-tract houses using low-cost, prefabricated construction techniques. These housing developments, called Levittowns, were specifically built for servicemen in locations such as New York, New Jersey, and Pennsylvania.

The new American family also took to the road with their new automobiles that conveyed speed, prosperity, and success. The American landscape was suddenly transformed by a new nation-wide interstate highway system, established by President Dwight D. Eisenhower (1890–1969) in 1956, built to take the driving family quickly from place to place—shopping malls, drive-ins, roadside motels, and fast-food restaurants, as well as family-oriented entertainment destinations such as Walt Disney's new theme park in Anaheim, California, and the U.S. national parks located throughout the country.

New technologies—television, transistors, automation, nuclear power, and plastics—coupled with new cultural movements—pop art, abstract expressionism, film, rock 'n' roll, pop music, and fashion—seized the imagination of Americans and helped define this time period as the American era.

Never before had every aspect of a nation's built environment symbolized its ideals and beliefs and transformed the daily lives of everyone who embraced the American way of life.

TAIL O' THE PUP

1946

TAIL O' THE PUP
Los Angeles, California, USA
Milton Black (1905–1970), Architect
Los Angeles, California, USA

For more than six decades, the Los Angeles streetscape was enhanced and made memorable by an iconic three-dimensional sign that functioned solely as a hot dog stand that captured the folly of a city that has always intrigued and surprised the public's imagination.

Built in 1946, Tail o' the Pup was a small, food stand that was a prime example of novelty architecture built throughout America in the 1950s and literally formed in the shape of the food that it sold—a bright-red hot dog weenie cradled in a golden-brown bun and slathered in yellow mustard. The structure itself measured 17 feet (5.2 m) wide and was fabricated from chicken wire and stucco.

Designed by architect Milton Black (1905–1970), the stand was located at the corner of La Cienega and Beverly Boulevards and opened in June 1946 to a star-studded, searchlight-lit fanfare typical of any Hollywood opening. Tail o' the Pup is a prime example of "duck" architecture—a term later coined by Robert Venturi in his 1970 manifesto *Learning from Las Vegas: The Forgotten Symbolism of Architectural Form* (see page 183)—in which business owners captured the attention of the ever-expanding automobile-oriented American family by creating structures that embodied graphic iconography and solely functioned as promotional signs that literally and symbolically advertised their wares and offerings.

In the mid-1980s, the stand moved to a new location before it was dismantled and placed in a storage warehouse in 2005. The City of Los Angeles has subsequently declared Tail o' the Pup a cultural landmark.

LAS VEGAS AND THE NEON DESERT

1946

BOULDER CLUB EXTERIOR SIGNS
Las Vegas, Nevada, USA
designer unknown

Fremont Street, named in honor of the American politician and explorer John Charles Fremont (1813–1890), is in the heart of downtown Las Vegas's casino corridor and dates back to as early as 1905 when the city was founded. It was the first paved street in Las Vegas and was nicknamed "Glitter Gulch" in the early 1950s due to an abundance of neon (see page 60) signs for casinos such as Binion's Horseshoe, Eldorado Club, Fremont Hotel and Casino, Golden Gate Hotel and Casino, Golden Nugget, the Mint, and

the Pioneer Club. It is the second most famous street in Las Vegas after the Las Vegas strip.

The Boulder Club, one of the earliest gambling establishments on Fremont Street, opened in 1929 and was the first to build and install a "spectacular" sign with animated elements on its building exterior in 1946.

The Golden Nugget, originally known as the Golden Nugget Gambling Hall, was the largest and most luxurious casinos located on Fremont Street in downtown Las Vegas at the time of its

opening in 1946. It was also one of the first establishments in Las Vegas to incorporate large animated lighting displays on its facade with more than 40,000 feet (12 km) of multicolored neon tubing.

"Vegas Vic" is the unofficial name for the towering cowboy erected in 1951 on the exterior of the Pioneer Club. This 40-foot- (12.2 m) high animated neon sign, designed with humanlike characteristics of a waving arm, moving cigarette, and an audio recording of "Howdy Podner"

1946

1951

GOLDEN NUGGET CASINO EXTERIOR SIGNS
Las Vegas, Nevada, USA
Young Electric Sign Company (est. 1920), Designers
Salt Lake City, Utah, USA

VEGAS VIC AND PIONEER CLUB
EXTERIOR SIGN
Las Vegas, Nevada, USA
Young Electric Sign Company (est. 1920), Designers
Salt Lake City, Utah, USA

that ran every fifteen minutes, was a departure at the time, since most signs introduced in the city during this era were letterform based, not figurative or character based. Perhaps the most recognized electronic sign in Las Vegas, Vegas Vic was designed and built by Young Electric Sign Company (YESCO) in 1951, and it became the unofficial greeter to Las Vegas visitors.

YESCO was founded in 1920 by Thomas Young (1895–1971), a sign painter who left England in the early 1900s with his family and immigrated to Ogden, Utah. He started a sign shop that specialized in coffin plates, gold leaf window lettering, lighted signs, and painted advertisements. As the science and technology of sign lighting and manufacturing evolved, so

did YESCO. The company erected the first neon sign in Las Vegas for the Boulder Club in 1947.

When the Stardust Hotel and Casino opened in 1958, it was located on 63 acres (25 ha) along the Las Vegas Strip and had the largest casino, the largest swimming pool, and was deemed the largest hotel in the Las Vegas area.

Its exterior neon signs were equal to its billing. The Stardust building sign provided the public with a panoramic graphic view of the solar system. A 16-foot- (4.9 m) diameter acrylic representation of the Earth was at its center with rays of neon and incandescent lights emanating from behind in all directions. Three-dimensional acrylic planets orbited among a galactic cloud of neon stars. Across this starlit

cloud was nestled a jagged composition of illuminated letterforms spelling out "Stardust." The sign was composed of 7,100 feet (2,200 m) of neon tubing with approximately 11,000 incandescent lightbulbs along its 216-foot- (66 m) long front fascia, with 975 incandescent lightbulbs contained in the "S" alone. At night, the neon-illuminated sign was reportedly visible from 60 miles (97 km).

Its freestanding roadside sign was composed of a circle constraining an amorphous cloud of cosmic dust encircled by an orbit ring of dancing stars. At night, incorporating neon and incandescent lamps in the animation se-

continued on page 122

Las Vegas and the Neon Desert, continued

1958

1959

STARDUST RESORT AND CASINO EXTERIOR SIGNS
Las Vegas, Nevada, USA

Young Electric Sign Company (est. 1920), Designers
Salt Lake City, Utah, USA

quence, light fell from the stars, sprinkling from the top of the 188-foot- (57 m) tall sign down over the Stardust name.

The iconic Welcome to Fabulous Las Vegas Nevada sign is in the center median of the Las Vegas Strip. This landmark sign, built in 1959, stands 25 feet high (7.6 m) and was designed by Betty Willis (b. 1924), a native Las Vegas graphic designer, who at the time worked for Western Neon Sign Company (est. 1936), a local sign manufacturer.

WELCOME TO FABULOUS LAS VEGAS ROADSIDE SIGN
Las Vegas, Nevada, USA

Betty Willis (b. 1924), Designer
Las Vegas, Nevada, USA

It is composed of a luminescent diamond panel bordered with flashing and chasing yellow incandescent lights around its perimeter. Across its top are seven circles backed with graphic representations of silver dollars, outlined in white neon, and each containing a bold, red, sans-serif letter collectively forming the word "Welcome." An eight-pointed, red star outlined in yellow neon crowns the sign.

The sign's translucent white panel displays "to Fabulous" in blue cursive letterforms with

"Las Vegas" in red sans-serif capital letterforms on the next line and "Nevada" in blue sans-serif capital letterforms directly below. On the back it says, "Drive Carefully" and "Come Back Soon."

The Welcome to Fabulous Las Vegas Nevada sign is characteristic of the "Googie" architecture movement that originated in southern California in the late 1940s through to the mid-1960s. It was a design movement influenced by car culture and the atomic age and characterized by the use of futuristic, space-age forms that communicated motion.

In 2009, the sign was listed on the U.S. National Register of Historic Places.

MORRIS LAPIDUS AND THE POPULIST HOTEL

1950

ALGIERS HOTEL
Miami Beach, Florida, USA
Morris Lapidus (1902–2001), Architect
Odessa, Russia

Morris Lapidus's (1902–2001) first hotel commission provided him with an opportunity to single-handedly redefine the modern hotel, as well as an entire district of Miami Beach that included the Sans Souci (1949), the Nautilus (1950), the Algiers (1950), the Biltmore Terrace (1951), and the DiLido (1952)—all in the center of the city on Collins Avenue.

In 1949, Lapidus received one of his largest commissions to date—the Algiers Hotel (1950), which was followed ten years later by the Summit Hotel (1960) in New York City.

The Algiers Hotel, one of the most historically and architecturally significant hotels in Miami Beach, Florida, is considered one of the first truly modern and populist hotels of the era. Its oceanfront location on Collins Avenue was distinguished by a turquoise tile-clad tower crowned with "scheherazade-like" letterforms

spelling out "Algiers." The hotel included 198 guest rooms, restaurant, ballroom, retail stores, pool, and beachfront cabanas. Lapidus created pure Hollywood cinematic glamour in a locale known for its cool and informal demeanor.

With the Summit Hotel in New York City, Lapidus adapted many of the design techniques and motifs he had successfully employed on his Miami Beach projects. For example, he preferred dramatic curvilinear and fluid forms such as an elongated "S" shape for the hotel's tower as opposed to the familiar box-like monolithic building masses of the modern era. The Summit was New York's first new hotel in more than thirty years and somewhat controversial due to its decorative characteristics, which were uncommon to hotels in urban centers.

The 21-story, 800-room hotel, completed in 1961 and located on the southeast corner

of Lexington Avenue and 51st Street, was clad in turquoise-glazed brick and dark green tiles. The most unconventional element on the facade was the hotel identification sign itself that dramatically spelled out the hotel name on vertically arranged, internally illuminated white plastic ovals held by highly stylized triangular metal brackets. At the top of this vertical composition was the word "the" set in lowercase, whimsical script-style letterforms, evocative of the styles used in his Miami Beach projects but on a larger scale, contrasted and coupled with bold, serif typography for the letters spelling out SUMMIT.

Influenced by his years of designing commercial retail stores and showrooms (see page 103), Lapidus's architecture and interiors not

continued on page 124

Morris Lapidus and the Populist Hotel, continued

1961

THE SUMMIT HOTEL
New York, New York, USA
Morris Lapidus (1902–2001), Architect
Odessa, Russia

only relied upon attention-getting elements such as sweeping curves, floating backlit ceilings, irregular-shaped forms, and perforated walls, but also on numerous graphic design elements to reinforce and enhance the overall building experience.

He used supergraphics throughout his interior spaces to create a mood as well as deemphasize aspects of architecture. Building facades were used as billboards for theatrical, dramatic, and overscaled letterforms that identified and branded each property and evoked the drama and spirit of the building experience. He was also one of the first architects to insist on "total architecture" with his clients. Lapidus ultimately conceived and directed every detail of each hotel project, inside and out, from the architecture, interiors, lighting, and graphics to table settings, upholstery, and staff uniforms.

Morris Lapidus's populist touch redefined the modern hotel experience during the 1950s and 1960s with a body of work that was an exuberant combination of spectacle, fantasy, and whimsy. He has been described as an "American original" who believed "too much is never enough."

ALVIN LUSTIG AND NORTHLAND SHOPPING CENTER

1952

NORTHLAND SHOPPING CENTER
SIGN PROGRAM
Southfield, Michigan, USA
Alvin Lustig (1915–1955), Designer
Denver, Colorado, USA

Following the end of World War II, coupled with the American public's increased reliance on the automobile, suburban shopping centers and malls—a modern adaption of the historical marketplace—started to take shape throughout the country far from the traditional retail environs of urban downtown.

Northland Shopping Center, designed by architect Victor Gruen (1903–1980), was the first mall to open in the United States and was quickly heralded as the future of shopping in postwar America following its opening in 1954.

Gruen, born Viktor Grunbaum, was an Austrian architect best known as a pioneer in the design of shopping malls in the United States. In 1951 founded his own firm, Victor Gruen Associates, which soon became one of the major architectural and planning offices of that time.

In 1954, he designed the first suburban open-air shopping mall—Northland Shopping Center in Southfield, a suburb of Detroit. It was a milestone for regional shopping centers in the postwar era because it was the first to rely upon one or more "anchors" or "big-box" retailers. Gruen pioneered the soon-to-be-enormously popular concept of a regional-sized, fully enclosed shopping complex and has been called "the most influential architect of the twentieth century" because of this development.

Northland Shopping Center was also one of the first collaborations of a major figure in American architecture with a major figure in American graphic design.

Alvin Lustig's (1915–1955) work with Gruen on the signing for the Northland Shopping Center was the first example of direct colla-boration between a graphic designer and an architect. Lustig designed a comprehensive set of coordinated signs for the center's main entrance, parking lots, and water tower. In his later years, Lustig would collaborate with influential American architect Philip Johnson (1906–2005) on the sign program for the modernist masterpiece Seagram Building (1958) in New York City.

Lustig was one of the first graphic designers to approach his craft and profession in a nonspecialized manner. He believed that all design was a matter of form and content and that the role of the designer was that of a synthesizer, not of a style maker. His diverse work included books, magazines, trademarks, letterheads, record albums, textiles, furniture, interiors, and environmental graphics.

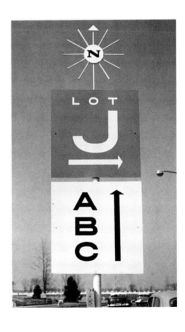

HOLIDAY INN

1953

HOLIDAY INN ROADSIDE SIGN
Memphis, Tennessee, USA

James A. Anderson (date unknown), Designer
Memphis, Tennessee, USA

In 1953, Kemmons Wilson (1913–2003) opened his first motor-court motel on a commercial strip outside of Memphis, Tennessee. The motel was named Holiday Inn and quickly became the American standard for all roadside motels, as well as becoming one of the world's largest hotel chains serving more than 100 million guests each year.

Wilson initially came up with his concept for a new type of motel after he and his family took a road trip to Washington, D.C., in which he was disappointed with the quality and consis-

tency provided by the roadside motels of the time. The name Holiday Inn was given to the original motel in reference to the 1942 musical film starring Bing Crosby and Fred Astaire of the same name.

The motel's distinctive and eye-catching roadside sign was originally based on movie marquees of the same time period—broad surfaces emblazoned with multicolored neon and incandescent chasing lights, illuminating letters, arrows, chevrons, and five-pointed stars animated in luminescent green, yellow, orange,

blue, red, and white. The iconic sign was also intentionally overscaled, measuring approximately 50 feet (15.3 m) high and 16 feet (4.9 m) wide, to catch the driver's attention. It was composed of a friendly script-based logotype originally designed by a Memphis-based commercial artist.

Since its beginnings in the early 1950s, the Holiday Inn sign was synonymous with road trips for the American driver and became a universal symbol and integral part of the American roadside experience during this era.

HOWARD JOHNSON'S

1954

HOWARD JOHNSON'S
Quincy, Massachusetts, USA

Rufus Nims (1913–2005), Architect
Pensacola, Florida, USA

One of the most familiar and recognizable symbols in American popular culture during the 1950s was the iconic orange roofs, blue cupolas, white weathervanes, and characteristic typography of the Howard Johnson chain of roadside restaurants and motels.

The name is derived from the company's founder, Howard Deering Johnson (1897–1972), an innovative entrepreneur and creator of the first franchise, who started the initial chain of restaurants and motels. The company's early beginnings started in Quincy, Massachusetts, in 1925 with an ice cream stand and small soda fountain in a local drugstore that expanded to a roadside empire with more than 100 locations from Maine to Florida, by the 1950s.

During the postwar building boom of interstate roadways across the country, Johnson's success catapulted when he won an exclusive food service contract along an initial 160-mile stretch of the Pennsylvania Turnpike—the nation's first superhighway. Subsequently, when the Ohio, Massachusetts, New York, Indiana, New Jersey, and Connecticut Turnpikes were completed, Johnson bid and won exclusive rights to serve motorists on these state turnpike systems. Just as the turnpike opened a new era of motoring throughout the United States, Howard Johnson's roadside restaurants and motels marked a new era of dining and lodging for the American driving public.

To appeal to the greatest number of motorists nationwide, Johnson relied upon a style and design of building that was well known throughout New England—the Colonial revival home, complete with painted white clapboards, multipaned windows, roof dormers, and a cupola. The only twist Johnson introduced was a brilliant orange roof guaranteed to catch the eye of the passing motorist. The distinctive, finned cupola was painted bright turquoise to intentionally complement and contrast the color of the roof and was topped off with a weathervane that featured a graphic silhouette of a man, a boy, and a dog called Simple Simon and the Pieman, their first trademark developed in the 1930s.

Howard Johnson's quickly became a familiar and welcoming graphic beacon and respite for the American motorist during the 1950s and 1960s that was well known for providing quality food at reasonable prices with the added plus of offering ice cream in twenty-eight flavors.

In 1954, Howard Johnson's opened its first motor lodge in Savannah, Georgia. By the 1970s, there were more than 1,000 restaurants and more than 500 motor lodges located throughout the world.

HOWARD JOHNSON'S — ON RIVER ROAD — HARRISBURG, PA.

LOS ANGELES'S WATTS TOWERS

1954

WATTS TOWERS
Los Angeles, California, USA

Simon Rodia (1879–1965), Designer/Builder
Ribottoli, Italy

The Watts Towers are one of a few primary examples of twentieth-century, nontraditional vernacular architecture and American naïve art evident in our urban built landscape. While the towers were originally created as a means of singular self-expression by the artist, following their completion they became an iconic landmark and visual symbol for the City of Los Angeles in the late 1950s and early 1960s.

Begun in 1921 and completed over a period of thirty-three years in 1954, the towers consist of seventeen interconnected structures and were singularly hand-built by Simon Rodia (1879–1965), an Italian immigrant construction worker, using reinforced concrete, steel rebar rods, mortar, shards of ceramic pottery, and a variety of found objects. The individual armatures of each tower are constructed from steel rebar pipes and rods, wrapped in wire mesh, coated with cement mortar, and then embedded with broken fragments of porcelain, ceramic tile, glass bottles, seashells, and scrap metal.

Rodia was born Sabato Rodia in Ribottoli, Italy, in 1879. In the early 1900s, he immigrated with his brother to the United States and settled in California. In his early years, he worked in rock quarries, logging, and railroad camps.

In 1921, he purchased a vacant lot running along the train tracks at 10th Street in south Los Angeles and began to construct what he called "Nuestro Pueblo" (meaning "our town" in Spanish). For the next thirty-four years, Rodia worked singlehandedly to build his towers without the benefit of machinery, scaffolding, bolts, rivets, welds, or drawings. His unbridled passion for his work, coupled with pipe fitter pliers and a window-washer's belt and buckle, provided Rodia with the tools to create a modernist masterpiece celebrating the human spirit and the pursuit of a singular vision.

While the towers have an imposing and constructivist-type presence as part of the urban streetscape, they also provide the pedestrian with a fantastical and dynamic spatial experience when they are walked in, around, and through as with any enveloping, larger-than-life sculpture. The tallest tower stands 104 feet (32 m) high, the second tallest 100 feet (30 m) high, and the next 52 feet (16 m) high.

In 1978, Watts Towers was restored and today operate under the City of Los Angeles's Cultural Affairs Department. They were designated a National Historic Landmark in 1990 and are listed on the U.S. National Register of Historic Places.

MCDONALD'S

1955

MCDONALD'S
Des Plaines, Illinois, USA

Stanley Meston (1910–1992), Architect
Los Angeles, California, USA

During the 1950s and 1960s, fast-food chains—epitomized by McDonald's—revolutionized the roadside restaurant by catering to young, affluent Americans who were part of the emerging and fast-growing automobile culture.

McDonald's, the world's largest fast-food chain with more than 30,000 restaurants worldwide, serving nearly 64 million customers daily, was founded by Ray Kroc (1902–1984) in 1955 after he purchased the rights to a small hamburger chain begun in 1940 by fast-food pioneers and brothers Richard (1909–1998) and Maurice McDonald (1902–1971). The McDonald brothers opened their first restaurant along

Route 66 in San Bernardino, California, featuring barbecue and carhops. In 1948, they made the switch to hamburgers and a self-service system of walk-up windows. They first introduced the "golden arches" in 1953 when they opened an outlet in Phoenix, designed by architect Stanley Meston (1910–1992).

In 1955, the first McDonald's under Ray Kroc opened in Des Plaines, Illinois, with an attention-getting red-and-white tiled building, distinctive sloped roof, and now-ubiquitous pair of stylized yellow arches at opposite sides of the building, projecting through the roof. Intended to be seen from miles away and glowing

brightly on any commercial strip when viewed from an angle, these poised, parabolic arches were meant to read as a letter *M*.

While the physical arches were dropped from all of their restaurants' building designs in the late 1960s, they have remained an integral graphic element of the McDonald's logotype. In just five decades, this worldwide, fast-food business phenomenon has become one of the most recognized brands of American popular culture.

WALT DISNEY AND
THE HAPPIEST PLACE ON EARTH

1955

DISNEYLAND

Anaheim, California, USA

Walt Disney (1901–1966), Designer
Hermosa, Illinois, USA

Walter Elias "Walt" Disney (1901–1966) was an American innovator and visionary who greatly influenced and reshaped the entertainment industry during the 1950s and 1960s. He was a film producer, director, screenwriter, voice actor, animator, entrepreneur, and one of the most imaginative minds of the twentieth century.

Disneyland, his lifelong dream, was the only theme park to be designed and built under his direct supervision. Located in Anaheim, California, "The Happiest Place on Earth" as Disney called it, is on an 85-acre (34 ha) site and was organized into five themed areas when it first opened in 1955: Main Street USA resembled an early-twentieth-century Midwest town; Adventureland featured jungle-themed adventures; Frontierland replicated an American Old West frontier town; Fantasyland brought real life to characters and places from Disney's movies; and Tomorrowland conveyed an optimistic vision of the future.

On entering a themed area, a guest was completely immersed in a themed environment—physically, visually, and experientially—and was unable to see or hear any other realm. The idea behind this was to develop theatrical "stages" with a seamless passage from one themed area to the next.

Additionally, various modes of transportation for moving people as well as for the fun of using unique and unusual means of transportation would be made available so that visitors would never have a need for their own car. .

Disney was born in Hermosa, Illinois, in 1901. He studied at the Chicago Art Institute and subsequently embarked on a career drawing political caricatures and comic strips.

In 1923, he and his brother Roy (1893–1971) established a cartoon studio in Hollywood, California, which ultimately became the Walt Disney Company.

Disney initially conceptualized Disneyland after visiting various amusement parks during the 1930s and 1940s, including Tivoli Gardens in Denmark; Efteling in the Netherlands; and Greenfield Village, Playland, and Children's Fairyland in the United States. He may also have been influenced by his father's memories of working at the World's Columbian Exposition of 1893 in Chicago. Its midway included attractions representing various countries from around the world, the first Ferris wheel designed by American engineer George Ferris (1859–1896), a passenger train that circled the fair's perimeter, and a Wild West Show starring showman Buffalo Bill Cody (1846–1917).

In 1955, Disneyland's annual attendance was one million visitors. It has a larger cumulative attendance than any other theme park in the world, with close to six hundred million visitors since it opened. In 2010, sixteen million people visited the park, making it the second most visited theme park in the world that year.

Disney achieved his goal of creating a different kind of park for people—a park that would have fun attractions set in a beautiful surrounding; a park that "would never be completed as long as there is imagination in the world."

It was also one of the primary examples of the twentieth century in which graphic design and architecture was planned from its initial inception as a seamless, cohesive experience in the built environment.

HOLLYWOOD WALK OF FAME

1958

HOLLYWOOD WALK OF FAME
Hollywood, California, USA

Pereira & Luckman (est. 1950), Architects
Los Angeles, California, USA

The Hollywood Walk of Fame, one of the most popular tourist attractions in Hollywood, California, for more than the last fifty years, consists of approximately 2,400 commemorative graphic stars embedded in eighteen blocks (1.6 miles; 2.6 km) of sidewalks running along Hollywood Boulevard and Vine Street. Each star, bearing the name of an actor, director, producer, musician, composer, or performer, functions as a permanent public monument celebrating the achievements of prominent individuals in the entertainment industry.

While it was originally conceived in 1953 as part of a long-term redevelopment plan for Hollywood Boulevard, the Hollywood Chamber of Commerce also proposed the idea as a means to "maintain the glory of a community whose name means glamour and excitement in the four corners of the world." Pereira & Luckman (est. 1950) was retained to develop the concept and draw up plans for city council approval.

The initial 1,558 honorees were selected between 1956 and 1957 by a committee including Cecil B. DeMille, Jesse Lasky, Samuel Goldwyn, Walt Disney, Hal Roach, Mack Sennett, and Walter Lantz. Construction on the walk began in 1958 with the first commemorative star for film director Stanley Kramer installed in its permanent location in March 1960.

As of 2010, the star-glittered sidewalks of the Walk of Fame are composed of 2,442 honorees. Each honoree's five-pointed star—a composite of coral and pink terrazzo framed in bronze and inlaid into a background field of speckled, charcoal-gray terrazzo—is located at 6-foot (1.8 m) on-center intervals. The name of each honoree is inlaid in sans-serif, all-capital, block-type bronze letters in the upper portion of the star.

Directly below each inscription, in the lower half of the star, is a round inlaid bronze graphic pictogram identifying the category or area of expertise of each honoree: a classic film camera for motion pictures; a television set for broadcast television; a phonograph record for music; a radio microphone for broadcast radio; and the masks of tragedy and comedy for theater. An average of twenty new commemorative stars are added to the walk each year.

In 1978, the City of Los Angeles designated the landmark Hollywood Walk of Fame a Los Angeles Historic and Cultural Monument.

MODERNISM AND
THE INTERNATIONAL STYLE
1950–1979

127 John Street Entrance Facade, 1968
New York, New York, USA
Rudolph de Harak (1924–2002), Designer
Culver City, California, USA

A new objective rationalism took hold of graphic design in the built environment during the postwar era of the 1950s to the 1970s. Modernism, void of style and of the outdated influence of prevalent art movements of the earlier part of the twentieth century—art nouveau and art deco—became a powerful and pervasive point of view for decades to come.

During this same era, a common movement in graphic design and architecture emerged from Switzerland and Germany and became one of the most influential design movements of the twentieth century.

The International Typographic Style, or Swiss Style, emerged from Switzerland during the 1950s and was based on the visual principles of order, function, and clarity. Its reliance upon pure geometry, asymmetrical compositions, sans-serif typography, mathematically defined page grids, and related proportional systems transformed graphic design with a new order. Its philosophy and tenets evolved directly from the de Stijl movement, the Bauhaus, and Jan Tschchold's (1902–1974) now classic *Die Neue Typographie (The New Typography, 1928)*.

In the built environment, the International Style was a major architectural movement that emerged during the 1920s and 1930s in Western Europe. Its moniker was originally coined by architectural historian Henry-Russell Hitchcock (1903–1987) and American architect Philip Johnson (1906–2005) for their 1932 groundbreaking exhibition at the Museum of Modern Art in New York City on what was considered at the time as avant-garde architecture. It was also rooted in the earlier developments of twentieth-century design, primarily from the modernist design principles of the avant-garde—de Stijl, constructivism, and the Bauhaus—characterized by a simplification of form, a rejection of ornament, and the use of functional, utilitarian materials such as concrete, steel, and glass coupled with an honest and obvious expression of a building's structure.

Both movements believed in "form follows function," which American architect Louis Sullivan (1856–1924) had proposed in 1896, and shared many characteristics that allowed them to transcend style, national identity, and an individual's point of view to become embraced worldwide.

Modernism and the International Style, now part of the mainstream's consciousness, provided graphic designers and architects with a unified language that has prevailed for the last ninety years and continues to resonate with many contemporary graphic designers and architects.

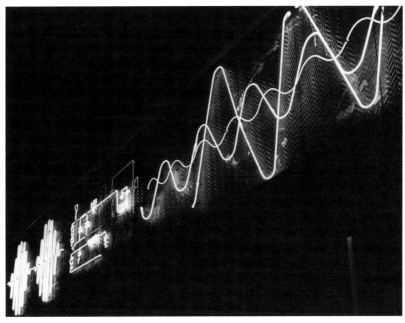

GYORGY KEPES
AND THE INFLUENCE OF LIGHT

1950

RADIO SHACK LIGHT MURAL
Boston, Massachusetts, USA
Gyorgy Kepes (1906–2001), Designer
Budapest, Hungary

One of the most influential and visionary minds of the early modernist era was Gyorgy Kepes (1906–2001)—a Hungarian-born painter, sculptor, filmmaker, planner, designer, writer, and educator.

He initially studied painting at Budapest's Royal Academy of Fine Arts, which in the early 1930s was a hotbed of political and artistic unrest. After the completion of his studies, he turned away from painting to filmmaking, which he felt was a more effective and impactful medium for an artist to express social beliefs.

Following his move to Berlin, he was invited to join the design studio of Laszlo Moholy-Nagy (1895–1946), the Hungarian painter and photographer who had taught at the Bauhaus (1919; see pg. 75) and then immigrated with him to London in 1936 during the political unrest of pre-Nazi Germany. The following year, Moholy-

Nagy became the director of the Illinois Institute of Technology (IIT)—the new American Bauhaus in Chicago—and invited Kepes to join him there to start a light and color department, the first of its kind in the United States. It was during his tenure there that he wrote his classic reference book on visual design and design education, *The Language of Vision* (1944). He subsequently was invited to establish a visual design program at the Massachusetts Institute of Technology (MIT) in Cambridge, which in 1968 became the Center for Advanced Visual Studies, dedicated to developing new technologies and to promoting creative collaboration between scientists, visual artists, and designers.

Kepes also designed numerous projects incorporating elements of light and illumination—most notably a programmable light wall mural in 1950 for Radio Shack in Boston.

This kinetic light wall was one of the first commercial installations to employ the graphic design principle of abstraction, coupled with neon tubing, in a dynamic and communicative manner, graphically representing radio and sound frequency waves that are not visible to the human eye. The mural, constructed of corrugated steel with a baked enamel surface, was illuminated with alternating neon tube light and black light.

Throughout his career and work Kepes believed that the language of graphic design could communicate facts, ideas, and stories in a meaningful and universal manner more than any other form of communication. His graphic design work for the built environment, such as his Radio Shack light mural, reminds us that his approach and interests were not limited to the two-dimensional world.

LUIS BARRAGÁN AND
TOWERS OF SATELLITE CITY

TOWERS OF SATELLITE CITY
Mexico City, Mexico

Luis Barragán (1902–1988), Architect

Guadalajara, Mexico

In 1957, Mexican architect Luis Barragán (1902–1988), in collaboration with German artist Mathias Goeritz (1915–1990), designed the Torres de la Ciudad Satélite (Towers of Satellite City) to serve as a promotional place marker for Mexico City's first planned residential real estate development—Ciudad Satellite. Little did the designers realize that it would subsequently become one of the most significant iconic landmarks introduced to an urban landscape created during the modern era.

Barragán is considered the most important Mexican architect of the twentieth century. He was self-taught and was highly influenced by the work of modernist architect Le Corbusier (1887–1965), as well as European modernism. The majority of his work is well known for its emotion and humanism reflected in his use of raw materials (such as stone and wood), color, and natural light. He is one of the few twentieth-century architects who succeeded in creating their own version of modernism by giving it a vibrant, sensuous aesthetic—an aesthetic derived from his native Mexico. Barragán worked for years with little acknowledgment or praise until 1975, when he was honored with a retrospective of his work at the Museum of Modern Art in New York City. In 1980, he became the second winner of the Pritzker Architecture Prize, considered to be one of the world's premier architecture prizes.

More than 100 feet (30.5 m) tall and constructed from reinforced concrete, the hollow, wedge-shaped, abstract towers of Satellite City were prime examples of a new form of monumental, minimalist art that emerged in Mexico during the 1960s. The towers stand 100 feet (30.5 m), 120 feet (36.6 m), 130 feet (39.6 m), 150 feet (45.7 m), and 165 feet (50.3 m) high respectively and are in the middle of one of the city's busiest thoroughfares—Periferico, Mexico City's main freeway.

Each tower was constructed, foot by foot, without scaffolding, using metal molds stacked one upon the other until complete. This construction process is clearly evident in the horizontal stripes, which modulate and visually enhance each tower's height and surface.

The towers appear monumental from a distance, whereas up close, they create an intimate and unusual public space that pedestrians can explore. Their primary colors contrast with the sky above, reflecting the ever-changing sunlight, constantly engaging the pedestrian as one of the first modernist signposts set in an urban environment. The towers also play optical games with the pedestrian as you move in and around them, shifting profiles and changing heights. At times, they appear to be flat planes suspended in space; other times, they appear to be square-based monumental forms, echoing the stone monoliths of Stonehenge (c. 3000 BCE; see page 26) in the United Kingdom.

JOSEF MÜLLER-BROCKMANN

1952

SWISS AUTOMOBILE CLUB
ACCIDENT BAROMETER
Paradeplatz, Zurich, Switzerland
Josef Müller-Brockmann (1914–1996), Designer
Zurich, Switzerland

During the 1950s, Josef Müller-Brockmann (1914–1996) explored the theories of nonrepresentational abstraction, visual metaphor, subjective graphic interpretation, and constructive graphic design, based on the sole use of geometric elements without illustration, nuance, or embellishment. He was one of the pioneers of functional, objective graphic design and the Swiss International Typographic Style, as well as a world-renowned graphic designer, author, and educator. Throughout his career, his rationalist work set the standard for modernism, constructivism, and for the use of pure geometry, mathematical systems, and the grid in visual communications.

In all of his work, he incorporated a precise mathematical plan, logically constructed, in which every compositional element had a reason for its size, proportion, placement, and position. While the majority of his work was print related, the few times he was involved in large-scale graphic design projects in the built environment, they were provocative, innovative, and memorable.

In 1952, Müller-Brockmann designed a large-scale public information display for his long-term client, the Automobile Club of Switzerland. This "accident barometer" informed and educated the public on the actuality of reckless driving throughout the country by presenting statistical data on the total number of automobile-related accidents and deaths.

The actual barometer was on the Paradeplatz, a major public plaza in central Zurich, thereby attracting a large amount of public attention from passers-by, as well as local media.

continued on page 138

1955

BALLY AROLA MURAL
Zurich, Switzerland

Josef Müller-Brockmann (1914–1996), Designer
Zurich, Switzerland

The display itself was composed of a series of large-scale, black-and-white, vertical and horizontal, three-dimensional intersecting planes. Narrative and statistical information was presented in the grotesque sans-serif typeface Akzidenz Grotesk (Gunter Gerhard Lange, 1896) on a large, centralized numerical display on one of the monolithic panels, updated on a daily basis. Below this centralized panel and visible at eye level were supplemental photographic images of accidents and detailed numerical-based statistics on annual fatalities.

Müller-Brockmann's modernist solution of intersecting planes and their integration to a large public space is reminiscent of information kiosks conceived by several avant-garde Russian constructivists in the 1920s, such as El Lissitszky (1890–1941; see page 69) and Aleksandr Rodchenko (1891–1956; see page 70), as well as modernist graphic designer and typographer Herbert Bayer's (1900–1985; see page 72) newspaper kiosk studies created at the Bauhaus.

Several years later, Müller-Brockmann designed a whimsical, large-scale mural for the Zurich-based shoe company Bally. Measuring approximately 50 feet (15.2 m) high, the mural was composed of various-scale footprints "walking" up and down the building facade. Singularly relying upon a simple graphic image, he created a colorful, kinetic, and rhythmic composition for a vacant wall in central Zurich.

Müller-Brockmann's use and integration of pure graphic forms in the built environment illustrates a timeless relationship between image and movement—vocabulary and message. His work is as current and communicative as it was more than a half-century ago when it was originally conceived.

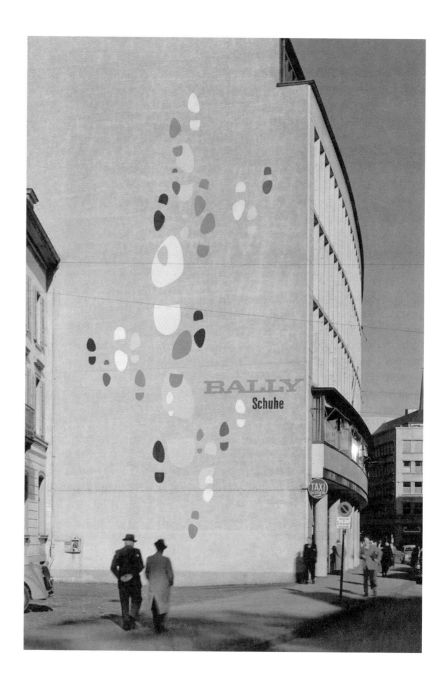

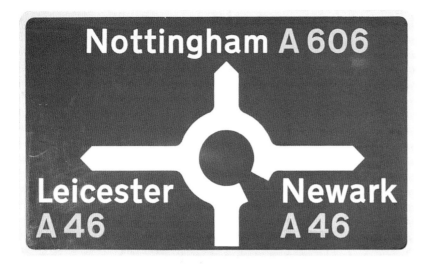

JOCK KINNEIR, MARGARET CALVERT, AND THE BRITISH TRAVELER

1957

BRITISH ROADWAY SIGN SYSTEM
United Kingdom

Kinneir, Calvert & Associates (est. 1964), Designers
London, United Kingdom

Born in 1917, Richard "Jock" Kinneir (1917–1994) was a British typographer and graphic designer who, with his colleague Margaret Calvert (b. 1936), were the first graphic designers, rather than civic engineers or road surveyors, to design cohesive national graphic systems for roadway and railway signs that are still used today throughout the United Kingdom.

Kinneir studied engraving at the Chelsea School of Art from 1935 to 1939. After World War II, he was employed as an exhibition designer with the United Kingdom's Central Office of Information and later by their Design Research Unit before starting his own design practice in London in 1956.

His first major commission was the design of the public information sign system for Gatwick Airport, London's second-largest international airport, in which he chose one of

his students from the Chelsea School of Art, Margaret Calvert, to assist him.

In 1957, he was asked to design a sign system for the new British roadway network. His objective was to design signs that could be read at speeds when driving in an automobile. For this sign system, Kinneir and Calvert designed a new typeface based on the influential sans-serif Akzidenz Grotesk (1896), an early grotesque designed by Gunter Gerhard Lange, released by the H. Berthold AG foundry, and the precursor to the ubiquitous sans-serif grotesque Helvetica (1956), designed by Max Miedinger (1910–1980) for the Haas foundry. Their new typeface was named Transport in 1963.

Typical signs used on main roadways rely upon a bold graphic road symbol, composed solely of line and letterform, alerting a driver to the actual layout of the upcoming road well

before a driver is close enough to read actual text information on a sign.

The components of the overall roadway network sign system are organized in three categories by function—informational, instructional, and regulatory, and based on pure geometric shapes. Instructional signs are circular; regulatory signs are triangular; and informational signs are either rectangular or square. Informational signs employ white lettering on a blue background; directional signs for primary routes employ white lettering on a green background, with road numbers indicated in yellow; and regulatory signs employ white lettering on a red background. Smaller signs on secondary local roads employ black lettering on a white background.

continued on page 140

Jock Kinneir, Margaret Calvert, and the British Traveler, continued

1965

BRITISH RAIL SIGN SYSTEM
United Kingdom

Kinneir, Calvert & Associates (est. 1964), Designers
London, United Kingdom

In the post–World War world, the needs of the modern driver increased exponentially due to better cars, an increase in the number of drivers on the road, and more opportunities for them to explore their surroundings on a regular basis. During this era, most public roadway sign systems did not meet the graphic standards of prominence, immediacy, and legibility to support drivers' planning and execution of safety-critical decisions—often made at fast speeds, sometimes under adverse conditions. Numerous sign proposals were tested by the government, including serif versus sans-serif typography, capital letters versus small capital letters, and size versus distance.

One of the most significant functional characteristics of Kinneir and Calvert's new sign system was that their modular system could be implemented by anyone throughout the country, either by local traffic authorities or trained graphic designers, each needing to follow the system's specifications and templates.

In 1964, the same year Calvert was made a partner of the firm, renamed Kinneir Calvert & Associates, they designed the British Rail sign system, which was based on their approach with the British Roadway program and later widely copied. Rail Alphabet, a new sans-serif typeface they designed for the project and based on a modified version of Helvetica (Max Miedinger, 1956) was ultimately used in both positive and negative forms. The typographic proportions of Rail Alphabet's capitals, ascenders, and descenders were minimized, and each letterform, standardized arrows, and the new British Railway symbol were all manufactured as individual artwork tiles for easy assembly and for maintaining optimum letterspacing.

More than fifty years after they were originally created, both of these sign systems still retain optimum functionality and aesthetic appeal and have also become organizational and design benchmarks for modern road and rail sign systems throughout the world.

THE FIRST AMERICAN MODERNIST— LESTER BEALL

1960

**INTERNATIONAL PAPER COMPANY
CORPORATE IDENTITY PROGRAM
New York, New York, USA**
Lester Beall (1903–1969), Designer
Kansas City, Missouri, USA

In the late 1950s, Lester Beall (1903–1969) became well known for his work in the area of corporate identity for several American corporations, including Emhart Manufacturing, Titeflex Inc., and International Paper Company. Beall was one of the first American graphic designers to adopt modernist design principles of pure geometry and abstraction in his broad-based consultant work. In 1937, he became the first American graphic designer to be honored with a one-man solo exhibition at the Museum of Modern Art in New York City.

He was born in Kansas City, Missouri, and later moved to Chicago where he studied at the University of Chicago and later at the Art Institute of Chicago. As a self-taught graphic designer, he initially designed exhibits and wall murals for the 1933 Chicago Century of Progress World's Fair. In 1935, he relocated to New York City and eventually opened his own design consultancy firm in Wilton, Connecticut.

Beall was deeply influenced by the European avant-garde, constructivism, and Bauhaus (1919; see page 75) aesthetics and produced award-winning work in a minimalist, modernist style. Throughout his work and career, he was well known for utilizing pure angled shapes, vibrant primary colors, minimalist forms, iconic arrows, silhouetted photography, and dynamic compositions in an innovative, functional, and communicative visual manner.

In 1955, Beall consolidated his design office operation in Connecticut, after commuting between New York City and his home at Dumbarton Farm for the past twenty years. Following this move, he increased his staff and started to receive design commissions for more comprehensive and complex projects in the expanding area of corporate identity. At this time, he not only designed corporate marks and logotypes but detailed corporate identity manuals outlining their use and regulations for clients such as Caterpillar Tractor Company, Martin Marietta, and International Paper.

While design standards manuals are commonplace today, they were pioneered by graphic designers such as Beall, Paul Rand (1914–1996; see page 142), and firms like Chermayeff & Geismar Associates (est. 1957; see page 144) during the 1960s. Beall's corporate identity manual for International Paper was one of the first to function as a comprehensive document that detailed an integrated corporate design program for a company. The manual itself specified design guidelines and rules of usage for all aspects of the company's corporate identity, including its symbol, stationery, administrative forms, vehicles, packaging, and building signs, and is still referred to today as a benchmark in the area of corporate design programs.

PAUL RAND AND WESTINGHOUSE

1960

WESTINGHOUSE
CORPORATE IDENTITY PROGRAM
Pittsburgh, Pennsylvania, USA

Paul Rand (1914–1996), Designer
Brooklyn, New York, USA

One primary example of early modernist thinking in graphic design and the built environment is evident in the corporate identity program developed for Westinghouse by Paul Rand (1914–1996) with Eliot Noyes (1910–1977), renowned architect and industrial designer, in the early 1960s. Donald C. Burnham (1915–2004), president of Westinghouse, introduced the program's new graphic style guide by stating that both Noyes and Rand ". . . had a real influence on our logotype, our advertising, our

graphics, our architecture, our packaging . . . leading Westinghouse toward good design across the board." The *Westinghouse Graphic Style Guide* was an informational and organizational benchmark in early-twentieth-century graphic identity programs, since it was one of the first design documents to illustrate building-mounted and freestanding letters, logotypes, and signs, as well as discuss the effective selection of a sign type that was appropriate to specific styles of architecture.

Rand was a graphic designer, author, and educator who shaped and influenced the course of twentieth-century American graphic design. With a career spanning more than sixty years, his work, writings, and teaching educated and inspired generations of graphic designers worldwide. He was educated at Pratt Institute, Parsons School of Design, and the Art Students League under George Grosz (1893–1959), a German émigré artist well known for his expressive drawings of Berlin life in the 1920s.

During the 1960s, Rand created some of the world's most memorable and enduring corporate identities, including IBM, UPS, Cummins Engine, ABC, and Westinghouse. At the time, Westinghouse was one of America's largest corporations with offices and plants throughout the world. It developed and manufactured transistors, power generation equipment, electronics, and atomic reactors for the needs of the modern era, yet its corporate logotype was conceived at the turn of the century by its founder, George Westinghouse (1846–1914). It was a block-style *W* framed in a circle and the word *Westinghouse* with a bold, lozenge-shaped bar directly underneath the *W*.

Although it was frequently updated, none of its iterations were any more modern or communicative than the original. Rand's solution—a circle framing a W, the points of which were topped with three dark circles referencing the

appearance of an electronic circuit board, and with a black lozenge underscore (a remnant from the old logotype).

Rand did not foresee the potential of the logotype when he first designed it, but the possibilities for bringing it to life became perfectly clear in the animated signs of 1962, when it first appeared on two huge electronic billboards—one in Pittsburgh and the other along the Long Island Expressway approach to New York City.

The Pittsburgh-located Westinghouse sign was a large, animated, electric billboard advertising the Westinghouse Electric Company and well known for the numerous combinations in which its individual elements could be illuminated. It was mounted on top of the WESCO (Westinghouse Electrical Supply Company) building in downtown Pittsburgh near Three Rivers Stadium on the banks of the Allegheny River. It consisted of 9 repetitions of the familiar

circle *W* logotype. Each circle was 18 feet (5.5 m) in diameter and divided into 10 sections—the top and bottom of the circle, the 4 diagonal strokes of the *W*, the 3 dots above the *W*, and the bar below.

Collectively, the entire billboard was composed of 90 individual elements, illuminated with argon and mercury vapor discharge tubing, and fitted on a 200-foot (61 m) aluminum structural grid. The billboard was computerized and programmed to generate the maximum number of graphic patterns and lighting combinations and sequences.

The Westinghouse billboard was demolished in 1998 when the WESCO building was razed to make way for PNC Park, the home of the Pittsburgh Pirates baseball team, but still remains a memorable historical beacon that was an integral part of the Pittsburgh skyline in the early 1960s.

CHERMAYEFF & GEISMAR AND CHASE MANHATTAN BANK

1960

CHASE MANHATTAN BANK
CORPORATE IDENTITY PROGRAM
New York, New York, USA
Chermayeff & Geismar Associates (est. 1957), Designers
New York, New York, USA

In the fall of 1960, the Chase Manhattan Bank began using their new corporate symbol—a simple octagon that is still in use today as the primary visual focal point of the JPMorgan Chase worldwide brand. Created by the design firm Chermayeff & Geismar Associates (est. 1957), it is one of the first corporate symbols to rely solely on an abstract modernist form and subsequently became a major influence on the widespread adoption of nonrepresentational and nonfigurative corporate identities throughout the modern business world since its introduction more than fifty years ago.

Ivan Chermayeff (b. 1937), with his partner Tom Geismar (b. 1931), have created some of the most memorable and recognizable images and identities of the twentieth century. Chermayeff was born in London, England, the son of the distinguished architect and educator Serge Chermayeff (1900–1996). He studied at Harvard University, Illinois Institute of Technology (IIT), and Yale University's School of Art and Architecture. In the early 1950s, he worked as a record album cover designer for CBS Records as well as an assistant to Alvin Lustig (1915–1955; see page 125). Geismar was born in Glen Ridge, New Jersey; studied concurrently at Brown University and Rhode Island School of Design; and worked for the U.S. Army's Exhibition Unit before pursuing his graduate degree at Yale University's School of Art and Architecture. Following their graduation, Chermayeff and Geismar moved to New York City to start their own design consultancy firm.

Since the early 1960s, Chermayeff & Geismar Associates has been at the forefront of the practice of corporate identity in the United States. Founded by Chermayeff, Geismar, and Robert Brownjohn (1925–1970), who subsequently left the partnership in 1960, their firm quickly became well known for their progressive and innovative approach to design problem-solving. They were masters in combining their background and training in modernist ideals with the visual language of the postwar era. Their early work explored a remarkable integration of type and image combined with expressive, intelligent, and literate visual storytelling.

In the past fifty years, Chermayeff & Geismar Associates have created more than 100 corporate identity programs for businesses worldwide, including Mobil (1964; see page 147), Xerox, PBS, NBC, Univision, Viacom, the Smithsonian, and *National Geographic*.

In 1959, the bank's chairman, David Rockefeller (b. 1915), selected Chermayeff & Geismar Associates to develop a contemporary and universal graphic symbol to reflect Chase Manhattan Bank's increasing global presence and to accompany the bank's new world head-quarters under construction in Lower Manhattan's Financial District—One Chase Manhattan Plaza—a modernist, 60-story (248 m) glass and anodized aluminum curtain-walled office building designed by Gordon Bunshaft (1909–1990), design partner at Skidmore Owings & Merrill (est. 1936).

At the time, the bank was using an ineffective symbol that was an amalgamation of related graphic elements and illustrative forms from their main heritage banks—the Bank of Manhattan Company and Chase National Bank—which had merged five years earlier to form Chase Manhattan Bank.

Chermayeff & Geismar created a nonrepresentational, geometric form that was simple, memorable, and timeless. The nonfigurative, graphic form is constructed of four rectangular, truncated wedges rotating around a central ground of an inner white square, creating an octagon. It was one of the first modern corporate icons to forgo reliance upon figurative interpretations, pictographic representations, or typographic solutions and immediately became a prototype for future corporate identity programs. The octagon was introduced in November 1960 to coincide with the completion of One Chase Manhattan Plaza and is still used in all of the bank's advertising, publications, stationery, and building signs.

ALEXANDER GIRARD AND LA FONDA DEL SOL

1961

LA FONDA DEL SOL RESTAURANT
New York, New York, USA
Alexander Girard (1907–1993), Designer
New York, New York, USA

Alexander Girard (1907–1993) is considered to be one of the most innovative and expressive designers of the twentieth century. Born in 1907 in New York City and raised in Italy, he studied at the Royal Institute of British Architects in London and then at the Royal School of Architecture in Rome. In 1932, he returned to New York City and opened his first architecture and interior design office.

By 1937, Girard moved to Detroit, where he continued his design practice. In 1949, he organized, designed, and curated "For Modern Living," a landmark exhibition at the Detroit Institute of Arts that comprised an array of objects from dog leashes and sunglasses to glassware, silver, and furniture displayed in site-specific room installations designed by modernists Alvar Aalto (1898–1976; see page 110); Eero Saarinen (1910–1961); Florence Knoll (b. 1917); George Nelson (1908–1986); and Charles (1907–1978) and Ray Eames (1912–1998).

From 1952 to 1973, Girard was the director of design for Herman Miller's textile division. He collaborated with leading Americans designers and influenced the fundamentals of modern interior, furniture, textile, and graphic design, as well as the way they were conceived and used throughout the United States and the rest of the world. He injected uninhibited color and visual playfulness to his work by referring to the handicrafts and folk art of countries like Mexico and India for inspiration. This inspired Girard to develop a new method of coloring and patterning that proved to be a long-lasting counterpoint to American modernist architecture.

One of his greatest contributions was his groundbreaking La Fonda del Sol restaurant at New York City's Time-Life Building, designed by Harrison, Abramovitz & Harris (est. 1941)

in 1959. At the time of its opening in 1961, it was the most completely integrated restaurant design in New York City.

The interior was rough, adobe-like white plaster walls punctuated with vibrant-colored niches displaying folk art and featured typographic wall murals composed of eclectic letterforms communicating the food offerings at the restaurant, as well as more than 80 different Sun motifs designed by Girard and found throughout the restaurant's interior. In addition to the interior, he designed every other detail of the restaurant, including menus, matchbooks,

tableware, furniture, uniforms, and the ceramic floor and wall tiles.

In many ways, Girard's design for La Fonda del Sol is a reinterpretation of Bauhaus (1919; see page 75) principles for a new, humanistic world. His solutions synthesized traditional handicrafts and materials with modernist forms, colors, textures, patterns, and typography—all set within a contemporary urban setting. La Fonda del Sol also symbolized a multicultural aesthetic that was groundbreaking for its time and extremely influential for future generations of architects and graphic designers.

MOBIL OIL AND
THE SUBURBAN LANDSCAPE

1964

MOBIL OIL SERVICE STATION
United States
Chermayeff & Geismar Associates (est. 1957), Designers
New York, New York, USA

In the 1950s and 1960s, Mobil Oil had to confront a new and critical issue that impacted their current graphic identity and brand. As more and more Americans migrated to the suburbs, oil companies such as Mobil realized that building of their service stations was being prohibited in new residential communities due to the less-than-graceful physical appearance of their retail outlets, long noted for visual chaos and clutter.

Recognizing this problem, Mobil commissioned Chermayeff & Geismar Associates (est. 1957) to revamp their entire graphic identity and to make their facilities and products more visually attractive and appealing to the modern American family now living in the suburbs.

First, they redesigned the logotype for Mobil in a geometric, sans-serif typeface based on Paul Renner's Futura (1927) specifically designed for the corporation and based on a circle and cylinder motif found throughout the design program earlier established by designer Eliot Noyes (1910–1977). Chermayeff & Geismar then reinforced this visual trademark by emphasizing the simplicity of the lowercase o (a pure geometric circle) of the logotype by coloring it bright red, the primary corporate color of the new graphic design program.

One of the critical components attributed to the success of this new comprehensive design program was that the new graphics were fully integrated to the new station architecture. Mobil's new logotype, which emphasized the *o* in their brand name, became the key element to the new program. Mobil's traditional symbol, the flying red Pegasus, was simplified graphically, framed in a white disk, and retained to give additional color, personality, and history to Mobil stations and products worldwide.

NEW YORK WORLD'S FAIR

1964

NEW YORK WORLD'S FAIR
Flushing, Queens, New York, USA

various designers and architects

The 1964 New York World's Fair was the third major world's fair to be held in New York City and hailed as "universal and international." Although it was best remembered as a showcase of mid-twentieth-century American culture and technology, twenty-four countries such as Spain, Vatican City, Japan, Mexico, Sweden, Austria, Denmark, Thailand, Philippines, Greece, and Pakistan also had presences at the fair.

It was located at Flushing Meadows Corona Park in the borough of Queens, which was also the site of the 1939 New York World's Fair and was one of the largest world's fairs ever to be held in the United States with a total area of 1 square mile (2.6 sq. km). The fair ran for two six-month seasons (April to October) in 1964 and 1965.

The symbol and physical centerpiece of the fair was a 12-story-high, three-dimensional stainless steel representation of the earth called Unisphere. Designed by American civil engineer and landscape architect Gilmore D. Clarke (1892–1982) and donated by United States Steel Corporation, it is the world's largest global structure, rising 140 feet (42.7 m). Built on the same structural foundation that supported the iconic Perisphere of the 1939 New York World's Fair (see page 109), the Unisphere was centered in a large, circular reflecting pool, accurately tilted at an angle of 23.5 degrees and surrounded by a series of water-jet fountains designed to obscure its tripod pedestal, reinforcing an appearance as if it is floating in space. Its stainless steel framework formed longitudinal and latitudinal lines with continents and large islands raised in steel mesh panels. National and state capitols were identified with colored blinking lights.

The most notable of the fair's pavilions was the egg-shaped IBM Pavilion designed by Eero

Saarinen (1910–1961), which contained a nine-screen film presentation conceived by Charles (1907–1978) and Ray Eames (1912–1998), the Chrysler Pavilion designed by George Nelson (1908–1986), the New York State Pavilion designed by Philip Johnson (1906–2005), and the Time Capsule Pavilion designed by Eliot Noyes (1910–1977).

In 1961, renowned American rationalist architects and designers Saarinen and Eames

started conceptualizing an exhibition pavilion to represent the IBM Corporation at the 1964 New York World's Fair. The IBM Pavilion, one of the most popular exhibitions at the fair, included a giant 500-seat grandstand that was hydraulically lifted up more than 50 feet (15.3 m) into an "egg-form" rooftop theater. There, a nine-screen film presented the inner workings of a computer to attendees of the fair. There were also demonstrations on handwriting recognition with a mainframe computer running a program to look up what happened on a particular date that a person wrote down—the first interaction for many with a computer. The Ovoid Theater, one of the main components of the pavilion, was one of the most unusual and provocative forms at the fair due to its shape, its raised placement off the ground, and its unique use of the IBM logotype, which appeared to be an embossed pattern fully integrated to the theater's facade.

The New York State Pavilion, a reinforced concrete and steel structure which supported the largest cable suspension roof in the world, played host to the fair as an open-air pavilion that consisted of an elliptical structure called the "Tent of Tomorrow," an orientation theater dubbed "Theaterama," and a grouping of three varied-height observation towers. Designed by influential modernist architect Philip Johnson (1906–2005), the pavilion contained the fair's

tallest structure and observation deck at 226 feet (68.9 m), as well as a large-scale terrazzo graphic representation of a Texaco road map of New York State on the main floor of the pavilion.

The most notable of the fair's pavilions was General Motors Corporation's Futurama—a show in which visitors seated in moving chairs glided past detailed scenery showing what life

continued on page 150

might be like in the "near future." It proved to be the fair's most popular exhibit with nearly 26 million people taking the journey into the future during the fair's two-year run.

The fair is also well remembered as the venue Walt Disney (1901–1966; see page 130) used to test, design, and perfect his newly conceived system of "Audio–Animatronics"—a combination of sound, mechanical electronics, and computers that controlled the movement of lifelike robots to act out scenes. The Walt Disney Company designed and created several shows at the fair.

In the "It's a Small World After All" attraction at the Pepsi-Cola Pavilion, animated dolls and animals frolicked in a spirit of international unity as fairgoers traveled on a boat ride around the world.

General Electric sponsored the "Carousel of Progress," in which the audience was seated in a revolving auditorium and viewed an audio–animatronics presentation of the progress of electricity in a typical American home.

Ford Motor Company presented Disney's "Ford Magic Skyway," which was the second most popular exhibition at the fair. It utilized Ford cars in an early prototype of what would become the People Mover ride system to move the audience through scenes featuring life-size audio–animatronics dinosaurs and cavemen.

The 1964–1965 New York World's Fair was attended by 51 million people and best remembered as a testament of American ideals and optimism in the mid-twentieth century.

CBS AND BLACK ROCK

THE POSTWAR WORLD 1950–2000

1965

**CBS HEADQUARTERS
CONSTRUCTION BARRICADE
AND SIGN PROGRAM**
New York, New York, USA

Lou Dorfsman (1918–2008), Designer
New York, New York, USA

In the 1960s, most major metropolitan cities throughout the world were in danger of becoming an urban oasis of innocuous aluminum and glass architectural structures. All of that changed in 1965 when a new headquarters building for the Columbia Broadcasting System (CBS), designed by the modernist architect Eero Saarinen (1910–1961) with interiors by Florence Knoll (b. 1917), was completed in New York City.

The 38-story (149.4 m) building, dubbed "Black Rock" due to its imposing appearance created by its massive Canadian black granite–clad facade, columns, and spandrels, conveyed an imposing, rocklike solidity that was extremely different from the majority of the glass-curtain walled buildings being built at that time. The building is the only skyscraper designed

by the Finnish-born Saarinen, designer of other well-known modernist structures including the TWA Terminal at Kennedy International Airport (1956), the St. Louis Gateway Arch (1960), the main terminal of Dulles International Airport (19), and the Vivian Beaumont Theater at Lincoln Center (1965).

Frank Stanton (1908–2006), then president of CBS, was determined that the visual character of the interior and exterior graphics for the new headquarters be equally elegant and distinctive as its architecture. Stanton gave Lou Dorfsman (1918–2008) the task of meeting this need as well as adding a critical and much-needed graphic design nuance to their new building that had not been achieved in any other headquarters building prior to this.

Following the completion of his undergraduate education at Cooper Union in 1939, Dorfsman worked as an exhibit designer for the U.S. Army until 1946, when he joined CBS under the guidance of William Golden (1911–1959), art director of the organization for more than two decades and graphic designer of one of the most universally recognizable trademarks of the era—the iconic CBS eye symbol. In 1951, Dorfsman was appointed art director for CBS Radio and eight years later succeeded Golden as vice president and creative director for the entire CBS Broadcast group.

Throughout his forty-five-year career at CBS, Dorfsman was the driving force and mediator for all visual forms at CBS, from print advertising, on-air graphics, and corporate identity to the sign program and graphics for the new headquarters building.

Initially, when the building was just an excavated corner along midtown's Avenue of the Americas, Dorfsman enclosed the construction site with a clear Plexiglas wall, rather than the traditional plywood fencing with peepholes, allowing passers-by to look in at any time to see

continued on page 152

CBS and Black Rock, continued

the progress of the new building. Loudspeakers located intermittently along the perimeter of this transparent wall informed the public about the future home of CBS and provided periodic CBS news reports.

As the building construction rose above sidewalk level, the Plexiglas wall was replaced with a protective walkway for pedestrians.

While this requirement was a New York City building code regulation, Dorfsman saw it as another creative opportunity that immediately became an informative, entertaining, and extremely memorable exhibitlike experience for the public. Instead of constructing the typical structure of scaffolding and painted plywood planking, he created a passageway consisting of thirty rear-illuminated panels, each equipped with a recess for a telephone, and that provided space for a series of special CBS promotions— the first was devoted to historic news broadcasts, the second promoted the summer's presidential nominating conventions, and the third previewed the new CBS fall program schedule.

For the building's sign program, Dorfsman brought a new level of visual quality and integrity to a corporate headquarters environment by reconsidering the importance and relationship of typography to all architectural forms and surfaces. He designed all aspects of typographic information found on the building's exterior, as well as within the building's interior, with a resolute consistency, rigor, and restraint.

Dorfsman collaborated with Freeman Craw (b. 1917), a major twentieth-century figure in the creation of comprehensive visual identity programs for some of the world's leading companies, on two proprietary typefaces for the new building. They redrew the typeface Didot, a seventeenth-century modern serif, and renamed it CBS Didot; as a supporting typeface, they designed a sans-serif gothic and

named it CBS Sans. CBS Didot was used for the bronze CBS logotype over the building's entrance doors, as well as for all interior sign requirements such as the identification of floor numbers, room numbers, directories, departmental and executive personnel names, mail chutes, fire alarm boxes, clock faces, and even exit signs. Every typographic element in and on the building relied solely upon one of these two new typefaces unifying the overall identity of this new corporate architectural symbol of the modernist era.

The CBS Building was the first project of the modernist era to achieve a "total design" through graphic design and architecture, all in the name of corporate image making. It quickly became a defining symbol for the company and for its continued commitment to excellence.

LOU DORFSMAN, HERB LUBALIN, AND GASTROTYPOGRAPHICALASSEMBLAGE

1965

**CBS HEADQUARTERS CAFETERIA MURAL
OR GASTROTYPOGRAPHICALASSEMBLAGE**
New York, New York, USA

*Lou Dorfsman (1918–2008), Herb Lubalin (1918–1981),
Designers*
New York, New York, USA

In September 1965, an employee cafeteria–lounge opened on the twentieth floor of CBS's new headquarters building in New York City. On the entire eastern wall of this public space was a seminal example of graphic design in the built environment—a 40-foot- (12.2 m) long by 8 ½-foot- (2.6 m) high typographic tour de force conceived and designed on an epic scale over a six-month period by CBS vice president and creative director Lou Dorfsman (1918–2008).

The *Gastotypographicalassemblage*, as Dorfsman called it, was devoted to the subject of food and based on an enlarged printer's job case—a wooden drawer composed of dozens of various-size compartments allowing the printer to sort fonts by letterform, with samples of metal and wood type. In this case, it would be multiple lockups of words and objects related to food.

This three-dimensional collage was organized in nine separate panels; words were jig-sawed out of thick pine wood, and blank spaces were filled with sculpted food items and culi-nary props. Most of its panels were composed in various typefaces totaling approximately 1,450 letterforms and spelling out culinary possibili-ties such as dill, banana, fudge, pumpernickel, hasenpfeffer, pizza, pâté de foie gras, and so on. The entire monochromatic assemblage was spray-painted in opaque white enamel. The only variations of color and texture that occurred along the expansive composition was a series of small figurative, sculptural, food-related items and utensils—a row of plastic bagels, a hero sandwich made out of wax, a composition of tin cans, a pair of wooden feet crushing a cluster of grapes, and a frying pan with a plastic egg.

Dorfsman collaborated with his longtime friend and colleague Herb Lubalin (1918–1981) and Tom Carnase (b. 1939), who were both responsible for refining the detail design of each typographic-based panel. Lubalin was a legend-ary art director and typographic master who brought humor, sensuality, and an expressive modernist flair to every letterform in his work. Born in Brooklyn, New York, he attended Cooper

Union, where he began his love affair with calligraphy, letterform, and formal typography. Immediately following his graduation in 1939, he joined the advertising agency of Sudler & Hennessey (later Sudler, Hennessey & Lubalin) as an art director. In 1964, he left the agency to start his own graphic design firm, where he ultimately worked in a broad range of areas including advertisements, editorial design, trademarks, typeface design, posters, packag-ing, and publications. In 1969, he and Carnase formed Lubalin & Carnase.

Throughout his career, Lubalin always treated space and surface as his most valuable visual communication tools. One designer noted that his work reminded him of a Claude Debussy quote—"music is the space between the notes." Lubalin embraced typographic characters as both visual and communicative forms—forms that became figurative and picto-rial and that invoked, informed, and ultimately

continued on page 154

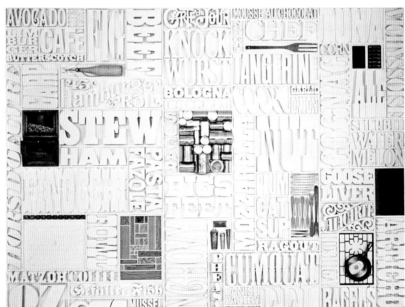

Lou Dorfsman, Herb Lubalin, and
Gastrotypographicalassemblage, continued

engaged the viewer. Rarely have complex typographic arrangements been so dynamic and so unified. The traditional rules and practices of typography were always abandoned for a more nontraditional and humanistic approach that made him a typographic genius.

Gastotypographicalassemblage's overall composition, bas-relief appearance, its popular content, and restrained treatment, as well as its unique presence within a modernist corporate headquarters environment, reinforced the wall mural's direct relationship in style, content, and theme to contemporary developments in sculptural assemblages by contemporary American artists such as Louise Nevelson (1899–1988) and Joseph Cornell (1903–1972), as well as the pop art movement that followed it in the coming years.

JOHN MASSEY AND
THE ART OF THE BANNER

1965

1966

THE MUSEUM OF MODERN ART
EXTERIOR BANNERS
New York, New York, USA

John Massey (b. 1931), Designer
Chicago, Illinois, USA

Born in 1931, John Massey studied fine art
in Hartford's Trinity College and editorial
illustration at the Chicago Academy of Fine
Arts. He then majored in advertising design
at the University of Illinois at Champaign–Ur-
bana, admittedly not knowing at the time what
advertising design was until his senior year
when he attended the 1953 Aspen International
Design Conference as a student intern and
met pioneering Swiss Style modernists Armin
Hofmann (b. 1920; see page 178) and Josef
Müller-Brockmann (1914–1996; see page 137).
This experience proved to be one of the most
influential of Massey's life and career.

Following that pivotal meeting, Massey
embraced Hofmann and Müller-Brockmann
as role models and immersed himself in the
history, principles, and challenges of advanced
modernist design thinking and practice. After
his graduation in 1954, he became a book
designer, then art director, at the University of
Illinois Press where Ralph Eckerstrom (1920–
1996) was its design director. Eckerstrom joined
Container Corporation of America (CCA) in 1957
as its director of advertising, design, and public
relations. In 1961, Massey followed as manager
of advertising and design, and then as Eckerstrom's replacement when he retired in 1964.

In 1983, Massey ended his tenure at CCA
and established an independent graphic design
consultancy, John Massey Inc., with clients that
included the Tribune Company in Chicago, The
Chicago Community Trust, American Library
Association, American Planning Association,
and Herman Miller.

His memorable work for New York City's
Museum of Modern Art and the Chicago Civic
Centre reflects his career-long interest in con-

CIVIC CENTER PLAZA EXTERIOR BANNERS
Chicago, Illinois, USA

John Massey (b. 1931), Designer
Chicago, Illinois, USA

sidering fine art and applied art as one singular
pursuit. Massey summarized this approach by
stating that "graphic design must satisfy the
problem it was conceived and planned to solve,
but it can achieve a life of its own, transcend-
ing the assignment. This autonomous life is
achieved because the creator imbues it with

a spirit." This spirit of melding art and graphic
design is nowhere better represented than in his
banner programs for these public institutions.

His abstract compositions of geometric
shapes and forms, combined with his use of
primary colors, used on these banners conveyed
light, movement, scale, and space and are
clearly based on the tenets of modernism—clarity, organization, and an affinity for communicating a visual story to a broad audience. A colleague and former staff member summarized
it best when he stated that Massey "created
abstract images to communicate with people."

BARBARA STAUFFACHER SOLOMON AND SEA RANCH

1966

SEA RANCH SUPERGRAPHICS
Sonoma County, California, USA
Barbara Stauffacher Solomon (b. 1928), Designer
San Francisco, California, USA

Barbara Stauffacher Solomon pioneered the use of Supergraphics* in 1966 with her work for Sea Ranch, a residential community in Sonoma County, California. Sea Ranch, noted for its distinctive contemporary architecture of simple timber-frame structures clad in wood siding and shingles, was designed by Charles Moore (1925–1993) of Moore, Lyndon, Turnbull & Whitaker and landscape architect Lawrence Halprin (1916–2009) in the vernacular style of the rugged coastline of northern California.

Born in San Francisco in 1928, Solomon initially studied fine art at the San Francisco Art Institute before traveling to Switzerland to study with renowned modernist graphic design and teacher Armin Hofmann (b. 1920; see page 178) at the Kunstgewerbeschule in Basel.

Supergraphics was the moniker given initially to an architectural movement in the 1960s and 1970s that gave architects (and, ultimately, graphic designers) the creative freedom to remove solidity, gravity, and even history by the application and manipulation of building surfaces. For most design historians, Sea Ranch represented the pivotal starting point of this movement; however, a precursor to this groundbreaking project occurred in 1962 with Robert Venturi's (b. 1925) Grand's Restaurant (1960; see page 183), where he integrated large-scale, mirror-image, stencil letterforms to the restaurant's interior.

The wall graphics at Sea Ranch were an obvious and direct extension of the architectural forms and profiles of the building architecture, as well as reflective of Solomon's rigorous, modernist education at Basel. They transformed the interior spaces with fundamental graphic design elements—bold stripes, geometric forms, vibrant primary colors, and truncated letterforms with obvious visual references to influential art movements of the time—pop art, op art, abstract expressionism, and the International Style. A critical characteristic to the success and brilliance of these supergraphics was that they moved up building surfaces, around corners, changing directions, making interior spaces appear larger and more engaging.

The art and architectural historian Sibyl Moholy-Nagy (1903–1971) summarized Solomon's influence on architecture and the built environment of this era best—"there are few things contemporary architecture needs more than a sensitive symbiosis with color, texture, and shape. There is a joyous element in Miss Stauffacher's art which lifts the spirit, and creates an environmental identity which is usually lacking in our Miesian heritage."

The term supergraphics is attributed to C. Ray Smith (1929–1988), architectural writer and critic, who described this new movement in architecture as "not a decorative device . . . but, a spatial experimentation."

UNIMARK AND
THE NEW YORK CITY SUBWAY SYSTEM

1966

NEW YORK CITY TRANSIT AUTHORITY
GRAPHICS STANDARDS
New York, New York, USA

Unimark International (est. 1965), Designers
New York, New York, USA

After completing his architectural studies in Milan and Venice in 1960, Massimo Vignelli (b. 1931) moved to the United States. In 1965, Vignelli became cofounder and design director of Unimark International, at the time, one of the largest graphic design consulting firms in the world, with more than 400 employees in forty-eight offices worldwide.

Unimark was created by Vignelli and Ralph Eckerstrom (1924–1996), former design director of Container Corporation of America

(CCA). The pair had first met in Chicago in 1958 while Vignelli was teaching at the Institute of Design at the Illinois Institute of Technology on a Moholy-Nagy Fellowship. Both men shared a similar design philosophy and were determined to bridge the gap between American marketing principles and European modernist graphic design. Unimark's philosophy was based on a disciplined and systemized approach for creating effective and rational mass visual communications for their clients; solutions that provided

the means by which an individual could implement any aspect of a graphic program in an efficient and effective manner. During the 1960s and 1970s, Unimark and Vignelli designed many of the world's most recognizable corporate identities and public information systems for clients such as American Airlines, Ford Motor Company, Knoll International, and the New York City Transit Authority.

In 1966, Unimark was asked to design comprehensive graphic standards for the New York City subway system—the oldest and largest complex networks of mass transit in the world. The system was originally formed in 1940, when the city's three independent railway lines merged—the Interborough Rapid Transit (IRT; see page 52), the Brooklyn–Manhattan Transit (BMT), and the Independent (IND). The current

continued on page 158

state of its public information sign system was in major disarray, since some of the individual railway lines dated back as early as 1885.

The new graphic standards were composed of four categories of signs—line identification, directional, informational, and station identification. The entire system initially used Standard Medium (also known as Akzidenz Grotesk, Gunter Gerhard Lange, 1896), an early sans-serif grotesque, and a precursor to the ubiquitous Helvetica (Max Miedinger, 1956), as the sole typeface used for all information requirements. Sign text was limited to black letterforms on a white background. Type sizes were limited to a set of three to reinforce a hierarchy of information throughout the system, and a modular set of sign panel sizes were employed for each of these categories, minimizing visual clutter and repetition throughout the subway stations. Signs were prefabricated and assembled like movable type to form sentences along suspended black metal channels. These main characteristics of the new system created an easy and cost-efficient method for a program earlier characterized for inefficiency and costly change-outs. A graphics standards manual was also produced, which functioned as the sole reference for the planning, design, and manufacture of all sign components in the system and was used extensively by graphic designers, architects, and contractors when planning the renovation and construction of subway stations system-wide.

Vignelli was also responsible for the redesign of the New York City subway system map, originally designed by George Salomon (b. 1920) in 1959. Influenced by the modernist approach taken by Henry Beck (1902–1974) with the London Underground Transport map (1933; see page 62), Vignelli rigorously maintained 45- and 90-degree lines that established the compositional framework for the map's color-coded graphic elements, layered with a simplified abstraction of the city's geography.

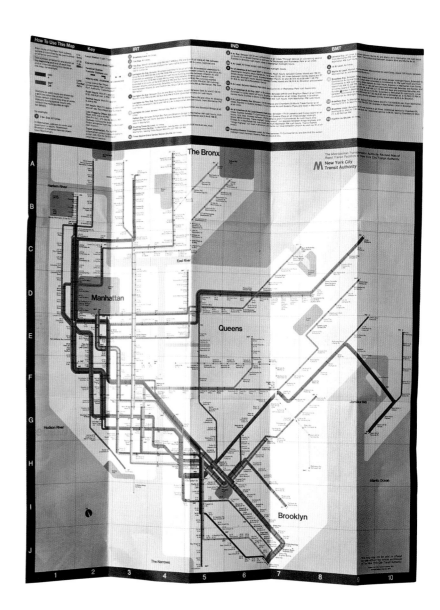

While the map gained wide attention when it was first introduced and became a renowned icon in modern graphic design history, it was not well received by the commuting public and was replaced by a more accurate and realistic version in 1979.

In 1971 following the closing of Unimark's New York offices, Vignelli and his wife Leila (b. 1934) cofounded Vignelli Associates, which continued a philosophy and approach firmly grounded in the modernist tradition and on simplicity through the use of fundamental elements and principles in all of their work. The firm's broad range of work and interests is based on a simple belief of Vignelli's: "If you can design one thing, you can design everything."

THE BOSTON T

1967

BOSTON TRANSIT AUTHORITY SIGN SYSTEM
Boston, Massachusetts, USA

Chermayeff & Geismar Associates (est. 1957), Designers
New York, New York, USA

In the mid-1960s, Boston's Massachusetts Bay Transportation Authority (MBTA) expanded to include both subway and surface transportation throughout the Greater Boston metropolitan area. This decision had an extraordinary impact on the City of Boston, as well as its surrounding cities and towns, which were now part of this new transportation system. The "T," as it came to be known, was one of the first combined regional transportation planning and operating agencies to be established in the United States. The newly created authority greatly expanded its services from the original fourteen cities and towns to encompass seventy-eight municipalities. Immediately, the T undertook a very aggressive advertising and marketing campaign to enhance its new image, to recapture lost ridership, build new customer usage, and expand its services with new equipment.

Cambridge Seven Associates (est. 1962), a multidisciplinary architectural and design firm led by architect Peter Chermayeff (b. 1936), was commissioned to redesign the overall system. Ivan Chermayeff (b. 1931) and Tom Geismar (b. 1937) of Chermayeff & Geismar Associates (est. 1957; see page 144), who were also design partners of Cambridge Seven Associates, were responsible for overhauling the overall graphic sign system.

As part of this system-wide expansion, the graphic designers created a new wayfinding sign system that introduced a simple, black sans-serif T framed in a black-bordered white circle as the overall system identifier. The four

continued on page 160

The Boston T, continued

system lines were renamed and color-coded (red, blue, orange, and green) rather than dentified by the names of their final station stops, providing flexibility for future system expansion.

A simplified diagrammatic system map comprising 45-degree diagonal lines and smooth transitional curves, reminiscent of Henry Beck's (1902–1974) seminal London Underground Transport map (1931; see page 62), also reflected the color-coding of the transit lines, which was consistently used on all sign elements throughout the system. Large-orientation wall maps of the surrounding neighborhoods were integrated into each station's architecture to guide exiting passengers. Helvetica Medium (1956), a sans-serif grotesque typeface designed by Max Miedinger (1910–1980) for the Haas foundry, was used on all system components, further unifying a typographic style throughout the extensive subway and bus system.

The new MBTA public-information sign system was introduced in 1965, with its first prototype station, Arlington Street, completed in October 1967.

RUDOLPH DE HARAK AND 127 JOHN STREET

1968

127 JOHN STREET ENTRANCE FACADE
New York, New York, USA

Rudolph de Harak (1924–2002), Designer
Culver City, California, USA

Designed by architects Emery Roth & Sons (est. 1947) in 1968, 127 John Street was a 32-story (97.6 m), multitenant commercial office building in New York City's financial district. The building's architecture was characteristic of the time period—a generic building mass clad in a standard glass and aluminum curtain wall with an open-floored structure for maximum flexibility for tenant build-out. Fortunately, the building came to be known as one of the most exciting projects of the early 1970s due to the innovative contributions of an independent-minded graphic designer—Rudolph de Harak (1924–2002).

While he had no formal training in graphic design, de Harak was a self-taught designer who honed his skills and vision over the years, as well as being strongly influenced by the work and writings of graphic design modernists Will Burtin (1908–1972), Gyorgy Kepes (1906–2001; see page 135), and Alvin Lustig (1915–1955; see page 125). Moving back East in 1950, de Harak subsequently started teaching at Cooper Union in 1952 and in 1958 opened his own graphic design studio. During the early 1960s, de Harak was immediately drawn to the rigor, simplicity, and rationalism of the International Style and European modernism, as well as the art movements of the era—abstract expressionism, op art, and pop art.

One of his most humanistic projects where he integrated these early influences was 127 John Street in Lower Manhattan, in which he literally transformed the identity of a faceless building into an unforgettable visual experience and an "atmosphere of pleasure, humor, and excitement for people."

Even before entering the building, a visitor was greeted by a huge digital clock measuring 40 feet (12.2 m) high by 50 feet (15.2 m) wide on a large blank wall of a building adjacent to the building's Water Street entrance. This kinetic supergraphic marked time by a series of rear-illuminated light boxes, 72 in all—12 for hours, 60 for minutes and seconds.

A structure composed of tubular stainless steel scaffolding, supporting brightly colored stretched canvas squares and platforms, served as protection and sun decks for passersby. At street level, love seats of welded, folded steel painted in bright, primary colors provided respite for pedestrians. A 12-foot (3.7 m) de Harak sculpture of a fishing lure was suspended above a small pool of water.

Entering the building, a corrugated steel tunnel illuminated by multiple rings of blue argon-gas-filled tubes guided visitors to the low- and high-rise elevators.

All identification signs throughout the public areas of the building were set in the sans-serif grotesque typeface Helvetica Medium (Max Miedinger, 1956) with the exception of building's exterior identification lettering. Here, "127 John Street" was composed of custom letterforms designed by de Harak and made up of individual 4-inch- (10 cm) diameter chromium spheres. It was the only instance of a sleek, shimmering material used by the graphic designer in contrast to the flat finished steel, textured canvas, and raw concrete evident throughout the exterior architecture.

The end result was a veritable visual playground that greatly enhanced the building architecture and ultimately redefined what a modern-day street-level entrance for a speculative office building could be.

LANCE WYMAN AND
THE MEXICO OLYMPICS

1968

MEXICO OLYMPICS GRAPHIC PROGRAM
Mexico City, Mexico

Lance Wyman (b. 1937), Designer
Kearny, New Jersey, USA

American graphic designer Lance Wyman (b. 1937) first gained worldwide recognition when he led an international design team for the graphic design system of the 1968 Summer Olympic Games in Mexico City.

Wyman majored in industrial design at Pratt Institute, graduating in 1960. He began his professional career as a staff designer at General Motors in Detroit and subsequently worked on the American Pavilion for the 1962 trade fair in Zagreb, Yugoslavia. In 1963, he moved back to New York City, where he joined

the firm of George Nelson (1908–1986) and designed the graphic elements for the Chrysler Pavilion at the 1964 New York World's Fair (see page 148).

For the Mexico City Games, he was determined that the overall graphic program reflect the cultural heritage of Latin America, as opposed to a direct design style or aesthetic. Following an extensive study of indigenous regional graphic motifs, ancient Aztec artifacts, Mexican folk art, regional arts and crafts, and adobe architecture, he ultimately focused on

two fundamental elements of graphic design for further development—line and color.

The core identity and logotype for the games was based on traditional iconographic forms found in Mexican culture, combined with 1960s op art, which created a vibrancy and unique visual language of concentric circles and lines. This parallel-line vocabulary was integrated with the official five-ring Olympic symbol and the number 68 for the games logotype and was also the basis of a custom display typeface that was applied to an extensive range of graph-

ics from tickets and postage stamps to giant color-coded balloons hovering over the arenas and radiating pavement patterns surrounding the Olympic stadium.

Color was also a key visual element to the overall system—decorative as well as functional. A bright color palette was used to codify all sporting events, motor and pedestrian routes, entry tickets, and seating sections for all venues. Wayfinding elements were vibrant, highly distinctive monoliths at various venues and displayed sets of color-coded pictograms used as universal communicators that eliminated cultural and language barriers. Routes to venues and events were also color-coded on the curbs of corresponding streets to assist attendees of the games.

The wayfinding components of the overall system consisted of modular, functional kit-of-parts with interchangeable elements that combined with directional and identification signs for mailboxes, telephones kiosks, water fountains, and so on.

Wyman stated that "graphic design became an important visual ambassador for the 1968 Mexico Olympic Games. It was the first time the games were hosted by a Latin American nation. In planning for the games, Mexico, an emerging third world nation, could not afford to make the extensive architectural statement made in Tokyo four years earlier. Graphic design contributed to the ambiance of the Mexican games and helped to make a meaningful visual impact for fewer pesos."

Following Wyman's success for the 1968 Olympics in Mexico City, he remained there for another four years, where he designed graphic programs for the Mexico City metro and the 1970 World Cup competition. In 1972, he returned to New York City and established his own graphic design practice.

The visual program for the 1968 Summer Olympic Games was a groundbreaking, innovative, and exuberant solution for the games, as well as for its locale, Mexico City, and quickly became a benchmark for future graphic designers of this worldwide event.

CROSBY/FLETCHER/FORBES AND A SIGN SYSTEMS MANUAL

1970

A SIGN SYSTEMS MANUAL
London, United Kingdom

Crosby/Fletcher/Forbes (est. 1965), Authors, Designers
London, United Kingdom

The groundbreaking reference book *A Sign Systems Manual* (Praeger Publishers) was the first publication written and designed by graphic designers that fully illustrated and described a simple, basic system for organizing, designing, constructing, and displaying signs, supported with examples of fully realized projects produced by some of the world's leading graphic design practitioners.

Crosby/Fletcher/Forbes was founded by Theo Crosby (1925–1994), Alan Fletcher (1931–2006; see page 218), and Colin Forbes (b. 1928) in 1962. Their clients included Pirelli, Cunard, Penguin Books, and Olivetti. The partnership evolved into the design consultancy firm Pentagram, when it was joined by Kenneth Grange (b. 1929) and Mervyn Kurlansky (b. 1936) in 1972.

A Sign Systems Manual was organized in eight sections—type alphabets, sign alphabets, measurement, scale, layout, organization, production, and sign programs.

The first part of the manual was a brief survey of typography—terminology, styles, proportions, measurement, scale—all essential for understanding how to effectively develop appropriate and functional lettering and typefaces on signs. Subsequent sections outlined alternative methodologies and systems for the layout, organization, design, and production of signs. The last section of the book showcased the work of other graphic designers, including Paul Rand (1914–1996; see page 142) for IBM, Kinneir Calvert Associates (est. 1964; see page 139) for British Rail, and Total Design (est. 1963) for Amsterdam's Schiphol Airport.

In the 1960s and early 1970s, environmental graphic design was in its infancy, and resources were extremely limited for graphic designers to thoroughly realize their work in the built environment. The authors clearly stated that the need for such a manual "arose from numerous inquiries from small manufacturers, public bodies, and students, who requested examples of schemes and design methods or advice on where they could obtain a comprehensive guide which could be of help. Apart from occasional articles in design journals and sign manuals produced exclusively for clients and therefore not usually obtainable, there appeared to be no such publication."

Although Crosby/Fletcher/Forbes never conceived this book to be a do-it-yourself manual, it provided the reader with practical insights to the basic principles of visual organization, specific skills and practices, and details necessary to conceive and produce a successful sign system. At the time it was published in 1970, *A Sign Systems Manual* was a much-needed design reference guide that proved extremely useful to many graphic designers now working in the modern built environment.

CORITA KENT AND BOSTON GAS COMPANY

1971

BOSTON GAS COMPANY MURAL
Boston, Massachusetts, USA
Corita Kent (1918–1986), Designer
Fort Dodge, Iowa, USA

One of the most prominent urban landmarks in the northeast United States is Boston Gas Company's gas tank mural, designed by Corita Kent (1918–1986).

Corita Kent (also known as Sister Mary Corita Kent) was an artist and educator who worked in Los Angeles and Boston. Her work, primarily silkscreen and serigraphy, contained messages of love and peace and was popular during the social and political unrest of the 1960s and 1970s.

She was admired by renowned architects and designers such as Buckminster Fuller (1895–1983), Charles Eames (1907–1978) and Ray Eames (1912–1998), and Saul Bass (1920–1996) for being one of the most innovative and controversial artists and designers of the era.

Kent was born Frances Elizabeth Kent in Fort Dodge, Iowa. At the age of eighteen, she entered the Roman Catholic order of the Sisters of the Immaculate Heart of Mary in Los Angeles, where she lived and worked from 1938 until 1968. She studied fine art at Otis (Otis College of Art and Design) and Chouinard Art Institute (California Institute of the Arts) before earning her undergraduate degree from Immaculate Heart College in 1941.

She was the chairperson of Immaculate Heart College's art department and completed postgraduate studies at the University of Southern California, where she received a master's degree in art history in 1951. After more than thirty years as a nun, she returned to private life in 1968, moving to Boston, where she devoted herself to creating art. For the next eighteen years, Kent created more than fifty commissions, in addition to more than 400 new editions of serigraphs. She initially gained critical acclaim and worldwide attention as a muralist for

her 40-foot- (12.2 m) high mural for the Vatican Pavilion at the 1964 New York World's Fair (see page 148).

In 1971, the Boston Gas Company commissioned Kent to design a mural for the exterior of a natural gas tank in the Dorchester neighborhood of South Boston. This storage tank was used for natural gas and was one of a few crucial storage facilities in the distribution system of Boston Gas, New England's largest natural gas company. Her 150-foot- (46 m) high, brightly colored, abstract rainbow swash painting immediately turned an industrial eyesore into a popular iconic landmark. Its scale and composition envelop the mass and form of the gas tank itself while simultaneously making it disappear and allowing the passerby to engage only with her graphic message.

During her later life, she was sometimes accused of being a "guerrilla with a paintbrush." Ultimately, she was a peace activist who created her own unique visual language for the betterment of the human spirit, and as with her work for the Boston Gas Company—for the betterment of the built environment.

THE "NEW" CONSTRUCTION BARRICADE

1971

PLAYBOY CLUB CONSTRUCTION BARRICADE
Chicago, Illinois, USA
Chermayeff & Geismar Associates (est. 1957), Designers
New York, New York, USA

1971

GEORG JENSEN STOREFRONT
CONSTRUCTION BARRICADE
New York, New York, USA
Herb Lubalin (1918–1981), Designer
New York, New York, USA

During the 1960s and 1970s, metropolitan areas across the free world were booming with building construction—New York City, Chicago, Los Angeles, London, Paris, and Tokyo all had major office buildings erected during this time period. As more and more commercial real estate development occurred, building owners realized that they needed to more effectively announce, promote, market, and ultimately brand their new real estate projects.

In the 1970s, temporary construction fences and barricades started to become communication vehicles for not only commercial exploitation, but for graphic designers to consider as new and dynamic surfaces for storytelling.

Some of the earliest and most innovative design solutions were created by Herb Lubalin (1918–1981; see page 153) and Chermayeff & Geismar Associates (est. 1957; see page 144), both based in New York City.

Lubalin was a legendary art director, graphic designer, and typographic master who brought humor, sensuality, and a modernist visual flair to every letterform and typographic element in his work. Throughout his career, he always considered space and surface his primary visual communication tools.

With his innovative solution for a George Jensen storefront in New York City, he easily made the transition from the two-dimensional printed page to the three-dimensional built environment. Here, he wrapped the construction barricade and lettering of the retailer's name in white vinyl sheathing, creating a provocative and curiosity-seeking story for any passerby to consider. Lubalin embraced typographic characters as both visual and communicative forms, forms that were meant to invoke, inform, and ultimately engage the viewer. The traditional rules and practices of typography were always abandoned for a more nontraditional and humanistic approach that made him a typographic and visual communication master.

Chermayeff & Geismar Associates visually reinterpreted Playboy's infamous bunny as a

1972

9 WEST 57 SOLOW BUILDING CONSTRUCTION BARRICADE
New York, New York, USA

Chermayeff & Geismar Associates (est. 1957), Designers
New York, New York, USA

series of broken vertical fragments displayed on angled, protruding fins for Playboy's first "membership-only" club on East Walton Street in downtown Chicago. These multiple, purely graphic images appeared abstract at first glance but came into focus as vehicles and pedestrians passed, engaging the public in an op-art-like game of "hide and seek."

The graphic designers relied upon a similar solution for the Solow Building Company's 9 West 57th Street construction barricade in New York City. This 280-foot- (85.3 m) long wall was fitted with projecting plywood fins painted red, white, and blue. Viewed from one direction, the wall read 9 West 57th Street; from the other

direction it read Solow Building Company. Both of these visually dynamic graphic treatments for building construction barricades were influenced by the work of Israeli-born artist Yaacov Agam (b. 1928), one of the modern era's leading pioneers of kinetic, optical art.

Lubalin and Chermayeff & Geismar redefined the function of the construction barricade as a new form of "canvas"—an archiectural surface that had a multitude of possibilities. It was viewed by moving vehicles and pedestrians and provided ever-shifting vantage points to ultimately imprint a building's identity in the public's minds long before building construction was completed.

OTL AICHER AND
THE MUNICH OLYMPICS

1972

**MUNICH OLYMPICS GRAPHIC IDENTITY,
PICTOGRAMS, AND WAYFINDING SIGN SYSTEM**
Munich, Germany

Otl Aicher (1922–1991), Designer
Ulm-Söflingen, Germany

Otl Aicher (1922–1991) was a type designer, graphic designer, author, and teacher who gained worldwide recognition during the post–World War II era for his corporate identity programs for international companies such as Braun (1954) and Lufthansa (1960). He was also well known for designing the sans-serif typeface Traffic (1974), which was used in the City of Munich and Munich Airport public transport systems. His best-known typeface, Rotis (1988), combined elements of serif, semi serif, sans serif, and semi–sans serif, and was produced in four weights—light, roman, bold, and black—with related italics for light and roman.

Aicher was born in Ulm, Germany, in 1922, where he later established his own graphic design studio, Buro Aicher, in 1947. He studied sculpture at the Munich Academy of Fine Arts and was a founding member with graphic designer Max Bill (1908–1994) of the Hochschule für Gestaltung (HfG) in Ulm, a design school for architects and product and graphic designers founded on the principles and practices of the Bauhaus (1919; see page 75).

One of his most prominent and influential commissions was the graphic identity, pictograms, and wayfinding sign system for the 1972 Summer Olympic Games in Munich. Aicher was commissioned to develop a comprehensive design program for all public information needs. He was also responsible for an extensive identification manual that defined all aspects of the design program, including design and

application standards for the use of the games' symbol—a radiant sunburst spiral, known as "the Universe," centered beneath the Olympiad rings and bracketed by two vertical lines. The humanist sans-serif Univers 55 (1957), designed by Adrian Frutiger (b. 1928; see page 172), was selected as the program's typeface, and a system of publication grids was also established. The bright color palette consisted of a partial spectrum composed of two blues, two greens, yellow, orange, and three neutral tones (black, white, and a middle-valued gray). Red was intentionally excluded so that a distinctive harmony of analogous colors was created, without a hint of aggression.

In addition to the program's graphic identity and wayfinding sign system, Aicher designed an extensive set of 180 pictograms for all sporting events, public services, and amenities. He based his groundbreaking design solution on a modular square grid divided by horizontal, vertical, and diagonal lines. Each pictogram, composed of a series of fundamental graphic elements—points and lines—was superimposed on a compositional framework, or grid, and emphasized the motion of the athletes and the diagrammatic indications of their equipment, ultimately communicating an immediate and universal identification that transcended language barriers. The full set of pictograms was widely used in printed graphics and identification signs throughout the games.

Aicher's approach to this set of pictograms reduced the number of design variables for each symbol to, as he called it, a "body alphabet" consisting of head, torso, arms, and legs. The result was a highly uniform graphic vocabulary for each sport—concise, efficient, and clear with an unmistakable visual dynamic inherent in each pictogram.

The pictograms were so well received by attendees that they were also used for the 1976 Summer Olympic Games in Montreal and for the 1980 Summer Olympic Games in Moscow, and subsequently established a valued precedent for the design of universal symbols, as well as comprehensive graphic programs for future Olympic Games.

TKTS TIMES SQUARE

1973

TKTS TIMES SQUARE THEATER CENTER
New York, New York, USA

Mayers & Schiff Associates (est. 1967), Architects
New York, New York, USA

New York City's TKTS (pronounced "Tee-Kay Tee-Ess," not "tickets") first opened in 1973 and was operated by the Theatre Development Fund, an organization that provided half-price day-of-performance tickets to the New York City's theater-going public.

The original TKTS pavilion in New York City's Duffy Square, the heart of the Great White Way (see page 48) and Broadway's Theater District, was designed by the architectural firm of Mayers & Schiff Associates (est. 1967)

and was inaugurated by Mayor John Lindsay (1921–2000).

At the time, New York City had allocated a capital budget of $5,000 to construct the pavilion, a sum that was obviously insufficient, even in the early 1970s. The city also had an operating budget for the pavilion that the building's architects used in an innovative manner to finance their design solution—a solution based on renting, rather than buying, the parts needed to construct the pavilion.

The pavilion was composed of a sales booth housed in a construction trailer punctured with multiple ticket-selling windows. Armatures wrapping around and over the construction trailer were made up of rented scaffolding components. White canvas panels were interwoven through the scaffolding, displaying large-scale, bright-red, sans-serif letterforms of the TKTS logotype. Foundations could not be dug under the sales booth due to the New York City subway located just below street level, so the architects used pile-driving test weights that were also rented to stabilize the structure.

For more than 25 years, this bold and visually striking pop-art-inspired landmark was a major focal point for theatergoers, as well as one of the most prominent and universally recognized typographic signs of New York City's Broadway theater district.

NUMBER 9

1974

NUMBER 9
Solow Building
New York, New York, USA

Chermayeff & Geismar Associates (est. 1957),
Designers
New York, New York, USA

The Solow Building at 9 West 57th Street in New York City was designed by Gordon Bunshaft (1909–1990), design partner at Skidmore Owings & Merrill (est. 1936), one of the largest and most successful architectural firms in the world, in 1974. It is located several hundred feet west of Fifth Avenue, between 57th and 58th Streets, and adjacent to several prominent neighbors including Bergdorf Goodman.

This 50-story (210 m) building has a distinctive concave vertical slope, giving it a "ski slope" appearance to passersby. A huge, sans-serif, bright red number 9 sits on the sidewalk in front of the building's entrance and appears to have come sliding down from the facade above. Designed by Ivan Chermayeff (b. 1937) of Chermayeff & Geismar Associates (est. 1957; see page 144), the 9 is constructed of ½-inch

(12 mm) plate steel and measures 10 feet (3 m) high and 5 feet (1.5 m) deep.

The scale, color, and placement of this novel three-dimensional numeral all contribute to its success over the last three decades as an overscaled, sculptural identifier for a prominent commercial office building, and as a timeless New York City landmark for New Yorkers and tourists alike.

HARPER & GEORGE

1974

**BRANIFF AIRLINES TERMINAL
ENVIRONMENTAL GRAPHICS
Dallas/Fort Worth International Airport
Dallas/Fort Worth, Texas, USA**

*Harper & George (est. 1963), Designers
New York, New York, USA*

Irving Harper (b. 1916), and Philip George (*dates unknown*) of Harper & George (est. 1963) were recognized in the 1970s for their dynamic and innovative use of color, pattern, and texture in the built environment. Well known for animating generic and bland architectural interiors, they often used flags, banners, and striking, colorful graphic compositions to enhance their projects.

Braniff International Airways was an American-based airline that operated from 1928 until 1982 primarily in the midwestern and southwestern United States, Mexico, South America, Panama, Asia, and Europe. During the 1960s, Braniff's senior management was determined to give the airline a more modern and attention-getting image that would appeal to a younger and more sophisticated clientele. Over the next fifteen years, Braniff worked with renowned American artists and designers such as Alexander Calder (1898–1976), Alexander Girard (1907–1993; see page 146), and Harper & George on this rebranding effort.

Plane exteriors were painted a single color, selected from a wide palette of bright hues. The new "jelly bean" fleet, as it was called at the time, consisted of bold colors such as primary red, beige, ochre, orange, turquoise, baby blue, medium blue, lemon yellow, and lime green.

In the early 1970s, Harper & George was commissioned by Braniff to redesign their airplane interiors and passenger terminals at various airports—Kansas City, Love Field (former Dallas airport), and Dallas/Fort Worth so that they would be more contemporary and appealing to the discriminating international traveler. In Kansas City, colorful banners of stainless steel and fabric hung from the ceilings, creating a continuous focal point and humanizing an otherwise cavernous and clinical-feeling interior public space. Bright and vibrant color schemes were introduced to all carpeting and upholstery, while textile-covered partitions with bold, graphic patterns divided the seating areas into intimate, private groupings. Even the luggage carousels were enlivened with rhythmic line-patterned supergraphics in bright, fluorescent-like hues.

Harper & George influenced future generations of architects, interior designers, and graphic designers in considering color, pattern, and texture as essential and engaging visual elements when realizing graphic design in the built environment.

ADRIAN FRUTIGER AND PARIS-ROISSY AIRPORT

1974

CHARLES DE GAULLE AIRPORT SIGN SYSTEM
Paris, France

Adrian Frutiger (b. 1928), Designer
Interlaken, Switzerland

Adrian Frutiger (b. 1928) is one of the most prolific typographers of the twentieth century and the designer of some of the most notable typefaces ever to be created during the modern era. He has created more than 175 typefaces, many of which have become notable fonts such as Univers (1957) and Frutiger (1976). He also was one of the first type designers to create type for film and photocomposition.

Frutiger has made an essential contribution to every typographic field in which he has worked. His other typefaces include Eqyptienne (1955), Serifa (1967), Iridium (1972), OCR-B (1968), and Centennial (1986). His adaptation of Univers for the IBM Composer (1966) revolutionized typewriting quality, and his exceptional improvement of typefaces for computers led to international standardization (1973) of his OCR-B typeface for optical character recognition.

As a young boy, he experimented with invented scripts and stylized handwriting as a rebellious response to the formal, cursive penmanship being enforced at the Swiss school he was attending at the time. At the age of sixteen, he began an apprenticeship as a compositor with an Interlaken lithographer, where he also learned woodcutting, engraving, letterpress, and calligraphy.

Between 1949 and 1951, Frutiger studied at the Kunstgewerbeschule (School of Applied Arts) in Zurich. In 1952, Charles Peignot (1897–1983) recruited Frutiger for Deberny & Peignot, one of the world's foremost type foundries in Paris. It was at Deberny & Peignot that Frutiger fully embraced the rationalist influences of the International Typographic Style and ultimately developed a typeface with remarkable visual uniformity and a flexible, integrated typographic system. He worked at the renowned foundry

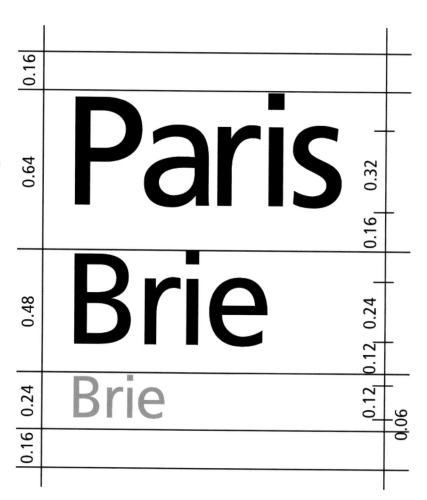

until 1962, the year he started his own graphic design studio in Arcueil, a Paris suburb.

The Charles de Gaulle Airport in Roissy—a suburb north of Paris—was at the time of its opening in 1968 France's largest international airport. Paul Andreu (b. 1938), the renowned French architect and designer of the new airport, commissioned the Swiss-born Frutiger to

design a new typeface for all signs and information displays throughout the airport, as well as establish the typographic criteria for its overall directional and wayfinding sign system.

Several years earlier, the RATP, Paris's public transport authority, had commissioned Frutiger to examine and improve the Paris Metro sign system. For this project, he had created a

version of his sans-serif Univers font—Metro (1973), with a set of capitals and numbers that would function optimally on white-on-dark-blue backgrounds in poor light. Based on the success of this project, the French airport authority approached him about this new commission.

Rather than relying upon one of his existing typefaces, Frutiger chose to design a new typeface that would fully meet the unique and demanding needs of the modern air traveler. Initially, Frutiger decided to develop a simple sans-serif typeface that made general use of its lowercase letterforms but also included initial capitals. His goal was to create a new sans-serif typeface that had the rational, clean profiles of Univers combined with the humanist characteristics of earlier-designed sans-serif typefaces. All signs within the system were dual language—French and English—and were based on thorough studies of letterspacing and character sizes at given distances to ensure optimum legibility and visual immediacy.

The result was an extremely distinctive and legible typeface that was an amalgamation of Univers tempered with the organic influences of Gill Sans (1927), a humanist sans-serif typeface designed by Eric Gill (1882–1940), Edward Johnston's (1872–1944; see page 62) typeface for the London Underground Transport (1916), and Roger Excoffon's (1910–1983) Antique Olive (1962). Originally named Roissy and completed in 1975, the typeface was renamed Frutiger when Mergenthaler Linotype released it in 1976 and subsequently was implemented throughout the new airport that same year.

While the typeface Frutiger is an obvious descendant of Univers, Frutiger wanted to explore new forms that would potentially redefine the sans-serif typeface. As a student at the Zurich School of Arts and Crafts, he had cut a sans-serif inscription in wood, which was subsequently published in 1951. Its letterforms were classical in profile and proportion and had a more humanistic appearance than the predominant sans-serif grotesques of the 1960s and 1970s, such as Max Miedinger's (1910–1980) Helvetica (1956). Frutiger has visual nuances derived from inscriptional lettering and old-style letterforms. Its ascenders and descenders are very prominent, and its counters are wide to easily distinguish letters from each other.

The resulting typeface is distinctive and extremely legible at various angles, sizes, and distances and was well suited for the needs of a modern public transportation facility such as the Charles De Gaulle Airport. Additionally, it is a typeface that possesses simple, warm, and accessible visual characteristics that immediately made it one of the most popular typefaces of the modern era.

AIGA SYMBOL SIGNS

1975

AIGA SYMBOL SIGNS
New York, New York, USA
Cook & Shanosky Associates (est. 1967), Designers
Princeton, New Jersey, USA

In the 1970s, a committee of graphic designers, under the auspices of the American Institute of Graphic Arts (AIGA), developed an extensive system of pictograms for the U.S. Department of Transportation called *Symbol Signs*. This set of passenger and pedestrian-oriented pictograms became the first U.S. symbol standard for airports, train stations, and other public transit facilities throughout the country. To encourage widespread adoption, the symbols were offered free of charge to any qualified users.

This landmark achievement represented the first time a cohesive and universal system of pictograms had been designed that communicated essential information across language barriers to international travelers in all bus stations, airports, railways, and ship terminals throughout the United States. It was also the first time a government agency (the U.S. Department of Transportation's Office of Facilitation) and a professional organization (AIGA) collaborated on a comprehensive design effort for the public good.

Prior to this effort, numerous civic and public organizations such as railways, airlines, and Olympic Games committees had developed sets of pictograms for use in guiding passengers, pedestrians, and visitors to transportation venues and international events. These efforts resulted in numerous well-designed graphic programs; however, none of them were suitable for the needs of U.S. travel facilities, nor did they address the needs of a diverse public made up of different ages and cultures.

Tom Geismar (b. 1931), partner of Chermayeff & Geismar Associates (est. 1957; see page 144) was invited to lead this effort by initially organizing a five-member committee of graphic designers—all with extensive experience in the design of symbols and signing. The group comprised Massimo Vignelli (b. 1931; see page 157), Seymour Chwast (b. 1931), Rudolph de Harak (1924–2002; see page 161), and John Lees (*dates unknown*).

Initially, a thorough process was undertaken to further guarantee optimum results. The Department of Transportation's Office of Facilitation and the AIGA committee members agreed upon an initial list of thirty-four messages they wanted graphically represented. Simultaneously, AIGA compiled an inventory of similar pictograms used at various times and locations throughout the world for further visual reference and evaluation. Following the committee's evaluation for clarity and effectiveness, a final set of pictograms was selected for adapting or redesigning and detailed design

Symbol Signs System

guidelines were established for subsequent refinement of each pictogram.

The actual task of designing the final set of pictograms in a cohesive and unified graphic style of consistent line, shape, weight, and form, based on the committee's analysis and findings, was completed by Roger Cook (b. 1930) and Don Shanosky (b. 1937) of Cook & Shanosky Associates (est. 1967). Cook and Shanosky followed these design guidelines and prepared drafts of each of the thirty-four symbol signs for committee review, testing, and final approval.

This final set of pictograms was released for public use in 1974; a supplemental set of 16 pictograms was subsequently developed by the same committee and graphic designers in 1979.

The project, as well as its designers, were recognized for Outstanding Achievement in Design for the Government of the United States of America in 1985 by President Ronald Reagan with one of the first U.S. Presidential Design Awards. Additionally, *AIGA Symbol Signs* are copyright free and have become the standard for off-the-shelf symbols in the reference catalogs of most U.S. sign companies.

PAGE, ARBITRIO & RESEN AND I. M. PEI

1975

NATIONAL AIRLINES TERMINAL SIGN PROGRAM
John F. Kennedy International Airport
Queens, New York, USA

Page, Arbitrio & Resen (est. 1966), Designers
New York, New York, USA

Page, Arbitrio & Resen (est. 1966) had its early beginnings as part of the internal graphic design department of renowned architect I. M. Pei & Partners (est. 1955) in New York City during the early 1960s. Charles "Don" Page (1917–2007) was an architect, graphic, and interior designer who joined Pei's office in 1961, where he became the head of its graphic design department. He remained with the firm until 1966 when he cofounded Page, Arbitrio & Resen with two other staff graphic designers from the I. M. Pei & Partners office—Dominic Arbitrio (b. 1931) and Ken Resen (b. 1934).

In the 1970s, Page, Arbitrio & Resen were involved in a wide range of design consultant work that included industrial design, corporate identity, annual reports, and environmental graphics. Two of their most important contributions to graphic design in the built environment are the building sign programs for the National Airlines Terminal at John F. Kennedy International Airport (1975) and the John Hancock Tower (1978) in Boston, with both buildings designed by I. M. Pei & Partners.

Due to their long-term working relationship with the I. M. Pei office, Page, Arbitrio & Resen were called in early in the architectural design of the National Airlines Terminal building—a 328-foot- (100 m) long by 30-foot- (9.1 m) high rectangular building capped with a large space-frame roof—which ultimately allowed their work to be as integral as possible to the building's modernist architecture.

For this project, the Pei office used broad strips of baked-enamel-finished white aluminum as trim throughout the building. These "sign bands" displayed large-scale typographic information that identified ticket counter func-

1978

JOHN HANCOCK TOWER SIGN PROGRAM
Boston, Massachusetts, USA

Page, Arbitrio & Resen (est. 1966), Designers
New York, New York, USA

tions, directions to amenities and departing gates, and information for exiting passengers. When an architectural surface was not available, freestanding or suspended sign bands were introduced throughout the terminal interior to display critical information.

Interior signs were set in the modernist sans-serif grotesque typeface Helvetica Medium (Max Miedinger, 1956) on painted white aluminum panels, identical to the architectural metal, color, and finish found in the building's interior architecture. All signs were dual language and color-coded; bright orange for English sign messages, black for Spanish sign messages.

Boston's landmark John Hancock Tower, a 62-story (241 m) monolithic glass skyscraper designed in 1978 by Henry Cobb (b. 1926), a founding partner of the architectural firm I. M. Pei & Partners, was the first commercial office building in the United States to introduce double-deck passenger elevators. While this type of vertical transportation system was an energy and core-space-saving measure at the time, it also demanded two-level loading of passengers and necessitated highly visible building signs to identify odd–and–even floor elevator service.

Page, Arbitrio & Resen's dramatic and colorful graphic design solution relied upon the introduction of yellow and red lobby and elevator graphics, which were greatly enhanced by their reflections seen in the polished stainless-steel-clad columns of the building's two-story lobby. Passenger elevators for odd floors, identified in primary yellow, were accessible only at street level; even floors defined by primary red were only accessible at mezzanine level. Both levels were connected by escalators for ease

of public access. White numerals and arrows on a colored wall directed the public from the escalators to the correct elevator bank. Elevator doors, cabs, and select core walls repeated the primary colors of red and yellow numerals. Visual clarity and immediacy were the obvious priorities in explaining this unique elevator system to the public.

The graphic designers also enlivened the cool, reflective sleekness of the building's interior public lobby by incorporating overscaled sans-serif numerals that read dramatically through the building lobby's street-level glass

facade, as well as reflected in the lobby's polished stainless steel clad columns. These 5-foot- (1.5 m) high Helvetica Extra Bold italic numerals were painted in epoxy enamel on existing core walls that were clad in black aluminum paneling.

Both projects by Page, Arbitrio & Resen exemplify the meaningful and fruitful collaborative process that started to occur in the mid-1970s between architects and graphic designers that achieved a seamless, appropriate, and integrated approach to graphic design in the built environment.

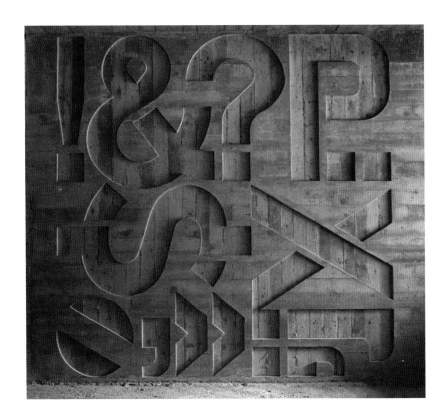

ARMIN HOFMANN AND DISENTIS

1975

DISENTIS SCHOOL MURALS
Basel, Switzerland

Armin Hofmann (b. 1920), Designer
Zurich, Switzerland

Armin Hofmann (b. 1920) began his career in 1947 as a teacher at the Allegmeine Gewerbeschule Basel School of Art and Crafts (later known as Schule fur Gestaltung or AGS) at the early age of twenty-six. He followed Emil Ruder (1914–1970), Swiss typographer, graphic designer, and educator, as the head of its graphic design department and was instrumental in developing the graphic design style known as the International Style or Swiss School.

For more than forty years, Hofmann devoted his life to teaching art, design, and the principles of visual perception and communications. His students' works are benchmarks of visual excellence, as well as the envy of students and teachers of graphic design worldwide.

His teaching methods and maxims were unorthodox and broad based, setting new standards that became widely known in design

education institutions throughout the world. His independent insights as an educator, married with his rich and innovative powers of visual expression, created a body of work enormously varied—books, exhibitions, stage sets, logotypes, symbols, typography, posters, sign systems, and environmental graphics.

Paul Rand (1914–1996; see page 142), one of the originators of the Swiss Style and a close friend and longtime colleague of Armin Hofmann, has described his contributions to the graphic design profession: "Few of us have sacrificed so much time, money and comfort for the sake of their profession as has Armin Hofmann. He is one of the few exceptions to Shaw's dictum, 'He who can, does; he who cannot, teaches.' His goals, though pragmatic, are never pecuniary. His influence has been as strong beyond the classroom as within it. Even those who are his critics are as eager about his ideas as those who sit at his feet. As a human being, he is simple and unassuming. As a teacher, he has few equals. As a practitioner, he ranks among the best."

While the majority of his print-related work is widely recognized for its modernist aesthetics and reliance on the fundamental elements

of graphic form—point, line, and shape—it also subtly conveys simplicity and complexity, and representation and abstraction. These same dynamic visual characteristics resonate in his graphic design work for the built environment. Over the course of his career, he has collaborated with Swiss architects on wall murals, ceiling frescoes, floor mosaics, theatrical sets, and public sculpture.

One seminal example is his wall relief murals for a high school in Disentis, Switzerland. While these murals primarily function as visual enhancements to an otherwise austere and sterile architectural environment, the altered direction of the wooden-panelized boards used to cast the concrete walls produced a vigorous, textured bas-relief that defined the large-scale sans-serif letterforms, numerals, and punctuation in an engaging and subtle manner. The final graphic solution was fully integrated to the building architecture, creating a timeless perfection of form and function.

JOHN FOLLIS AND ARCHITECTURAL SIGNING AND GRAPHICS

1979

ARCHITECTURAL SIGNING AND GRAPHICS
New York, New York, USA

John Follis (1923–1994), Author, Designer
Los Angeles, California, USA

John Follis (1923–1994) is considered by many to be one of the founding fathers of environmental graphic design. He was born in Pasadena, California, and studied under Alvin Lustig (1915–1955; see page 125) at the Art Center School (est. 1930) in Los Angeles, now known as Art Center College of Design.

From 1950 to 1960, he was the art director of *Arts & Architecture* (1929–1967) magazine—an American design, architecture, landscape architecture, and arts publication that played a significant role both in California's cultural history and in the development of American modernism. While it was the first American magazine to recognize the work of such twentieth-century notables as Hans Hofmann (1880–1966), Charles (1907–1978) and Ray Eames (1912–1988), Frank Lloyd Wright (1867–1959; see page 54), Hans Hollein (b. 1934), and Frank Gehry (b. 1929), it was also one of the first publications of its time to achieve a high standard of editorial graphic design, assisted in its early years by Alvin Lustig, Herbert Matter (1907–1984), and John Follis. In 1960, Follis left *Arts & Architecture* to start his own design consultant firm, John Follis & Associates.

His groundbreaking book, *Architectural Signing and Graphics* (Watson-Guptill Publications, New York), was, in 1979, the first comprehensive how-to reference book on an emerging design discipline—environmental graphic design. The book was organized in fourteen sections and covered topics such as human factors, project analysis and planning, design, bidding and documentation, construction engineering, installation and supervision, as well as twenty-five case studies that featured design solutions of leading graphic designers working in this new discipline. In his introduction, Follis outlined

the need for this book by writing "in an area of design which is growing and changing swiftly, there is a need to provide guidelines where none now exist. The intent is to establish these guidelines in the form of a process and methods that have been found to be successful and which are sufficiently flexible to be applicable to any project. Design is not art, nor is it science; it involves aspects of both. Design should be an effective blending of creative intuition, logical analysis, and technical knowhow. The result

of this synthesis can be signing and graphics programs that communicate efficiently while enhancing the architectural environment."

Architectural Signing and Graphics was a much-needed design reference book that proved extremely useful to many graphic designers for more than thirty years before it was replaced with several other publications that were more relevant with technologies and processes current with the demand and needs of our ever-evolving built environment.

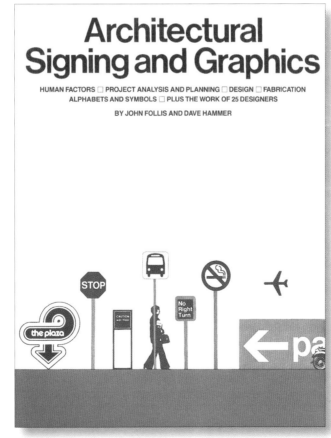

POSTMODERNISM AND BEYOND
1966–1995

At the onset of the worldwide information age and digital revolution, a new era in graphic design in the built environment began to
take form in the late 1960s and 1970s with the exploration of new
theories, tenets, and practices. In the latter part of the twentieth
century, modernism and the International Style began to wane in
favor of a new point of view—the postmodernist movement.

Postmodernism brought focus and value to freedom of expression and individualism. It represented the rejection of order and
clarity and what is "modern" for a more individualized approach to
style, aesthetics, and design. Its stylistic conventions ranged from
an amalgamation of diverse motifs and iconography, the use of
unconventional historicist references, and a freedom of expression
that was not possible or acceptable with modernist tenets that
grew out of the Bauhaus.

Early supporters of this movement included American writer
and activist Jane Jacobs (1916–2006), who criticized the "soulless-
ness of the urban environment" in her 1961 book *The Death and Life
of Great American Cities*, and American architect Robert Venturi
(b. 1925), whose 1966 dictum "Less is a bore" from his treatise
Complexity and Contradiction in Architecture (The Museum of Modern Art Press, New York) became an anthem for future generations
of graphic designers and architects.

Pop art, popular culture, new wave typography, the Memphis
style, retro design, and vernacular expression were also major influences on this movement and functioned as pluralistic counterpoints
to the now familiar world of modernism and objective rationalism.

In the early 1980s, American architects such as Michael
Graves's (b. 1934) Portland Building (1982) in Portland, Oregon, and
Philip Johnson's (1906–2005) AT&T Building (1984, now known as
the Sony Building) in New York City were seminal examples of early

postmodernism. These groundbreaking buildings were radical departures from the pervasive International Style; they illustrated the movement's preference for visual elements and references culled from history and reintroduced color, pattern, shape, and symbol to the built environment.

American architectural theorist Charles Jencks (b. 1939) described the postmodernist movement as "one half modern the other one as something different (which refers to the traditional style), linked with an attempt to communicate with a wide public and a dedicated minority . . ."

At the close of the twentieth century, postmodernism offered graphic design in the built environment opportunities for individualism and nonconformity, whereas modernism symbolized uniformity and conformity. Coupled with the widespread proliferation of new digital technologies, the possibilities in the new millennium for graphic design in the built environment became boundless.

VENTURI SCOTT BROWN AND ASSOCIATES

1967

GRAND'S RESTAURANT
Philadelphia, Pennsylvania, USA
Venturi Scott Brown and Associates (est. 1964),
Architects
Philadelphia, Pennsylvania, USA

Since the early 1960s, Robert Venturi (b. 1925) has challenged our existing assumptions about graphic design and the built environment. He has been a controversial critic of corporate modernism and elitist architecture and a proponent of graphic iconography found in the modern landscape. For many, his unorthodox approach marked the advent of the postmodernist era and redefined the course of contemporary graphic design and architecture. Venturi is an American architect, founding principal of

Venturi Scott Brown and Associates (est. 1964), and a major figure in twentieth-century architecture. Together with his wife and partner, Denise Scott Brown (b. 1931), he has helped shape the way architects and graphic designers think about architecture and experience the modern world.

Venturi attended Episcopal Academy in Merion, Pennsylvania, and studied architecture at Princeton University from 1947 to 1950. In 1951, he briefly worked at the architectural

offices of American modernist architects Eero Saarinen (1910–1961) in Bloomfield, Michigan, and Louis Kahn (1901–1974) in Philadelphia.

One of Venturi's first projects that explored the integration of graphic iconography with architectural form was Grand's Restaurant, completed in 1967 and located in Philadelphia. This project involved the renovation of two adjacent dilapidated row houses into a modest neighbor-

continued on page 184

Venturi Scott Brown and Associates, continued

1972

LEARNING FROM LAS VEGAS
Cambridge, Massachusetts

*Robert Venturi (b. 1925), with Denise Scott Brown
(b. 1931) and Steven Izenour (1940–2001)
Philadelphia, Pennsylvania, USA; Nkana, North
Rhodesia; New Haven, Connecticut, USA*

hood restaurant that catered to local students. In keeping with its purpose and limited budget, Venturi Scott Brown and Associates used conventional means and elements that took on new meaning when used in a new context.

On the restaurant's exterior, a porcelain-enameled sign band composed of large-scale stencil cut-out letterforms and a three-dimensional stylized graphic representation of a cof-fee cup directly above the entrance reinforced the dual physical identity of the building's entrance, as well as unified it as a total graphic and architectural expression. The sign, painted in two colors—blue and yellow—spanned the entire width of the storefront and was dramatically illuminated at night with letterforms appearing translucent white and the cup outlined in white neon tubing.

The graphic ornamentation of the interior walls consisted of giant yellow stencil letterforms spelling out "GRAND'S" painted on the plaster wall surfaces directly above the wainscoting of the booths.

Both of these simple typographic treatments greatly altered the overall identity and scale of the restaurant's facade and interior space, as well as reinforced Venturi's maxim "Less is a bore"—a counterpoint to architect Mies van der Rohe's (1886–1969) famous modernist dictum "Less is more."

Following the release of his first book in 1966, *Complexity and Contradiction in Architecture* (The Museum of Modern Art Press, New York), Venturi was hailed as a theorist and counterrevolutionary with radical ideas. That same year, he taught a series of design studios at the Yale School of Architecture in which he started to consider a set of new design principles based on a graduate student project that studied the archetypal American main street—the Las Vegas Strip.

The culmination of this study became his highly influential and widely read manifesto of

1978

**INSTITUTE FOR SCIENTIFIC INFORMATION
BUILDING FACADE**

Philadelphia, Pennsylvania, USA

Venturi Scott Brown and Associates (est. 1964),
Architects
Philadelphia, Pennsylvania, USA

1972, *Learning from Las Vegas: The Forgotten
Symbolism of Architectural Form* (MIT Press,
Cambridge), written with his wife and Steven
Izenour (1940–2001), which called for a recon-
sideration of our built environment and what
Venturi called its "messy vitality." Here, they
celebrated and fully supported the transformation of the ordinary into the extraordinary
and the idea of applying decorative, graphic

imagery to conventional buildings. In the book,
the authors also coined the terms "duck" and
"decorated shed"—descriptions of the two
predominant ways of embodying iconography
in buildings. Venturi Scott Brown ultimately
adopted the latter strategy, designing formal
yet simple "decorated sheds" with complex and
sometimes shocking ornamental flourishes.

A seminal example of this strategy is
clearly evident in the design of their 1977 corporate headquarters for an international scientific
information services corporation that used
advanced computer technology.

The Institute for Scientific Information
corporate headquarters, completed in 1979, is
a 132,000-square-foot (12,263 sq m) building
in Philadelphia. Here, the architects imposed a

pure geometric pattern of colored brick and porcelain enamel paneled tiles on the flat, square
facade of the building. This tight, rigorous
colored graphic pattern is visually kinetic and
energetic, forcing the flat facade to come alive
with movement, color, and an ever-changing
presence depending upon the viewer's approach
and vantage point to the building.

In this project, Venturi Scott Brown branded
the building with a simplistic representation of
the developing world of information technology,
as well as created a building that symbolized
image over form.

JAMES WINES AND BEST PRODUCTS

1970   1974

BEST PRODUCTS CO. "PEELING FACADE"
SHOWROOM
Richmond, Virginia, USA
James Wines/SITE (est. 1970), Architects
New York, New York, USA

BEST PRODUCTS CO. "INDETERMINATE
FACADE" SHOWROOM
Houston, Texas, USA
James Wines/SITE (est. 1970), Architects
New York, New York, USA

In the 1970s, James Wines (b. 1932) and his architectural firm SITE (est. 1970), introduced postmodernist iconography to the American suburbs with a series of nine showrooms for Best Products Co., one of the largest merchandising showroom firms in the United States.

Wines studied architecture at Syracuse University and worked as a sculptor between 1955 and 1968 before founding his multidisciplinary design firm SITE (Sculpture in the Environment) in 1970.

SITE's groundbreaking prototype showrooms for Best Products, described by Wines as a "rectangular brick shoebox on an asphalt parking lot," were used as the ideal form for the application of what he called "de-architecture"—an attack on urban conformity or in his words a "radical subversion of normal expectations in architecture."

The first showroom, in Richmond, Virginia, was designed in 1970 to have the same visual characteristics of any standard shopping center building, however, on closer inspection the brick veneer facade appeared to be peeling precariously away from the structure of the building mass itself. Rather than focusing on developing new architectural forms or utilizing new materials, Wines and SITE injected this building with a new visual appeal by creating an effect they described as "architecture in a state of tentativeness and instability."

With their next project for Best in Houston, SITE created the "Indeterminate Facade"

1975

BEST PRODUCTS CO. "NOTCH PROJECT" SHOWROOM
Sacramento, California, USA

James Wines/SITE (est. 1970), Architects
New York, New York, USA

in 1974. The roof of the existing building was arbitrarily extended upward, thereby creating the impression that the building was arrested between construction and demolition. At one point, a cascade of apparently loose bricks was made to flow down the caducous-looking facade. A building inspector could not believe that this effect was intentional and officially ascribed it to "hurricane damage."

In 1975, Wines continued his exploration of "an architectural iconography of negation" for

Best with its "Notch Project" located in Sacramento, California. Here, one of the building's corners at its base appears to have broken off and separated from the building proper. This 14-foot– (4.3 m) high, 45-ton wedge-shaped building fragment, mechanically displaced at a maximum distance of 40 feet (12 m), creates an unusual main entrance to the showroom with its distinctive and somewhat disturbing raw, jagged edge. While these showrooms were disturbing and even shocking to some when

they were first completed, they established a new set of values that became increasingly prevalent in the graphic design and architectural professions during the later part of the twentieth century.

STUDIO OF RICHARD HAAS

1974

112–114 PRINCE STREET MURAL
New York, New York, USA
Richard Haas (b. 1936), Designer
Spring Green, Wisconsin, USA

Richard Haas (b. 1936) is considered one of the most prominent American muralists of the twentieth century, acclaimed for his architectural murals and use of the trompe l'oeil style.

Haas was born in Spring Green, Wisconsin, and attended the University of Wisconsin–Milwaukee from 1954 to 1959, earning a bachelor of arts degree in art education. In the years following his studies, he worked as a stonemason apprentice at Taliesin, the home of Frank Lloyd Wright (1867–1959; see page 54).

In 1968, he relocated to New York City, where he developed an obsession with nineteenth- and early-twentieth-century American architecture and its history that has remained the driving force in his lifelong career.

Haas completed his first large-scale trompe l'oeil mural in 1974 on the east blank wall facade of a cast-iron building at the corner of Prince and Greene Streets in Soho in New York City. This memorable mural is an exact two-dimensional architectural replica of the building's north facade and subsequently led Haas to numerous outdoor commissions throughout the United States and Europe.

Haas completed his next major mural commission in 1975 for Boston Architectural College (est. 1889). This mural, on the west facade of an innocuous 1960s-era concrete building on Newbury Street, celebrates the work of eighteenth-century French neoclassical architects—Étienne-Louis Boullée (1728–1799) and Claude-Nicolas Ledoux (1736–1806). The entire facade is a neoclassical architectural cross-section cutaway drawing in which a hypothetical building interior is revealed in trompe l'oeil and also provides the passerby with imagery that is a notable and memorable contrast to the brutalist style of the existing building.

1975

BOSTON ARCHITECTURAL SOCIETY MURAL
Boston, Massachusetts, USA

Richard Haas (b. 1936), Designer
Spring Green, Wisconsin, USA

At 1211 North LaSalle Street in Chicago, a sixteen-story apartment building originally built in 1929, Haas created a trompe l'oeil mural in homage to Louis Sullivan (1856–1924) and the Chicago School of Architecture. The mural, completed in 1980, draws on the work of Sullivan, an American Beaux-Arts architect who strongly influenced Chicago design and architecture and culled from several of his Midwestern bank buildings of the early twentieth century. Portraits of Sullivan, Frank Lloyd Wright (1867–1959), John Root (1850–1891),

1980

1211 LASALLE STREET MURAL
Chicago, Illinois, USA

Richard Haas (b. 1936), Designer
Spring Green, Wisconsin, USA

and Daniel Burnham (1846–1912)—all prominent Chicago-based architects from the late nineteenth and early twentieth centuries—are represented at the base of the mural.

For more than four decades, Haas has functioned as an urban graphic artist and visual storyteller, providing us with imaginative and unique ways of reconsidering and reshaping our visual landscape in the built environment.

JEAN WIDMER AND
CENTRE GEORGES POMPIDOU

1977

CENTRE GEORGES POMPIDOU
SIGN PROGRAM
Paris, France
Visuel Design (est. 1980), Designers
Paris, France
Renzo Piano (b. 1937) and Richard Rogers (b. 1933),
Architects
Paris, France

Jean Widmer (b. 1929) was born in Frauenfeld, Switzerland, and studied at the Kunstgewerbeschule in Zurich, where he was influenced by the teachings of the color theorist Johannes Itten (1888–1967), a former "master" instructor at the Bauhaus (1919; see page 75). In 1952, he moved to Paris to study at the École des Beaux-Arts before becoming an art director at the department store Galeries Lafayette in 1959. In 1961, he became art director for the fashion magazine *Jardin des Modes*.

Widmer's work for the Centre de Creation Industreille (CCI) in 1968 marked a radical change in his visual style as well as the projects he undertook. His desire for simplicity and minimalist graphic forms can be seen in his posters for the CCI, as well as in his pictograms for the French Tourism Sign System (1970) and his analytical work for French Motorway Sign System (1978). Together, with Adrian Frutiger (b. 1928; see page 172), Widmer was part of the first generation of Swiss graphic design émigrés in Paris.

In 1970, Widmer started to work on visual identity and sign programs for numerous French cultural institutions that included the Musée d'Orsay (Gae Aulenti, 1986), the Institut du Monde Arabe (Jean Nouvel, 1987), the Conservatoire national superieur de musique et de dance (Christian de Portzamparc, 1995) in Paris, the Cite de la Musique (Christian de Portzamparc, 1995), and the Centre Georges Pompidou.

With his groundbreaking work for the Centre Georges Pompidou in 1977, he created a simple, clear, and elegant program that became

a critical turning point for the role of graphic design in public spaces, universities, and cultural institutions throughout France.

The iconoclastic Pompidou Centre, designed by Renzo Piano (b. 1937) and Richard Rogers (b. 1933) in 1977, turned the architectural world upside down with its exposed steel skeleton of brightly color-coded and functional structural elements—green pipes for plumbing, blue ducts for climate control, yellow for electrical, and red for circulation and safety

devices. The building design not only revolutionized the design of future museums, but also transformed the world of museums from what had once been perceived as elitist monuments into popular and engaging public spaces for social and cultural exchange.

Widmer's sign program conformed to two criteria: information was organized and displayed vertically to ensure full integration to the building's architecture, and was color-coded to clearly distinguish each of the four departments within the museum. All graphic components utilized a new sans-serif typeface, Beaubourg 77, specifically designed for the Pompidou by Adrian Frutiger (b. 1928; see page 172).

Although challenging the museum-going public with vertically oriented typography, this innovative solution required less physical space, facilitated the efficient flow of visitors through the museum's interior spaces, and ultimately became such a success that it was used as a wayfinding benchmark for graphic designers worldwide on subsequent institutional projects.

MILTON GLASER AND THE BIG KITCHEN

1978

THE BIG KITCHEN SIGN PROGRAM
New York, New York, USA

Milton Glaser (b. 1929), Designer
New York, New York, USA

Milton Glaser (b. 1929), one of the most celebrated graphic designers of the twentieth century, attended the High School of Music and Art and graduated from Cooper Union in New York City. In 1951, he traveled to Italy on a Fulbright scholarship to study with Italian painter and printmaker Giorgio Morandi (1890–1964) at the Academy of Fine Arts in Bologna. Shortly after his return to the United States, Glaser and his fellow Cooper Union classmates Seymour Chwast (b. 1931), Reynold Ruffins (b. 1930), and Edward Sorel (b. 1929) cofounded Push Pin

Studios in 1954, where his illustrations and design work helped define one of the most influential and prolific collaborations of American graphic design practitioners during the 1960s.

In 1974, Glaser established his own design firm and is best known for the Bob Dylan poster (1967), the "I Love New York" logotype (1977), and as the cofounder of *New York* magazine (1968) with editor Clay Felker (1925–2008).

One of his earliest collaborations on a project for the built environment was the Big Kitchen at the World Trade Center's concourse in New York City. Here, the integration of graphic design and architecture was the result of a creative four-year process between Glaser, architect James Lamantia (1923–2011), restaurateur Joseph Baum (1920–1998), and interior designers Harper & George (est. 1963).

Glaser introduced large-scale, freestanding 7 ½-foot- (2.3 m) high sculptural sans-serif let-

terforms that announced "Big Kitchen," as well as functioned as seating, counter space, and privacy "hedges" for enclosing the café and dining areas of the restaurant. Each monumental letterform, based on a custom typeface also designed by Glaser, was covered in a checkerboard motif as a graphic reference to old-fashioned dining establishments. This comprehensive sign program also included signs, menus, promotional and advertising materials, logotypes, and the commissioning of art for interior spaces.

This team of expert designers and culinary artists succeeded in transforming a lower-level public concourse of New York City's World Trade Center into a series of visually exciting eateries that provided stimuli for the public's eye as well as their palate.

DAN REISINGER AND YAD VASHEM

1979

YAD VASHEM TYPOGRAPHIC FACADE
Jerusalem, Israel

Dan Reisinger (b. 1934), Designer
Kanjiza, Serbia

Dan Reisinger (b. 1934) is Israel's most accomplished and innovative graphic designer. He was born in Kanjiza, Serbia, into a family of painters and decorators working in Austria-Hungary and the Balkans. The majority of his family perished in the Holocaust. As a teenager, he became active in the partisan Pioneer Brigade, and with his mother and stepfather immigrated to Israel in 1949.

In 1950, he was accepted as a student, its youngest at the time, at the Bezalel Academy of Art and Design in Jerusalem. Following his graduation in 1954, he traveled and worked throughout Europe between 1958 and 1960. Upon his return to Tel Aviv, he was appointed chief art director of Israel's largest ad agency. From 1964 to 1966, Reisinger studied stage and three-dimensional design at the Central School of Art and Design (today the Central Saint Martins College of Art and Design) in London. In 1966, he returned to Israel, where he established his own design studio in Tel Aviv.

One of his most memorable and dramatic large-scale works is a 164-foot- (50 m) long cast-aluminum bas-relief in Hebraic letter-forms, completed in 1978, of a biblical quotation on the exterior of the Yad Vashem, Israel's official museum and memorial to Holocaust victims in Jerusalem. Up close, these rectangular blocks appear pitted, rusted, and weather beaten as weary, individual units, but at a distance they collectively coalesce into words from the Old Testament.

Established in 1953 and located on the Mount of Remembrance in Jerusalem, Yad Vashem, the second-most-visited tourist site in Israel, after the Western Wall, is a 45-acre (18.2 ha) campus that also houses the Holocaust History Museum, the Children's Memorial, the Hall of Remembrance, the Museum of Holocaust Art, the International School for Holocaust Studies, as well as a synagogue, archives, a research institute, library, publishing house, and an educational center.

The quotation reads, "And to them will I give in my house and within my walls a memorial and a name . . . that shall not be cut off." Its imposing, brutalistic, and worn appearance symbolizes, as well as eternalizes, the import of the events commemorated within the walls of Yad Vashem.

TURIN'S LINGOTTO

1983

TURIN VENT PRORATE PER ILL FUTURE DEL LINGOTTO
Turin, Italy

Gregotti Associati (est. 1974), Designers
Milan, Italy

When Fiat's Lingotto car plant opened in Turin, Italy, in 1920, it quickly became an international landmark for the industrial revolution and technological progress due to its sheer size, rationalist architectural design, and famous rooftop test track. Over its sixty-year life, many of Fiat's best-known car models were designed and manufactured at Lingotto.

In 1982, the plant ceased production, and Fiat began to search for new uses for this enormous facility. As part of their process, the car company invited twenty internationally-known architects to submit design proposals with the only requirement being that their proposals respect the architectural integrity of the original plant. The result was called "Venti progetti per il futuro del Lingotto" (Twenty projects for Lingotto's future), an exhibition that displayed all the proposals for the public's consideration.

Italian graphic designer Pierluigi Cerri (b. 1939) of Gregotti Associates (est. 1974) was responsible for the project's program design that included a sign system to exhibit the twenty submitted projects.

The project's main identification sign consisted of a group of large-scale sculptural sans-serif letterforms strategically located outside the factory's main entrance, which spelled out "Lingotto." These three-dimensional, monumental 12-foot (4 m) letters rose in the air and formed a dynamic visual and spatial presence due to their varied orientations to one another—some upright, some placed at an angle. Lingotto's utilitarian architecture of concrete, metal, and glass provided an appropriate and contrasting backdrop for this sculptural grouping of vibrant blue, green, red, and yellow monolithic letterforms.

MAYA LIN AND
THE VIETNAM VETERANS MEMORIAL

1983

VIETNAM VETERANS MEMORIAL
Washington, D.C., USA
Maya Lin (b. 1959), Architect
Athens, Ohio, USA

In the 1980s, the concept of memorial architecture in the United States dramatically changed due to the controversial contributions of architect Maya Lin. Traditional and cliché figurative imagery that had dominated memorials since the founding of the republic were replaced with metaphor, abstraction, and spatial engagement.

Maya Lin (b. 1959) is an American artist and architect known for her work in sculpture and landscape art. She was born in Athens, Ohio, and studied architecture at Yale University, where she received her undergraduate degree in 1981 and a master's degree in architecture in 1986.

In 1981, at age twenty-one and while still an undergraduate at Yale University, Maya Lin won a public design competition for the Vietnam Veterans Memorial in Washington, D.C., from more than 1,441 competition submissions.

Lin shunned the historical precedents set by most national memorials that traditionally and physically reached for the heavens by creating a dramatic opening or a "wound" in the earth that symbolized the import of the loss of each and every soldier in one of the most controversial wars in American history.

The design is deceptively simple yet emotionally powerful. Its granite walls bear the inscribed names of 58,261 American soldiers, listed chronologically (1959–1979) as they fell. The open V-shaped granite wall appears as a bold slash beneath the earth with one side oriented toward the Lincoln Memorial and the other to the Washington Monument. The memorial is virtually invisible with its highest point almost even with the lawn of the National Mall. Each facet of the wall is composed of 40-inch- (1 m) wide continuous polished black granite

panels graduating from 12 inches (30 cm) above ground angled down to 10.1 feet (3 m) at its base.

Lin believed from the beginning that the memorial needed to be solely based on the power of the name. "The names would become the memorial. There was no need to embellish," she stated.

In reading the names, visitors are immediately aware that they have become detached from the world above and have come face to face with their own reflection in the polished wall—a symbolic and solitary embrace of their loved ones. Here, visitors can trace the names of their loved ones and leave personal tokens and mementos at the foot of the wall.

There is also an obvious and symbolic relationship of the design of the memorial to the design and organization of a book—the names,

set in Optima (1952), a humanist sans serif typeface designed by Hermann Zapf (b. 1918), on the right-hand panels are set ragged right, and on the left they are set ragged left—both creating a spine at the apex of the wall as in a book. Even the intimate scale of the names is reminiscent of reading a book, as opposed to a conventional memorial where the typography is treated more like a billboard.

Each name is preceded (on the west wall) or followed (on the east wall) by one of two graphic symbols—a diamond or a cross. A diamond denotes that a serviceperson's death was confirmed; a cross symbolizes those individuals who are missing in action or prisoners at the end of the war. When a serviceperson's remains are returned, the diamond symbol is superimposed over the cross. If a serviceper-

son returns alive, an outline circle is inscribed around the cross.

Since its opening in 1983, the Vietnam Veterans Memorial has become an essential pilgrimage for veterans, family, and friends of American military lost in the Vietnam War.

TAKENOBU IGARASHI AND
THE ARCHITECTURAL ALPHABET

1983

ALUMINUM ALPHABET SERIES
Tokyo, Japan

Takenobu Igarashi (b. 1944), Designer
Tokyo, Japan

Takenobu Igarashi (b. 1944) is a graphic designer who has continually explored the fusion of graphic design with the built environment. Following the completion of his undergraduate studies at Tama University of Fine Arts in Japan, he traveled to the United States and earned his graduate degree from the University of California in Los Angeles.

While the majority of his work for the last thirty years has been in graphic identity, environmental graphic design, and product design, his exploration and experimentation

with letterform and isometric grids has brought him international attention and recognition. In the 1980s, his two-dimensional, isometric alphabets, first conceived as a series of poster calendars for the Museum of Modern Art in New York City, quickly evolved into three-dimensional alphabetic structures that Igarashi called architectural alphabets.

The Aluminum Alphabet Series, the first to involve alphabet sculptures, comprises twenty-six three-dimensional, aluminum letterforms. Each sculptural form consists of a series of

aluminum plates of varying thickness joined together by flat-head, aluminum fasteners. Here, Igarashi used letterform as a means to explore the potential of three-dimensional form. He says, "One of the charms of the Roman letter is its simple form. The wonderful thing is that it is created with the minimum number of elements; the standard structure is based on the circle, square, and triangle, which are the fundamentals of formation."

Letterforms are basically symbols or signs written on paper in a flat, two-dimensional

world. Design variations of letterforms can be achieved by extending their two-dimensional characteristics into a three-dimensional world. Letterforms can also be considered as simple graphic compositions made up of basic geometric elements—circles, triangles, and squares—and within these simple compositions are hidden possibilities for the development of a greater set of shapes and forms.

Igarashi's approach was to conceive letterforms as solid volumes divided into positive and negative spaces. A three-dimensional

composition is realized when the form of the letter is extended in both its positive and negative directions; in other words, by generating spatial tensions in both directions. The objective was to liberate each letter's form while still maintaining its readability. He states, "This is one example of my attempt to find a geometric solution between meaning and aesthetic form. Based on a 5-millimeter (⅛ in.) three-dimensional grid system, the twenty-six letters of the alphabet from A to Z were created by adding and subtracting on the x-, y-, and z-axes."

The Aluminum Alphabet Series is a unique, groundbreaking result of taking a conceptual, spatial, and mathematical view of letterforms and revealing some of the many possibilities of shape and mass. It is the ultimate study in typography, material, detailing, visual interpretation, and three-dimensional form, as well as a representative microcosm of how graphic design can be realized in the macrocosm of the built environment.

LOS ANGELES SUMMER OLYMPICS

1984

**LOS ANGELES SUMMER OLYMPICS
GRAPHIC PROGRAM
Los Angeles, California, USA**

Sussman/Prejza & Co. (est. 1968), Designers
Los Angeles, California, USA

Since 1980, Deborah Sussman (b. 1931) and Paul Prejza (b. 1936), and their firm Sussman/Prejza & Co. (est. 1968), have advanced the field of environmental graphic design, creating urban sign programs for numerous cities in California as well as environmental graphics for Disney (1989; see page 212), Hasbro, and Apple.

In the 1960s, Sussman worked with two pioneers of twentieth-century American design, Charles (1907–1978) and Ray Eames (1912–1988), whose creative imprint revolutionized the look of postwar America. It was during this mentoring period that she became rooted in an Eamesian joy of color, pattern, cultural influences, and ethnic design.

Her environmental graphics program for the 1984 Los Angeles Summer Olympics literally changed the way we experience graphic design in an urban environment. This comprehensive program guided an enormous international audience through a series of twenty-eight athletic facilities, forty-two cultural locations, and three Olympic villages, while visually celebrating the games and the surrounding city on a grand scale and in a festival-like manner. Sussman's system of temporary structures, scaffolding, columns, arches, large-scale graphics, banners, and bright colors coupled with an eclectic assemblage of stars, stripes, geometric shapes, and confetti-like patterns were inventive, functional, and extremely accessible.

A kit of parts composed of simple, basic forms was assembled to provide each venue with a unifying design common denominator. For example, Sonotubes, traditionally used as molds for casting concrete columns, were used

as columnar forms themselves and adorned with program graphic standards such as colorful painted stripes. They were then organized in multiples to form entrance colonnades, combined with either tent structures or topped with flat graphic pediments reminiscent of architectural forms from earlier Olympics.

Color made the 1984 Los Angeles Summer Olympics a truly visual event. It transformed one of the largest cities in the world into an intimate, cohesive experience, as well as the manner in which visual communications would be approached for all future Olympics. The color scheme, which Sussman called "festive Federalism," was unexpected, exciting, and distinct from the everyday visual fabric of an urban city. Hot magentas and oranges were the base colors on which the color palette was built. Sports pictograms were white on magenta; freeway

signs were magenta with aqua; the interaction of magenta against yellow, vermilion, and aqua was the most important interrelationship of the palette. The colors also had strong ties to the region—magenta and yellow are of the Pacific Rim, Mexico, and the Far East. Aqua is Mediterranean and a strong counterpoint to the warmer Pacific colors.

Colors were generally used in combinations of three or more, and the palette was divided to produce enormous visual variety. Each venue had its own palette that related to the character of its specific sport and to the ambient color and lighting of its surroundings. For example, gymnastics was represented by vermilion, yellow, and green; swimming by aqua and white. The colors worked very effectively in southern California light, appearing brilliant and vibrant at different times of the day.

"My work with color is informed by content. It has roots in contextual sources and is inspired by geography, cultural history, user's needs, architecture, urban characteristics, and available materials. I work intuitively when selecting the actual palettes, often relating them to musical iconography. Ray Eames and Alexander (Sandro) Girard were my mentors. Wassily Kandinsky said, 'In general, color is a medium that has a direct impact on the soul.' This has been my experience and remains my belief," explains Sussman.

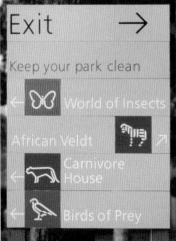

CINCINNATI ZOO

1984

CINCINNATI ZOO GRAPHIC PROGRAM
Cincinnati, Ohio, USA

Schenker, Probst & Barensfeld (est. 1981), Designers
Cincinnati, Ohio, USA

In the 1980s, many zoos around the world started to redefine the habitats for their animals from tiny wire-mesh, iron-barred, and concrete cages to simulations of their own natural habitats. One of the first institutions to embrace this groundbreaking approach in the United States was the Cincinnati Zoo, the nation's third largest zoo (65.4 acres, 26.5 ha).

As zoos and animal habitats evolved, so did graphic design's role in directing, identifying, and informing visitors of different species and the regions they inhabited.

In 1984, the Cincinnati Zoo commissioned graphic designers Schenker, Probst & Barensfeld (est. 1981) to develop a comprehensive graphic program for all of the zoo's visual communication needs, from wayfinding and informational signs to interpretive exhibition graphics and printed material.

Modular informational signs were organized in two categories—one that identified species and enabled visitors to recognize them, and interpretive and educational signs that provided visitors with detail information on migration,

flight patterns, endangered species, and so on. For example, in the Swan Lake and the habitat for the Birds of Prey, sign structures consisted of a series of panels set into a metal channel system fastened to a treated wood post set in the ground or near water. Its top unit functioned as the primary identifier with a stylized graphic illustration of the species and supporting interpretive narrative text. Directly below were fiberglass-embedded photographic images of different bird species, each with accompanying narrative text.

Cincinnati Zoo

For directional signs, a color-coded palette (red for caution, yellow for traffic, green for general information, white for exhibitions, and black for facilities) was applied against a monochromatic painted gray aluminum background on standardized wood posts and aluminum panel structures.

Frutiger (1976), a humanist sans-serif typeface designed by Adrian Frutiger (b. 1928; see page 172) was used throughout the program in combination with an extensive set of custom-designed pictograms that was a perfectly integrated extension to the humanist graphic profiles of the typeface.

The end result was an extensive series of program elements that appeared sensitively integrated to their natural environment, were flexible enough to accommodate the constantly changing zoo environment and population, and provided a wealth of detailed and illustrated documentary information to the visitor.

THE NEW AMERICAN MARKETPLACE

1985

SOUTH STREET SEAPORT SIGN PROGRAM
New York, New York, USA

Sussman/Prejza & Co. (est. 1968), Designers
Los Angeles, California, USA

During the 1960s and 1970s, most urban waterfronts throughout the world were seen as long-neglected industrial wastelands. That perception, held by civic leaders, real estate developers, and inhabitants of those cities, started to drastically change in 1985 with the opening and revitalization of New York City's South Street Seaport.

Prior to 1985, this reclaimed 3.5 acre (1.4 ha) area of lower Manhattan was overrun with wholesale fish markets, unadorned clam bars, and abandoned warehouses. Following

its redevelopment by the Rouse Company (est. 1956), an innovative real estate developer that introduced a new era of the "festival" retail marketplace based on European-style markets, it is now one of the most bustling business, residential, and tourism areas of New York City, full with restaurants, indoor and outdoor cafés, pubs, and boutiques.

Working with Rouse, the overall master plan for the new South Street Seaport was designed by Benjamin Thompson and Associates (est. 1967), architects and planners well known

for their work for major waterfront developments such as Boston's Faneuil Hall (1976) and Baltimore's Harborplace (1980). The project's expressive graphic design was the responsibility of Sussman/Prejza & Co. (est. 1968).

Their graphics were wide ranging, covering overall identification of the South Street Seaport, logotypes for two new buildings—Fulton Market and Pier 17—and informational and wayfinding signs for the interior public spaces, as well as for the individual shops and stalls of some 200 retail tenants.

The Bluefish, the seaport's symbol, was realized in various materials and integrated to directories, as well as informational and wayfinding signs in both buildings. The Pier 17 Pavilion displays large-scale slab-serif typography on its south and north facades, reminiscent of nineteenth-century rail terminal piers and clearly visible from passing boats and the Brooklyn side of the East River.

The program's materials palette was responsive to the industrial and market aesthetics of the new seaport, recalling the earlier metal,

porcelain enamel, and painted wood signs that were a prevalent part of the area's history. Metal panels, standard angles, and exposed fasteners were used for all signs, since they were natural extensions of the existing industrial buildings that were designed with exposed steel frames and other utilitarian, functional details. This level of design restraint provided an environment for individual retail tenants to create a more idiosyncratic and distinct counterpoint with their own identity and signs, as well as further convey the spirit of this historic locale.

To achieve a visual diversity throughout, Sussman/Prejza allowed individual retail tenants and vendors to design their own identification signs based on a set of preestablished design and material guidelines.

The collaborative efforts of both design disciplines further guaranteed a seamless integration of graphic design and architecture that was evident throughout South Street Seaport so that signs were not so assertive that they became a dominant feature within this new retail environment.

COMMUNICATION ARTS AND BAYSIDE

1987

BAYSIDE MARKETPLACE SIGN PROGRAM
Miami, Florida, USA

Communication Arts (est. 1973), Designers
Boulder, Colorado, USA

Bayside Marketplace is a festival marketplace along the shores of Biscayne Bay in downtown Miami. Developed by the Rouse Company (est. 1956), an innovative real estate developer that introduced a new era of the "festival" retail marketplace to the United States based on European-style markets, this 230,000-square-foot (21,368 sq m) retail center opened in 1987 and attracts more than 15 million people annually.

Designed by Benjamin Thompson and Associates (est. 1967), architects and planners well known for their renowned work for major

waterfront developments such as Boston's Faneuil Hall (1976) and New York City's South Street Seaport (1985), Bayside combines Caribbean vernacular architecture, the resort history of Miami Beach, and the Anglo/Latin cultural influences of the region into one cohesive experience for the public. The project's eclectic and expressive graphic design was the responsibility of Communication Arts (est. 1973).

With its multitude of shops, restaurants, and specialty food stores, Communication Arts designed a comprehensive graphic program that

included identification and wayfinding signs, project identity, specialty area identity, as well as the design of the Pier 5 market merchandising system.

Some of Bayside's unique graphic design features included a monolithic entrance sign composed of 12-foot- (3.7 m) high bold, sans-serif letterforms that changed from opaque and graduated pastel colored forms during the day to jukebox-like, neon-illuminated edged objects at night. In one of the main public corridors of the interior is a suspended 20-foot- (6.1 m) long

three-dimensional, papier maché swordfish that has a dual function as a dramatic sculptural icon located in the public space as well as an thematic and memorable identification marker for the Pier 5 Market.

As one of the premier design consultants in the world that created visual "placemaking" in the built environment during the 1970s and 1980s, Communication Arts built an international reputation with large-scale projects that balanced curiosity, emotion, and intellect with a strong understanding of real-world needs.

712 FIFTH AVENUE

1987

**712 FIFTH AVENUE
CONSTRUCTION BARRICADE
New York, New York, USA**

Vignelli Associates (est. 1971), Designers
New York, New York, USA

In 1987, Vignelli Associates (est. 1971) redefined the construction barricade for 712 Fifth Avenue, a new skyscraper designed by architects Kohn Pedersen Fox Associates (est. 1976) under construction in New York City, as "a delightful visual diversion for passerbys" by creating a 76-foot- (23.2 m) high elevation blueprint of the two historic building facades at the base of the new building and concealed by the barricade while under restoration.

The former Coty Building, designed in the neo–French Classic style by American architect Woodruff Leeming (1871–1919), was completed in 1908. In 1910, perfumer Francois Coty (1874–1934) commissioned the world-renowned glassmaker René Lalique (1860–1945) to design glass windows on the building's facade facing Fifth Avenue. The former Rizzoli Building, also an exemplary example of neo–French Classic architecture, was designed by American architect Albert Gottlieb (1870–1942) in 1908. Both of these buildings had to be incorporated into the building design due to the landmark status of their facades.

Basic utilitarian materials such as MDO plywood and fiberglass coupled with the use of bright primary colors and Helvetica (Max Miedinger, 1956) were used to create a super-graphic that also provided high visual impact along New York City's prestigious Fifth Avenue. A bold red horizontal strip below the oversize blueprint displayed project information in white vinyl lettering, while an immense yellow square directly above identified the project itself. This yellow square conveyed the greatest visual impact on the barricade as it appears to have slipped in front of the blueprint, giving it a greater sense of import.

Vignelli's intent was to create a highly visible announcement for this new building on one of the world's most prestigious addresses, to turn a potential eyesore into an asset, and to ultimately create an informative and memorable experience for the passerby. Additionally, with the buildings hidden in mystery, this unusual barricade provided a once-in-a-lifetime opportunity to unveil the finished project with an inevitable sense of dramatic license for promotional and marketing purposes.

SOLANA

1988

SOLANA SIGN PROGRAM
Westlake, Texas, USA
Debra Nichols Design (est. 1991), Designers
San Francisco, California, USA

Solana is a 900-acre (364 ha), 7 million-square-foot (650,032 sq m) office park near the Dallas/Fort Worth Airport in Westlake, Texas, designed by architects Ricardo Legorreta (1931–2012), Mitchell/Giurgola Architects (est. 1958), and Barton Myers Associates (est. 1984).

Despite the office park's vastness, Solana is well integrated and unified due in part to its innovative sign program designed by Debra Nichols Design (est. 1991). Solana announces itself from a distance, not only by its buildings but also by a set of visual landmarks set in the landscape—singular monolithic forms in vivid tones of purple, magenta, and yellow.

These striking figurative elements are multifunctional—art, landmark, and guidepost—marking streets and major intersections throughout the campus. Sculptural prairie animals—steer, wolf, horse, and bird—are inspired by native American Southwest Huichol folk art and are made of oxidized bronze and aluminum painted hot pink, turquoise, and yellow.

In addition to transmitting information to the thousands of people who work at and visit Solana every day, this imaginative and highly distinctive design solution to wayfinding blurs the fine lines between art and craft and celebrates regional themes and signs as functional symbols that mark places and distances in the built environment.

HOLD EVERYTHING
PROTOTYPE STORE

1988

HOLD EVERYTHING PROTOTYPE STORE
San Francisco, California, USA

Gensler (est. 1965), Designers
San Francisco, California, USA

The design program for Williams-Sonoma's Hold Everything prototype stores, a United States–based specialty retail chain that sold home organization and storage solutions, was based on a dynamic visual branding presentation of a line of products designed to organize one's life. The product line included shelving, containers, timesaving gadgets, and storage systems for kitchen, bedroom, bath, laundry, and closet.

The prototype store , designed by the San Francisco office of Gensler (est. 1965) in 1988, used fundamental graphic elements—vibrant hues of blue, red, yellow, and green—coupled with the basic shapes of squares, circles, and triangles for every program component: shopping bags, gift boxes and tags, merchandise tags, business cards, gift certificates, product display systems, promotion display panels, interior product identification, and exterior store signs. For example, a merchandise wall system composed of three-dimensional squares or boxes painted in bright colors displayed a wide range of gadgets. Each box display also contained descriptive text and visual diagrams that further demonstrated the use and function of each product.

Bodoni (Giambattista Bodoni, 1798) and Futura (Paul Renner, 1927; see page 80), two classic serif and sans-serif typefaces that have simple and clean graphic characteristics, were used solely and extensively throughout.

While the majority of the products displayed did not necessarily have a consistent design aesthetic, the retailer's branding program unified this disparity; identified, marketed, and promoted each and every item displayed; and collectively created a lively and memorable retail experience throughout the store.

STUDIO DUMBAR AND PTT

1989

PTT GRAPHIC PROGRAM
Netherlands

Studio Dumbar (est. 1977), Designers
Rotterdam, Netherlands

Since the 1920s, the Dutch postal and telecom-munications authority or PTT has been a avid supporter of twentieth-century graphic design and therefore has had a strong visual presence throughout the Netherlands. Their new graphic program, influenced by the tenets of de Stijl and constructivism, was designed by Studio Dumbar (est. 1977) to mark the company's privatization in 1989. It visually reinforced the relationship between the post and telecom companies to their parent holding company by celebrating their differences, as well as their common bond to one another.

Studio Dumbar was founded by graphic designer Gert Dumbar (b. 1940) in 1977 and has offices in Rotterdam and Shanghai. The agency has created corporate images for many renowned international brands such as Shell, City of Delft, TNT China, and Dutch PTT.

Simple, basic graphic design elements such as color, shape, and typography made this versatile and flexible program extremely acces-sible and understandable to the public. The PTT family of logotypes, all based on one design solution with subtle deconstructed variations, included PTT Post, PTT Telecom, and the hold-ing company PTT Nederland. Univers (1957), a neo-grotesque sans-serif typeface designed by Adrian Frutiger (b. 1928; see page 172), was used for all three logotypes, set in lowercase, in white, and contained within a colored square. The PTT Post logotype was red, PTT Telecom was green, and the PTT Netherland blue with two squares, one green and one red, which indicated its connection to both companies.

These logotypes functioned as conceptual springboards for the realization of a comprehen-sive visual brand that appeared on printed ma-terial, vans, uniforms, trains, buses, billboards, buildings, and signs. For example, its individual elements—bars, squares, and circles—provided a structured grid that were used collectively or as sole graphic elements on advertisements or on building facades as PTT identifiers.

An extensive sign system used for all facilities followed the same flexible geometry and graphic criteria, making it one of the most sophisticated and innovative graphic identity programs of the modern age.

MUSÉE DU LOUVRE

1989

MUSÉE DU LOUVRE SIGN PROGRAM
Paris, France

Carbone Smolan Agency (est. 1980), Designers
New York, New York, USA

Musée du Louvre, one of France's national trea-sures, is one of the largest buildings in Europe and the most visited museum in the world.

It is located on the Seine's Right Bank in Paris, housed in the Palais du Louvre, which began as a fortress built in the late twelfth century under Philip II and covers an area of 652,300 square feet (60,600 sq m). The mu-seum opened in 1793 and is comprised of the Sully Wing to the east, the Richelieu Wing to the north, and the Denon Wing to the south, parallel to the Seine.

The current renovated and expanded Louvre was one of the Grand Projets proposed in 1983 by French president François Mitterrand (1916–1996). Renowned American architect I. M. Pei (b. 1917) was awarded the project and proposed a controversial glass pyramid to func-tion as a new entrance in the main court, the Cour Napoléon.

Carbone Smolan Agency (est. 1980) won the coveted international competition to design a comprehensive visitor information system and sign program for the Musée du Louvre. Ken Carbone (b. 1951) graduated from the Philadel-phia College of Art in 1973 with a degree in graphic design. Following his graduation, he accepted a position at Chermayeff & Geismar Associates (est. 1957; see page 144) and

subsequently joined Gottschalk & Ash Ltd. (est. 1966) in Toronto, Canada, to work on the 1975 Montreal Olympics. He subsequently estab-lished a New York office for Gottschalk & Ash with graphic designer Leslie Smolan (b. 1952) and eventually purchased the company that was renamed Carbone Smolan Agency in 1980.

The final design solution to guide visitors throughout Musée du Louvre is architectural based, rather than collection based, correlating to the buildings that were fixed, rather than to collections, exhibitions, or art that would always be changing. Signs are in French, with hand-held printed guides made available in multiple languages for visitors.

The framework of the new wayfinding system is based on treating the museum like

the City of Paris, culled from its own *arrondisse-ment* (neighborhood) numbering system. Each of the museum's three wings—Sully, Richelieu, and Denon— is divided into ten arrondisse-ments. This numbering or address plan, when keyed to a handheld guide, accommodates for the constant relocation of the museum's collections and ultimately makes the museum accessible to millions of visitors. Arrondissements are organized horizontally, whereas vertical access is organized by color-coded floors—blue for ground, red for first, and yellow for second. This information is presented on the printed guides as well as on all wayfinding signs, which were fabricated brake-formed aluminum painted metallic gray panels. A simplified version of the museum's plan was also developed both for the printed guides and wayfinding signs. Each museum wings is identified by a single large alpha metal letter adhered to suspended glass panels, whereas each arrondissement is identi-fied with a single number.

The primary typeface used throughout the program is Granjon (1928), designed by British typographer George William Jones (1860–1942). While this Garamond revival typeface was once the official typeface of the French government, it was specified for its old-style characteristics and for its conveyance of culture and authority appropriate to the Louvre.

Univers 55 (1957), a neo-grotesque sans-serif designed by Adrian Frutiger (b. 1928; see page 172), is used as a secondary typeface throughout the nonpublic areas and on sign elements that function solely as internal opera-tional elements.

In response to the dual presence of clas-sical and modernist architecture, the graphic designers specified a materials vocabulary for all signs that reflected both sensibilities—stone, marble, bronze, glass, and steel.

The new I. M. Pei–designed pyramid and the museum's new entrance and underground public lobby were completed in 1988. As of 2010, attendance had more than doubled since its completion.

SUSSMAN/PREJZA AND
WALT DISNEY WORLD

1989

WALT DISNEY WORLD
EXTERIOR SIGN PROGRAM
Orlando, Florida, USA
Sussman/Prejza & Co. (est. 1968), Designers
Los Angeles, California, USA

Walt Disney World, located in Orlando, Florida, is a sprawling site covering approximately 44 square miles (114 sq km) that contains the Magic Kingdom, a fantasy theme park modeled after Disneyland; Walt Disney Village and Pleasure Island, a mammoth resort and shopping mall; Epcot Center, a world's fair–like projection of the future; and Disney/MGM Studios (now known as Hollywood Studios), a Hollywood movie lot come to life.

Each of these primary thematic areas is separated by large greenbelts and connected by an extensive north–south axial highway and arterial road system, which, like any small suburban city, requires a functional and accessible wayfinding system.

When Sussman/Prejza & Co. (est. 1968), creators of the acclaimed graphics for the 1984 Los Angeles Summer Olympics (see page 198), were commissioned to redesign Disney World's extensive sign system for roads, buses, and gateways, the task underscored Disney's quest for distinctive ways to communicate its time-honored spirit. Ultimately, Sussman/Prejza relied upon the universal symbols of entertainment and escapism that embodied Disney World's most prominent and famous resident—Mickey Mouse.

The simplest graphic vocabulary was developed for the program that relied solely on three fundamental graphic design elements—color, form, and typography.

The color palette specified for all sign components was taken from the colors of Mickey Mouse—red and yellow, and black and white, supplemented with a vibrant purple, green, and blue.

The final vehicular program ranged from hotel and radio information signs to regularity signs, such as stop signs and signs posting speed limits to directional signs, overhead signs, street signs, and trailblazer signs. To address this wide range of varied sign components, Sussman/Prejza created a kit of parts that was applied in different ways depending on sign function, location, and information.

For example, a white arrow contained in a black circle serves two functions, one obvious,

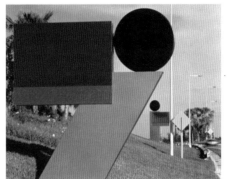

one subtler—a clear and emphatic directional sign and a suggestive and symbolic mouse ear. Two plain black circles were used to suggest Mickey Mouse's head. Along with a red command panel and decorative painted pole sleeves, the graphic designers devised a varied but simple and distinct vocabulary of parts. Collectively, this kit of sign parts, described as "just wonderful toys sitting in the landscape," not only became an effective and efficient way of creating a system of functional wayfinding signs, but it also engaged the visitor's memory and imagination along their vehicular route.

Materials used included aluminum posts and panels, painted PVC pole sleeves, and 3M Scotchlite high-intensity vinyl to enhance nighttime legibility on sign panel fascias. An angular post form was used for the majority of highway signs that instilled a postmodernist identity to

the signs, but it was the spirit of Mickey Mouse who had the most profound influence on these sign forms. Without literally looking like the famous cartoon character, the black circle (in which directional arrows are located) became an immediately identifiable graphic signature.

At the beginning of the project, Disney's corporate typeface Times Roman (1932), a transitional serif based on George William Jones's (1860–1942) Granjon (1928) and designed by British typographer Stanley Morison (1889–1967), was considered to identify each individual district name; however, Plantin (1913), a transitional serif typeface designed by American typographer Frank Hinman Pierpont (1860–1937), was ultimately used throughout the program. Univers (1957), a neo-grotesque sans-serif typeface designed by Adrian Frutiger (b. 1928; see page 172), was also used exten-

sively throughout the program for its wide range of variations in size and weight.

One of the most distinctive, playful, and nostalgic set of signs in the program was a special series of highway messages featuring Mickey on three sequential overhead signs spread over a few miles. The first panel shows two yellow gloved hands reaching over the top of the overhead sign panel; the second, two round black ears peek up; and finally the third, Mickey's smiling face peers over. Based on the same teaser premise as the Burma-Shave signs (1925; see page 61) of the 1920s, these signs span Disney World's main highway and approach to the park's main entrance gate.

The remaining signs, totaling 700-plus throughout the site, run the gamut in function from site identification and directional to utilitarian markers for stop, yield, and speed limit.

SHEA STADIUM

1989

SHEA STADIUM NEON EXTERIOR MURALS
Flushing, New York, USA

Poulin + Morris Inc. (est. 1989), Designers
New York, New York, USA

Jack L. Gordon Architects (est. 1969), Architects
New York, New York, USA

The seven simplified profiles of baseball players depicted in neon and designed in 1989 by Richard Poulin (b. 1955) of Poulin + Morris Inc. (est. 1989) for New York City's Shea Stadium, home of the New York Mets from 1964 to 2010, celebrated America's favorite pastime with simplicity, light, and scale.

Shea Stadium, a 60,000-seat multipurpose stadium located in Flushing Meadows, Corona Park in Queens, New York, was designed by architects Praeger-Kavanagh-Waterbury (est. 1953) in 1964.

Each baseball figure, measuring 90 feet (27.4 m) high by 60 feet (18.2 m) wide, was reduced to the fewest number of essential lines that were then rendered in two vibrant colors—the dominant one applied to the lines in the composition that were the most suggestive of the figure's movement—the batter's swing, the fielder's stretch, the runner's gait.

They were based on one of the most fundamental and expressive elements of graphic design—line—and not only communicated the identity of "baseball" to fans, pedestrians, and motorists who passed by the stadium, but also celebrated the spirit and energy of a favored American pastime.

These minimalist figures were fabricated in double neon tubing (two neon colors per windscreen mural) framed and contained within aluminum u-channels and painted the same color as its illumination, allowing the same colors to be experienced during the day, as well as at night.

Here, neon illumination (1915; see page 60), traditionally used for advertising and commercial needs, was used to create prominent and iconic signs, as well as large-scale public art, in keeping with the energetic and exuberant atmosphere of the American ballpark.

CHICAGO O'HARE'S UNITED TERMINAL WALKWAY

1989

UNITED TERMINAL WALKWAY
O'Hare Airport
Chicago, Illinois, USA
Michael Hayden (b. 1943), Designer
Toronto, Ontario, Canada

The subterranean walkway that carries passengers to and from their arrival and departure gates between concourses at O'Hare International Airport's United Airlines Terminal 1, designed by architects Murphy/Jahn (est. 1981), is not only a tunnel but also a visual adventure unto itself.

This 860-foot (262 m) public moving underground passageway is framed on each of its sides by undulating, backlit, multicolored walls. Floating directly above under a mirror-paneled ceiling is an illuminated sculpture installation titled *Sky's the Limit*, designed by Michael Hayden (b. 1943) and composed of more than 1 mile (1.6 km) of neon glass tubing (1915; see page 60).

For more than three decades, Hayden has utilized and manipulated neon lighting in architectonic-scaled installations. Controlled and animated by a computerized digital program, *Sky's the Limit's* color spectrum and lighting effects progress in a varied fashion from one end of the passageway to the other along the path of its moving walkways—two in each direction—with pedestrians walking along its perimeters if they choose to do so.

As skillfully as this neon lighting installation was handled, it is by no means the only attraction. One only has to observe the passengers engaging with this kaleidoscopic light show to understand the impact and influence of a fundamental principle of graphic design when sensitively integrated to the built environment.

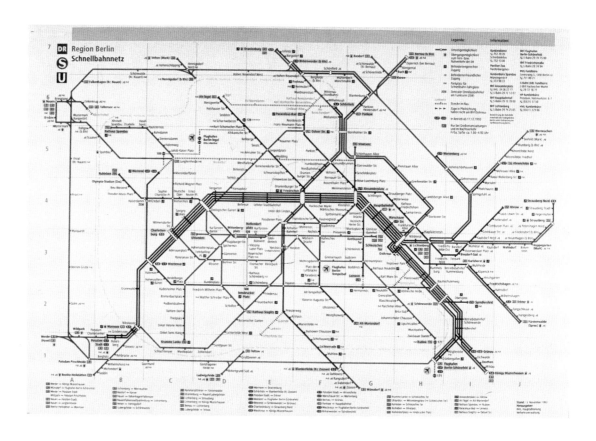

ERIK SPIEKERMANN AND
THE BERLIN TRANSPORTATION SYSTEM

1990

BERLIN TRANSPORTATION AUTHORITY
SIGN PROGRAM
Berlin, Germany

MetaDesign (est. 1979), Designers
Stadthagen, Germany

Erik Spiekermann (b. 1947) is an accomplished type designer, graphic designer, and typographic consultant. A native of Hanover, Germany, Spiekermann studied art history at Berlin's Free University and simultaneously ran a printing and metal type business from his basement. In 1973, he moved to London, where he lectured at the London College of Communication (formerly called the London College of Printing) and worked as a freelance graphic designer. In 1979, he returned to Berlin and founded MetaDesign,

which grew into Germany's largest design firm, with more than 200 employees by 2000.

Spiekermann is also a principal of the Font-Shop (est. 1989), a company dedicated to selling high-quality PostScript fonts from all major manufacturers. FontShop, through its subsidiary FontFont, creates and promotes new fonts from up-and-coming type designers and includes several of Spiekermann's own typefaces, including Berliner Grotesk (1979), Info (1996), Meta (1991), Unit (2003), and Transit.

Transit (1990) was designed by Spiekermann as part of MetaDesign's extensive work for the Berlin Transport Authority. This highly legible sans-serif typeface possesses a large x-height, narrow proportions, and broad versatility when used in both small-scale text and large-scale display settings. It was designed to blend a visual aesthetic quality with legibility and was based on the Frutiger (1976) type family designed by Adrian Frutiger (b. 1928; see page 172).

In 1992, Spiekermann and MetaDesign were asked by the Berlin Transport Authority to develop a comprehensive corporate identity and wayfinding sign system that would unify every aspect of one of the largest public transportation systems in the world. The Berliner Verkehrsbetriebe (known as BVG; est. 1928) is Berlin's integrated public transportation system and manages the city's U-Bahn underground railway, tram, bus, and ferry networks. The system has a network of 1,703 kilometers (1.064 mi) of bus lines, 190 kilometers (119 mi) of tramlines, and 479 kilometers (299 mi) of underground train lines.

This five-year commission included a complete overhaul of every type of public passenger information displayed inside and outside system vehicles and stations. MetaDesign also redesigned all system-related maps, including the newly unified system network map—a color-coded diagram of Berlin's transit system based on the iconic Henry Beck–designed map for the London Underground (1933; see page 62). The subway map was a new interpretation of Beck's modernist masterpiece, utilizing the same design principles and forgoing geographical accuracy, without complaints from governmental agencies or users of the system.

The overall end result is an outstanding, functional, and accessible graphic design solution for the one of the world's most effective integrated urban rapid-transit systems in the modern built environment.

ALAN FLETCHER'S HOUSE GATES

1990

ALAN FLETCHER HOUSE GATES
London, United Kingdom
Alan Fletcher (1931–2006), Designer
Nairobi, Kenya

Alan Fletcher (1931–2006) has been described as one of "the most highly regarded graphic designers of his generation and probably one of the most prolific" and is the founder of Fletcher/Forbes/Gill (est. 1962; see page 164) and one of the original founders of the international design group Pentagram (est. 1972).

He was born to a British family in Kenya in 1931 and grew up in East London in the United Kingdom. Fletcher attended the Hammersmith School of Art, the Central School of Art where he met his future Pentagram partners Colin

Forbes (b. 1928) and Theo Crosby (1925–1994), and Yale University.

After the founding of Pentagram, he spent the next two decades expanding the firm from five partners to eleven, from one office in London to offices in New York and San Francisco, and working for clients such as Reuters, the Victoria & Albert Museum, and Lloyd's of London.

In 1999, he left Pentagram to work independently as a design consultant at his home in London's Notting Hill. It was there he decided to redesign the entrance gates to the driveway

of his home. These custom-forged black metal letterforms, also designed by Fletcher, are based on early condensed wood typefaces and held together by metal hinge straps with the tail of the Q acting as the gate stop.

This simple solution has become one of the most memorable and enduring design solutions that Fletcher had ever conceptualized. It reflects his love and passion for letterforms, his intimate understanding of scale and material, and his inventive approach with integrating graphic form to an architectural setting.

CORNING GLASS

1992

CORNING GLASS
CORPORATE HEADQUARTERS ENTRANCE
New York, New York, USA
Donovan & Green Inc. (est. 1974), Designers
New York, New York, USA

Glass and light were the subject and media used by graphic designers Donovan & Green Inc. (est. 1974), for the Corning Glass Corporate Headquarters in New York City. Here, graphic designers transformed an innocuous entrance corridor into an engaging visual experience based on optical principles and state-of-the-art technology that literally and symbolically reflected Corning's pioneering advancements in fiber optic communications.

This spectral painting was an active composition of point-source light, dichroic filters, prisms, and optical mirrors that greeted staff and visitors on a daily basis. The dynamic light patterns that appeared along this 50-foot

(15.3 m) wall were created by different filters that separated white light through mirrors and prisms into its various projected colors along a visible spectrum. Their ultimate effect was to paint and repaint the corridor with an ever-changing light show of dramatic and subtle color patterns and hues.

This entrance corridor, described as an "artful, engaging visual presentation that communicated the essential aspects of Corning's corporate values wrapped in a memorable visual experience" expressed both the company's past innovations in light transmission and the spirit of its future developments in the field of light science.

NORTH HOLLYWOOD PUMP STATION

1992

NORTH HOLLYWOOD PUMP STATION
BUILDING FACADE
Los Angeles, California, USA

Barton Phelps & Associates (est. 1984), Architects
Los Angeles, California, USA

The North Hollywood Pump Station, designed by architects Barton Phelps & Associates (est. 1984), is a massive poured and cast concrete box adjacent to the Hollywood Freeway in Los Angeles. The 1.7-acre (0.69 ha) facility houses eleven turbine pumps that provide much of the water for central Los Angeles via aqueduct from snow runoff in the Sierra Nevada Mountains 340 miles (547 km) away.

The building facade functions as a public information mural composed of a car-scaled map with topographic features that visually communicates the building's story and furthers the City of Los Angeles's Department of Water and Power's water awareness program. Incised lines in the concrete and stainless steel lettering—offset from the blue and green tiled ocean and inlaid at the concrete land mass—trace the aqueduct systems that convey water hundreds of miles to Los Angeles. The City of Los Angeles appears on the map as an illuminated bright-green LED light.

While the building was designed to shield much of the loud machine noise generated by the turbine pumps housed within, it also functions as a large-scale civic billboard for passing pedestrians and motorists.

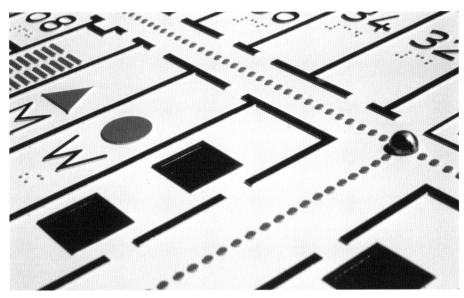

THE INFLUENCE OF UNIVERSAL DESIGN

1994

**LIGHTHOUSE INTERNATIONAL
HEADQUARTERS SIGN PROGRAM**
New York, New York, USA
Whitehouse & Company (est. 1978), Designers
New York, New York, USA

Lighthouse International headquarters in New York City, designed by Mitchell/Giurgola Architects (est. 1958), is one of a small number of buildings in the United States specifically designed to address the needs of individuals who have a broad range of vision, hearing, and mobility impairments. The building design was developed in collaboration with graphic designer Roger Whitehouse (*dates unknown*) of Whitehouse & Company (est. 1976), a multidisciplinary design firm based in New York City.

This 170,000-square-foot (15,794 sq m) facility is a model of universal design and accessibility and had been planned to meet and exceed the recommendations of the Americans with Disabilities Act of 1990. It was conceived as a "working laboratory" where many of its design features were designed, tested, and evaluated

for the first time with input from Lighthouse staff, researchers, and users who provided input regarding lighting, signs, color contrast, audible communications, safety, orientation, and mobility issues.

For example, at the main reception desk, tactile and large-print maps of all public floors help visitors plan their travel routes within the building. Since loss of the ability to perceive color contrast is one of the most common effects of vision impairment, strong contrasting colors are used for walls and doorframes. Floor tiles point out elevators and safe travel paths, and color and texture contrast between walls and floor, on stair treads, and along edges of desks also assist with maximized ease of use.

An integrated wayfinding system includes large-print white-on-black sign panels; tactile

signs identify locations in raised letters and braille, positioned at an angle to optimize readability; and audio "talking signs" identify conference rooms, restrooms, and stairwells to visitors carrying special handheld receivers. Elevators feature a special enunciation system that identifies each floor and directs people toward the reception desks, where floor-specific tactile maps are located.

Whitehouse's pioneering work for this headquarters facility, in which he further defined universal design and wayfinding principles for individuals with disabilities, formed the basis for the sign and graphic sections of the amended Americans with Disabilities Act (2009).

DISNEY'S ALL-STAR RESORTS

1994

DISNEY'S ALL-STAR RESORTS
Lake Buena Vista, Florida, USA
Communication Arts (est. 1973), Designers
Boulder, Colorado, USA

The All-Star Resorts were Disney's first foray in developing economically priced hospitality accommodations for the entire family.

Located at Walt Disney World in Lake Buena Vista, Florida, All Star Resorts is an immense motel complex, designed by Arquitectonica (est. 1977) in collaboration with graphic design firm Communication Arts (est. 1977), composed of 5,760 rooms organized among a sprawling campus of thirty low-profile buildings.

Its visual themes were culled from American pop culture iconography found in sports, music, and the movies and reinterpreted into popular "decorated sheds" (1970; see page 183). All-Star Sports and All-Star Music have themed sections for guests relating to basketball, tennis, surfing, jazz, calypso, and rock 'n' roll. The design team described their design solution

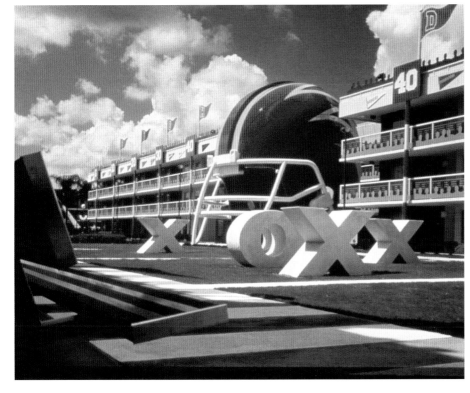

as "three-dimensional collages" in which the building's standard elements such as parapets, balcony railings, columns, and exterior stairs are surfaces in which oversize three-dimensional iconography was attached—baseball caps, basketball hoops, surfboards, football helmets, referee whistles, team banners, megaphones, banjos, top hats, and sheet music. Most of the icons were fabricated of metal or fiberglass sprayed onto metal mesh.

This approach of embodying graphic iconography in buildings was strongly influenced by earlier postmodernists such as architects Venturi Scott Brown and Associates (est. 1964, see page 183) and James Wines/SITE (est. 1970, see page 186) in the 1960s and 1970s.

The final visual effect created by Communication Arts and Arquitectonica is a surprising play on scale that ultimately created a memorable live-in playground and a larger-than-life version of reality for anyone staying at one of these unusual motels at Disney World.

FREMONT STREET EXPERIENCE

1995

FREMONT STREET EXPERIENCE
Las Vegas, Nevada, USA

The Jerde Partnership (est. 1977), Architects
Los Angeles, California, USA

During the 1940s and 1950s, Las Vegas's Fremont Street (see page 120) was considered the city's center of fantasy, licentiousness, and gambling. However, as casinos toward the south end of the Strip grew larger and more extravagant in the 1980s, downtown Las Vegas, including Fremont Street, started to fade. In 1992, downtown casino owners joined with the City of Las Vegas to develop an ambitious plan for saving this landmark area.

The Fremont Street Experience, designed by the Jerde Partnership (est. 1977), is a pedestrian mall and attraction in downtown Las Vegas. Located along the westernmost section of Fremont Street that includes the area known for years as "Glitter Gulch," the Fremont Street Experience is composed of a 90-foot- (27.4 m) high by 1,500-foot- (457.2 m) long LED display barrel-vaulted, steel-framed canopy covering five city blocks.

The LED or light-emitting diode, a semi-conductor electroluminescent light source created by photons, was invented by Nick Holonyak (b. 1928) while he was working as a consult-ing scientist at General Electric's Syracuse research laboratories in 1962.

Today, the Fremont Street Experience solely functions as an animated urban theater that comes to life every evening with a show of 12 million LED lamps that illuminate the over-head canopy and a 550,000-watt sound system comprising 220 audio speakers that produce an hourly multimedia visual and audio extrava-ganza. Since its opening in 1995, it remains one of the most popular and highly attended tourist attractions in the city.

This groundbreaking project, which became the cornerstone for the redevelopment of downtown Las Vegas, marks the first time civic leaders and casino owners collectively invested in the urban renewal of their city.

MORGAN STANLEY IN TIMES SQUARE

1995

MORGAN STANLEY
WORLD HEADQUARTERS BUILDING FACADE
New York, New York, USA

Poulin + Morris Inc. (est. 1989), Designers
Gwathmey Siegel & Associates (est. 1977), Architects
New York, New York, USA

With the purchase of the 42-story, 1.3 million-square-foot (121,000 sq m) office tower at 1585 Broadway by Morgan Stanley in 1995, the company inherited strict requirements under Times Square Redevelopment Area zoning regulations, that the building facade carry large-scale, illuminated, kinetic signs. The result—a giant information display—was one of the first illuminated and animated facades in New York City's Times Square area, and is made up of several large-scale sign elements.

Graphic designers Richard Poulin (b. 1955) and Douglas Morris (b. 1962) of Poulin + Morris Inc. (est. 1989) were responsible for the design of a series of "supersigns" integrated to the building facade of this Gwathmey Siegel & Associates (est. 1977)–designed postmodernist tower in the heart of Times Square.

During all hours of the day and night, the building's five-story-high podium facade is alight with bright signs. Two rear-illuminated cylinders at the building corners, each measuring 44 feet (13.4 m) in height, feature the Morgan Stanley brand in a kinetic typographic composition. Directly above are three 140-foot- (42.7 m) long electronic ticker panels, stacked atop each other, which use LED/light-emitting diodes for transmitting information in real time, as opposed to traditional traveling message boards, which are programmed in advance. News bulletins are carried on one panel, with stock market quotations on the other two. At each end of the building's southeast and northeast corners are 30-foot (9.1 m) by 60-foot (18.3 m) LED-based information panels displaying financial charts and other advertising-based images and text. Ten 44-foot- (13.4 m) high perpendicular fins along Broadway are clad in black mirrored glass, edged in purple neon, and rear-illuminated with large-scale sans-serif letterforms that spell out "1585 B'WAY."

This unique design scheme not only brought new life to a building that had long been dormant, it added to the resurgence of the Times Square area and brought a new brand identity to one of the largest securities and financial management firms in the world.

IV

THE BEGINNING
OF THE 21ST CENTURY

THE BEGINNING OF THE 21ST CENTURY

GreenPix Zero Energy Media Wall, 2008
Beijing, China
Simone Giostra & Partners (est. 2006), Architects
Brooklyn, New York, USA

Since the 1990s, the influence of postmodernism has provided graphic designers and architects with an eclectic range of styles and idioms. Popular culture, graffiti, and new nontraditional forms of visual communications such as film, video, and digital media all began to have a tremendous influence on not only graphic design, but also on how graphic design could be realized in the twenty-first-century built environment.

Globalization, fueled by the Internet and social media, now allowed people from all corners of the world to communicate on a level that they never experienced before. New and innovative technologies were quickly embraced, inevitably empowering graphic designers and architects to gain more control over the realization of their ideas.

At the start of the new millennium, the digital revolution advanced at an extraordinary pace, transforming every aspect of human life around the world. Comparable to the profound changes and innovations that occurred at the beginning of the twentieth-first-century, the beginning of the twenty-first-century has brought about radical changes throughout the world and its built environment.

Coupled with the rapid development of new electronic, computer, and digital technologies, the distinction between graphic design and architecture has now started to evolve into one singular and impactful point of view.

LAX AIRPORT

2000

LAX AIRPORT GATEWAY
Los Angeles, California, USA
Selbert Perkins (est. 1982), Designers
Playa Del Rey, California, USA

Los Angeles International Airport is the primary airport serving the Greater Los Angeles area, the second-most populated metropolitan area in the United States. It is most often referred to by its airport code, LAX, with the letters pronounced individually.

In 2000, prior to the City of Los Angeles hosting the Democratic National Convention, fifteen monumental acrylic glass pylons, each ten stories high, were placed in a circle around the intersection of Sepulveda Boulevard and Century Boulevard, with additional pylons of decreasing height following Century Boulevard eastward, evoking a sense of departure and arrival. Illuminated internally by LED lighting technology, the pylons slowly cycle through a rainbow of colors that symbolize the multiculturalism of the city and can be customized to celebrate events, holidays, or seasons.

Designed by Selbert Perkins (est. 1982), a multidisciplinary graphic design firm, the LAX Airport Gateway project is reminiscent of landmark monuments created by graphic designers and architects throughout the twentieth century. The cylinders, echoing the scale and function of Luis Barragán's Towers of Satellite City (1957; see page 136) in Mexico City, provided a gateway to the airport and offered a welcoming landmark for visitors arriving to Los Angeles.

UNIVERSAL CITY WALK

2000

UNIVERSAL CITY WALK
GRAPHIC STEETSCAPE
Orlando, Florida, USA
Sussman/Prejza & Co. (est. 1968), Designers
Los Angeles, California, USA

Universal City Walk, completed in 2000, is a 30-acre (12.1 ha) series of entertainment and retail districts totaling 23 acres (57 ha) adjacent to the theme parks of Universal Studios in Orlando, Florida.

Freestanding structures and graphic scrims functioned as primary character elements for City Walk's public spaces and introduced verticality, illumination, animation, and visual play to its urban streetscape. Abstract design motifs and refined hardware details were used in its towers, banners, canopies, directional signs, and tenant identification systems, which were fully integrated throughout the City Walk districts.

As part of a comprehensive urban streetscape for the new venue, environmental graphic design firm Sussman/Prejza & Co. (est. 1968; see page 212) highlighted the Florida locale as its primary inspiration for creating a citified visual language for this new venue.

NJPAC
LUCENT CENTER

2001

**NJPAC LUCENT TECHNOLOGIES CENTER
FOR ARTS EDUCATION BUILDING FACADE
Newark, New Jersey, USA**

Pentagram (est. 1972), Designers
New York, New York, USA

The Lucent Technologies Center for Arts Education in Newark, New Jersey, is an arts education school affiliated with the New Jersey Performing Arts Center (NJPAC). Directly adjacent to the NJPAC site, the school's masonry edifice was originally constructed in the early 1940s and covers an area of about 30,139 square feet (2,800 sq m).

By painting the building's exterior white and covering it with bold inline letterforms, Paula Scher (b. 1948) of Pentagram (est. 1972) used large-scale sans-serif typography to give the building a fresh and unmistakable identity of its own. Evocative words such as *poetry, music, drama, dance,* and *theater* run across the facade in a kinetic pattern and are complemented with bright and colorful banners that transform this otherwise generic school building into a lively symbol for the city of Newark.

NATIONAL MUSEUM OF EMERGING SCIENCE AND INNOVATION

2001

NATIONAL MUSEUM OF EMERGING SCIENCE AND INNOVATION SIGN PROGRAM
Tokyo, Japan

Hiromura Design Office Inc. (est. 1987), Designers
Kisho Kurakawa (1934–2007), Architect
Tokyo, Japan

Tokyo's National Museum of Emerging Science and Innovation or *Miraikan* (meaning "future museum") opened in 2001 and provides hands-on exploration of the latest developments in cutting-edge science and technology, including the interaction of robots, virtual-reality rides, and displays that suggest future applications of these new and innovative developments.

Throughout this 436,896-square-foot (40,589 sq m) museum and its surrounds, a system of sign panels is integrated into the floor and pavement surfaces, directing visitors to various destinations—information desk, galleries, shop, café, terrace, restrooms, elevators, escalators, and parking. Sign panels are made of translucent laminated glass, rear illuminated, and treated with dotted glass grains to prevent visitors from slipping when wet.

While this approach provided unobtrusive views of the museum's interiors as well as reinforced a sense of transparency throughout, the sign program also provided visitors with an immediate and intuitive vehicle for wayfinding. Information is multilingual and displayed in black and white so as to not compete visually with the exhibits. Alphanumeric identification codes and pictograms are used so that information is communicated succinctly and immediately. A new typographic monospace font with rounded terminals was developed for all informational requirements and was based on the humanist sans-serif typeface Frutiger (Adrian Frutiger, 1976; see page 172).

The design solution from Hiromura Design Office Inc. (est. 1987) for the museum's sign program is as innovative as the museum experience itself.

BIBLIOTHECA ALEXANDRINA

2002

**BIBLIOTHECA ALEXANDRINA
BUILDING FACADE
Alexandria, Egypt**
*Snøhetta (est. 1989), Architects
Oslo, Norway*

In 2002, the new library of Alexandria in Egypt, known as Bibliotheca Alexandrina, reopened its doors for the first time in 2,000 years. The new building was the culmination of an international effort lasting more than twelve years that created one of the most contemporary libraries in the world.

Designed by the Norwegian architects Snøhetta (est. 1989), the Bibliotheca Alexandrina is located on the shores of the Mediterranean Sea in Alexandria, Egypt. The dimensions of the library are vast, with shelf space for more than 8 million trilingual (Arabic, English, and French) books and a main reading room that covers 753,474 square feet (70,000 sq m) on eleven levels. The building complex also houses a conference center; specialized libraries for maps, multimedia, the blind and visually impaired, young adults, and children; museums; temporary exhibition galleries; a planetarium; and a manuscript restoration laboratory.

The library's architectural design is equally striking, with its main reading room directly beneath a 105-foot- (32 m) high glass paneled roof, tilted out toward the sea like a sundial and measuring 525 feet (160 m) in diameter.

The exterior walls of the Bibliotheca Alexandrina are grey Aswan granite from Egypt's Nile Valley. These monumental stone walls are covered with sandblasted scripts, signs, letters, and symbols from many of the world's cultures and represent the multitude of languages contained within the walls of this twenty-first-century sanctuary.

TOWERS OF LIGHT

2002

**TOWERS OF LIGHT
New York, New York, USA**
*various architects and designers
New York, New York, USA*

The Towers of Light was a commemorative art installation comprising eighty-eight searchlights at the original site of the World Trade Center that created two vertical columns of light in remembrance of the September 11 attacks on New York City.

While initially planned as a temporary lighting installation, the Towers of Light was continued annually through to the tenth anniversary of the attacks in 2011. It was described by its creators as an ". . . emotional response

more than anything . . . the towers are the ghost limbs, we can feel them even though they're not there anymore."

Initially conceived by architects John Bennett (*dates unknown*) and Gustavo Bonevardi (b. 1960) of PROUN Space Studio (est. 1996) and artists Julian LaVerdiere (b. 1971) and Paul Myoda (b. 1967) this emotionally dramatic installation, composed of high-intensity searchlights, was visible throughout New York City as well as most of the tristate area of New York, New Jersey, and Connecticut.

THE NEW YORK PUBLIC LIBRARY
FOR THE PERFORMING ARTS

2003

**THE NEW YORK PUBLIC LIBRARY
FOR THE PERFORMING ARTS
AT LINCOLN CENTER SIGN PROGRAM
New York, New York, USA**

*Poulin + Morris Inc. (est. 1989), Designers
New York, New York, USA
Ennead Architects (formerly Polshek Partnership;
est. 1963), Architects
New York, New York, USA*

The New York Public Library for the Perform-ing Arts at Lincoln Center houses one of the world's most renowned collections of resource materials on theater, dance, music, and the performing arts.

In 2000, the library underwent an extensive three-year renovation of its 140,000 square feet (12,600 sq m) of public reading rooms, galleries, auditorium, and preservation labs, led by Ennead Architects (est. 1963). The multi-disciplinary design firm of Poulin + Morris Inc. (est. 1989) was responsible for the design of the renovation's comprehensive environmental graphics, donor recognition, and wayfinding sign program.

Bold and vibrant colors, large-scale typog-raphy, and iconographic images culled from the library's extensive research collections were used throughout the newly renovated interior spaces to create a more engaging and relevant visual experience for the library user. A major component of the program is a typographic wall mural (Times New Roman, 1932) that identifies the names of composers, musicians, actors, playwrights, dancers, and other performing artists represented in the library's collections. The mural spirals up a five-story primary circu-lation staircase, serves as a vehicle for interior wayfinding, and is a visual celebration of the performing arts.

MOMA QNS

2003

MOMA QNS SIGN PROGRAM
Queens, New York, USA

Two Twelve Associates (est. 1980), Designers
New York, New York, USA
Cooper Robertson & Partners (est. 1979), Architects
New York, New York, USA
Michael Maltzan (b. 1959), Architect
Levittown, New York

In 2002, the Museum of Modern Art's (MoMA) midtown location in New York City underwent extensive renovation and expansion, reopening in 2004. During this two-year period, a portion of MoMA's world-renowned collections were placed on display in what was dubbed MoMA QNS, a former Swingline staple factory in Long Island City, Queens.

This 25,000-square-foot (2,323 sq m) temporary utilitarian facility, designed by architects Cooper Robertson & Partners (est. 1979) and exhibition architect Michael Maltzan (b. 1959), was strategically selected for its proximity to midtown Manhattan.

The building exterior was treated like a large-scale canvas with painted MoMA QNS supergraphics covering the rooftop and building facade. This economical and distinctive typographic feature appeared on a bright blue facade and communicated the museum's visual identity in a consistent manner with its perma-

nent home in midtown Manhattan. Additionally, these large-scale, monumental letterforms made it easy for visitors to locate MoMA QNS in the dense cityscape of Long Island City from a distance, especially when approaching the building via the elevated trains of the New York City transit system.

A modernist typographic system comprising two typefaces—Franklin Gothic (Morris Fuller Benton, 1903), culled from the MoMA logotype, and a contemporary sans-serif Office (Stephan Muller, 1999)—was used throughout the program.

The building's interior sign program was based on new MoMA QNS identity standards and implemented by environmental graphic design firm Two Twelve Associates (est. 1980). In this architectural context, the graphic designers utilized a common museum technique of silk-screening identification and directional information directly onto interior wall surfaces of the facility. This economical solution not only communicated essential information to the public in an immediate and no-nonsense fashion, but also preserved the visual integrity of the building's interior spaces.

MELBOURNE EXHIBITION CENTRE

2003

MELBOURNE EXHIBITION CENTRE
SIGN PROGRAM
Melbourne, Australia

Emerystudio (est. 1999), Designers
Melbourne, Australia
Denton Corker Marshall (est. 1972), Architects
Melbourne, Australia

The Melbourne Exhibition Centre, designed by architects Denton Corker Marshall (est. 1972), is a 322,917-square-foot (29,062 sq m) facility located prominently on a bend in the Yarra River at the edge of central Melbourne.

Bold graphic elements, designed by graphic design firm Emerystudio (est. 1999) mark the Melbourne Exhibition Centre, beginning on its rooftop and extending throughout the building's interiors with overscaled, monumental sign elements and supergraphics. A ½-kilometer- (⅓ mi) long colonnade of immense, slanted planes juts through walls and ceilings, creating a display armature for primary public information. Each graphic plane denotes the entry to exhibition halls in bold, condensed sans-serif stencil letterforms along the public corridor. Bright colors and oblique angles provide a dynamic visual character for the building, making it difficult for anyone to understand where graphic design ends and architecture begins.

SEATTLE CENTRAL LIBRARY

2004

SEATTLE CENTRAL LIBRARY SIGN PROGRAM
Seattle, Washington, USA

Bruce Mau Design (est. 1985), Designers
Toronto, Ontario, Canada
Office of Metropolitan Architecture (est. 1975),
Architects
Rotterdam, Netherlands

The Seattle Public Library, covering an area of 355,209 square feet (33,000 sq m), was designed by the Office of Metropolitan Architecture (OMA) under the direction of Rem Koolhaus (b. 1944) and opened in 2004. This striking and innovative building, a central feature of the city's cultural and communal life, houses a vast number of books, official publications, periodicals, audiovisual materials, and the technical facilities to gain access (also online) to the current library catalog. Each day, between 6,000 and 8,000 visitors use the library to take advantage of all that the city has to offer, publicly, culturally, and scientifically.

Bruce Mau Design (est. 1985), a multidisciplinary design firm, collaborated with the building architects to create an identity and wayfinding sign program that they described as "big strong made friendly."

The basic concept underlying this program is a balance between the signs themselves and the building architecture, with materials and dimensions made to fit in with their surroundings. Unconventional elements, such as playful, oversize supergraphics and lettering on the inner and outer walls, echo the unique structure of the building.

Surfaces of desks and walls become part of the signs, rather than the other way around. Overscaled sans-serif letters in Futura (Paul Renner, 1927) make it impossible to overlook the book stacks for fiction or the checkout desk.

Letterforms wrap around library counters, run up the sides of brightly lit escalators confirming where you are going, and appear on floors and within the book stacks. Even the Dewey decimal system appears in large-scale floor panels that are movable as the inventory of books changes and evolves.

Ultimately, the success of this design solution is due to the fact that it makes the user feel as though they are inside the navigational system of a real-world library—engaging, accessible, understandable—and designed for the flow of real people.

BLOOMBERG
HEADQUARTERS

2005

BLOOMBERG HEADQUARTERS
SIGN PROGRAM
New York, New York, USA

Pentagram (est. 1972), Designers
New York, New York, USA
STUDIOS Architecture (est. 1985), Interior Designers
New York, New York, USA

Bloomberg Tower, designed by Pelli Clark Pelli Architects (est. 1977), is a 806-foot- (246 m) tall, 55-story, 1,400,000-square-foot (130,000 sq m) building on the east side of midtown Manhattan in New York City. The building houses the headquarter offices of Bloomberg LP—a financial news, data, and analytics provider, as well as retail outlets, restaurants, and residential condominiums.

Working with STUDIOS Architecture (est. 1985), design consultancy Pentagram (est. 1972) created an interior wayfinding sign program, combined with environmental graphics and several dynamic, superscale, electronic media installations, that seamlessly communicated Bloomberg's product brand and services—data, news, and information—to employees, clients, and visitors.

S. I. NEWHOUSE SCHOOL
OF PUBLIC COMMUNICATIONS

2007

**S. I. NEWHOUSE SCHOOL
OF PUBLIC COMMUNICATIONS
ENVIRONMENTAL GRAPHICS
AND DONOR RECOGNITION WALL**
Syracuse, New York, USA

Poulin + Morris Inc. (est. 1989), Designers
New York, New York, USA
Ennead Architects (formerly Polshek Partnership;
est. 1963), Architects
New York, New York, USA

In 2007, the S. I. Newhouse School of Public Communications complex at Syracuse University in New York State expanded to include a new 74,000-square-foot (6,900 sq m) building, designed by Ennead Architects (est. 1963). This glass-wrapped building addition houses community spaces, high-tech media labs, and research centers, designed specifically to foster collaboration through natural gathering places for students, faculty, alumni, and guests of the premier journalism school in the country.

A unique donor recognition wall in the building's entrance lobby acknowledges the digital evolution of public communications by using a kinetic medium to communicate donor names and their personal messages to passers-by. More than 100 staggered, horizontal LED digital panels display this information in a fluid, synchronized pace simulating multiple news zippers communicating simultaneously as if real-time information were being displayed. In this context, LED technology was used in a nonconventional setting to symbolize the tenet "the medium is the message."

A sans-serif typographic wall mural (Din, 1905) in the "heart" or atrium of the building spans three stories identifying NEWHOUSE and its programs such as media studies, journalism, and graphic design. This monumental mural is a visual metaphor composed of CMYK-colored halftone dots celebrating "NEWHOUSE" and its pursuits of traditional and nontraditional forms of public communications in the new digital era.

Designed by Poulin + Morris Inc. (est. 1989), these dynamic visual solutions not only inspire but also connect with the spirit, energy, diversity, professionalism, and creativity of past, present, and future generations of this premier school of communications.

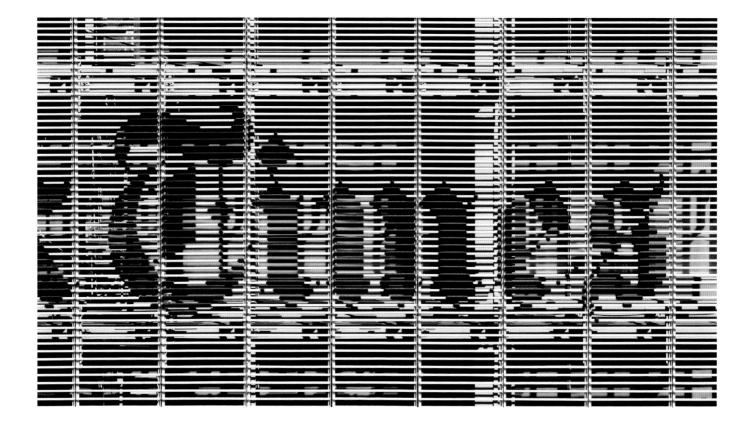

THE NEW YORK TIMES BUILDING

2008

THE NEW YORK TIMES BUILDING FACADE
New York, New York, USA

Pentagram (est. 1972), Designers
New York, New York, USA
Renzo Piano Building Workshop (est. 1981), Architects
Genoa, Italy

Completed in 2008, the New York Times Building is a 52-story, 1,046-foot- (319 m) high, 1,540,000-square-foot (143,070 sq m) tower on the west side of midtown Manhattan in New York City. The building was designed by architects Renzo Piano Building Workshop (est. 1981) and houses its main tenant, the New York Times Company, publisher of the *New York Times*, the *Boston Globe*, and the *International Herald Tribune*.

The steel-framed building utilizes an exterior screen of 1 ⅝-inch (4 cm) ceramic rods mounted on the exterior of the glass curtain walls of the east, west, and south building facades. The rod spacing increases from the base to the top, providing greater transparency as the building rises.

Located on the western facade at the lower portion of this screen, *The New York Times* iconoclastic blackletter logotype, 110

feet (34 m) long, is integrated to each of these ceramic rods as an intricate assemblage of approximately 1,000 extruded painted aluminum sleeves.

Designed by Michael Bierut (b. 1957) of Pentagram (est. 1972), this dynamic and optically innovative treatment provides the building with an extremely integrated building identification sign, as well as provides a meaningful and resonant symbol for the publisher.

NEWSEUM

2008

NEWSEUM BUILDING FACADE
Washington, D.C., USA

Poulin + Morris Inc. (est. 1989), Designers
New York, New York, USA
Ennead Architects (formerly Polshek Partnership; est. 1963), Architects
New York, New York, USA

Newseum, located between the Capitol Building and the White House and adjacent to the Smithsonian museums on the National Mall, is a seven-level, 643,000-square-foot (60,000 sq m) interactive museum designed by Ennead Architects (est. 1963) and dedicated to news and journalism. As one of nation's capital's most popular destinations, Newseum's mission is to "raise public awareness of the important role of a free press in a democratic society."

The building's principal facade is a glass curtain wall punctuated by a 74-foot- (22.5 m) high monolithic plane of sandblasted limestone engraved with the forty-five words of the First Amendment of the U.S. Constitution. Designed by Douglas Morris (b. 1962) of the multidisciplinary design firm Poulin + Morris Inc. (est. 1989), this exterior monumental feature accentuates large-scale typography set in all-capital serif Trajan (Carol Twombly, 1989) letterforms as a bas-relief and permanently displays the First Amendment as a timeless element set in a modern context.

This visual theme is also carried over to the graphic identity, environmental graphics, wayfinding, and branding program developed by the graphic designers. The end result reflects a strong marriage between past and present, reinforcing Newseum's political, social, and historical mission.

GREENPIX ZERO ENERGY MEDIA WALL

2008

GREENPIX ZERO ENERGY MEDIA WALL
Beijing, China

Arup (est. 1946); Simone Giostra & Partners
(est. 2006), Architects
Boston, Massachusetts,USA; Brooklyn, New York, USA

GreenPix was a groundbreaking project that applied sustainable and digital media technology to the curtain wall of the Xicui Entertainment Center in Beijing, near the site of the 2008 Summer Olympic Games.

It featured the world's largest LED light wall display and the first photovoltaic system that harvested solar energy during the day integrated into a glass curtain wall. The 197-foot (60 m) by 108-foot (33 m) laminated glass facade is composed of 2,292 individually programmable LED color nodes that display moving images and offer video artists an almost infinite range of lighting and animation choices.

Through the use of this new technology, the building itself became a self-sufficient organic system that harvested solar energy during the day and used it to illuminate the building's curtain wall display at night. Additionally, the photovoltaic cells that were laminated to the building's curtain wall fed energy into the building systems during the day, reduced build-ing energy costs, and functioned as an effective shading device that protected the building from excessive heat gain. At night, the curtain wall displayed the energy accumulated throughout the day in bursts of light, transforming the facade into a glowing beacon and making the building an overwhelming visual experience within the nightscape of Beijing.

The project was designed and engineered by Arup (est. 1946) and Simone Giostra & Partners (est. 2006), an architectural and engineering collaboration with an international reputation for developing innovative solutions for the built environment.

GreenPix was launched in 2008 with a series of video art installations that immediately galvanized an energetic art movement in Beijing and produced an ever-changing public work of art that became a part of the everyday lives of Beijing's residents.

BROOKLYN BOTANIC GARDEN

2008

BROOKLYN BOTANIC GARDEN ENTRANCE
Brooklyn, New York, USA

Poulin + Morris Inc. (est. 1989)
New York, New York, USA
Ennead Architects (formerly Polshek Partnership;
est. 1963), Architects
New York, New York, USA

From the top of its 50-foot- (15.2 m) high, green-tinted, cast-glass cone, down to the embracing arms of its stainless steel–sheathed, leaf-patterned walls, the Eastern Parkway entrance at the Brooklyn Botanic Garden links 52 acres (21 ha) of theme spaces, including the Japanese Hill and Pond, an herb garden, a fragrance garden, and 12,000 varieties of plants harbored inside with sky, light, and earth.

Brooklyn Botanic Garden opened in 1910 and was designed by the Olmsted Brothers (est. 1898), the sons of American landscape architect Frederick Law Olmsted (1822–1903), with its original buildings designed by American Beaux-Arts architects McKim, Mead & White (est. 1872).

In collaboration with Ennead Architects (est. 1963), the multidisciplinary design firm of Poulin + Morris Inc. (est. 1989) created 12-foot- (3.6 m) high, curved walls rising on both sides of the entrance sheathed in stainless steel with an etched cherry tree leaf pattern. The garden's logotype (Requiem, 1992) is dimensionalized in two-tone stainless steel and appears to float in front of the entrance walls. A pair of 16–foot (4.9 m) wide gates located between them are of the same material; however, the leaf pattern here is water-jet cut, creating a stainless steel grille for viewing into the garden when the gates are closed. Behind the gates, the garden's ticket and information booths are sunken into an earth berm. The entrance's centerpiece is a 50-foot- (15.2 m) high, cast-glass cone that functions as a sundial.

THE COOPER UNION

2010

**THE COOPER UNION ACADEMIC BUILDING
SIGN PROGRAM**
New York, New York, USA
Pentagram (est. 1972), Designers
New York, New York, USA
Morphosis (est. 1972), Architects
Santa Monica, California, USA

The sign program for the Cooper Union's new 175,000) square foot (16,258 sq m) academic building on Cooper Square in New York City's East Village, is an essential and fully integrated component of the building's innovative and dynamic architecture, designed by Pritzker Prize–winning architect Thom Mayne (b. 1944) of Morphosis (est. 1972).

Designed by Abbott Miller (b. 1963) of Pentagram (est. 1972), typography throughout the program has been manipulated and dimensionalized in different ways, engaging multiple surfaces, appearing cut or extruded across corners, and extended through varied building materials. The geometric sans-serif typeface Gridnik (Wim Crouwel, 1974), with its strong angularity and futuristic appearance, was used throughout the program.

The building canopy features optically extruded letterforms that appear "correct" when seen in strict elevation but distort as their profiles recede backward in space. An expansive installation of donor recognition signs is displayed above a main circulation staircase that descends through the building's central public space.

This bold, iconic building, as well as its integrated graphic design elements, embodies the values and aspirations of an institution well known for advanced education in graphic design and architecture.

GOUGH STREET BANNERS

2010

GOUGH STREET BANNERS
Hong Kong, China
Eric Chan Design Co. Ltd. (est. 1991), Designers
Hong Kong, China

Gough Street, one of the oldest streets in Hong Kong, is occupied mostly by small commercial and residential buildings several stories high and built during the 1950s and 1960s.

Eric Chan Design Co. Ltd. (est. 1991) used the ever-present idea of residents hanging out their wash to dry on bamboo sticks to create a memorable and kinetic identification. Scale, material, color, and composition all reinforce the celebratory nature of these banners as welcomed additions to any urban streetscape.

X EXHIBITION

2010

X EXHIBITION
Shenzhen, China
Sense Team (est. 1999), Designers
Shenzhen, China

X Exhibition features the talent of eleven young designers from five countries. The design concept for the exhibition explores the idea of semipermanent identity installations located all over the city that would express the creative energy of the exhibition and the work of its up-and-coming designers.

Sense Team (est. 1999), the graphic designers of X Exhibition, employed fluorescent light installations as the sole identifier for each venue, as well as for the names of each

designer and discipline. Custom stencil-like letterforms, composed of fluorescent lights, were used as the sole light source for the exhibition, as well as the principle design element in the

exhibition that symbolized the creative "spark." These "characters of light" expressed the creative power and energy of this group of eleven designers throughout the city of Shenzhen.

IV

PHOTOGRAFFEUR JR

2010

URBAN PHOTOGRAPHIC MURALS
Rio de Janeiro, Argentina

JR (b. 1983), Designer
Paris, France

JR (b. 1983), an anonymous Parisian street artist who identifies himself as a photograffeur —a hybrid of photographer and graffiti artist— illegally pastes his huge, close-up photographic portraits on walls, roofs, bridges, and embankments in downtrodden locales around the world. Personal identity is a central theme in his "guerrilla art," and he frequently uses the expressive human face to question racial stereotypes, preconceptions, and injustices. The scale of these installations is so vast that you can see the eyes of his subjects from the sky above.

He is an elusive visual communicator and political and social commentator whose photographic graffiti work has captivated and changed the world.

His "Women Are Heroes" installation was plastered all over trains, rooftops, and other public places throughout strife-torn countries in an effort to empower women around the world. In the urban slums of Brazil, Cambodia, and Kenya, his oversize portraits of their inhabitants were printed on waterproof digital vinyl and also doubled as new roofs for their ramshackle and rundown homes.

This monumental and highly emotional photographic work is much more than familiar graffiti or advertisements that envelop entire buses in urban centers around the world. It uses architecture and the built environment in a subversive manner to reach a worldwide audience with his humanitarian goals.

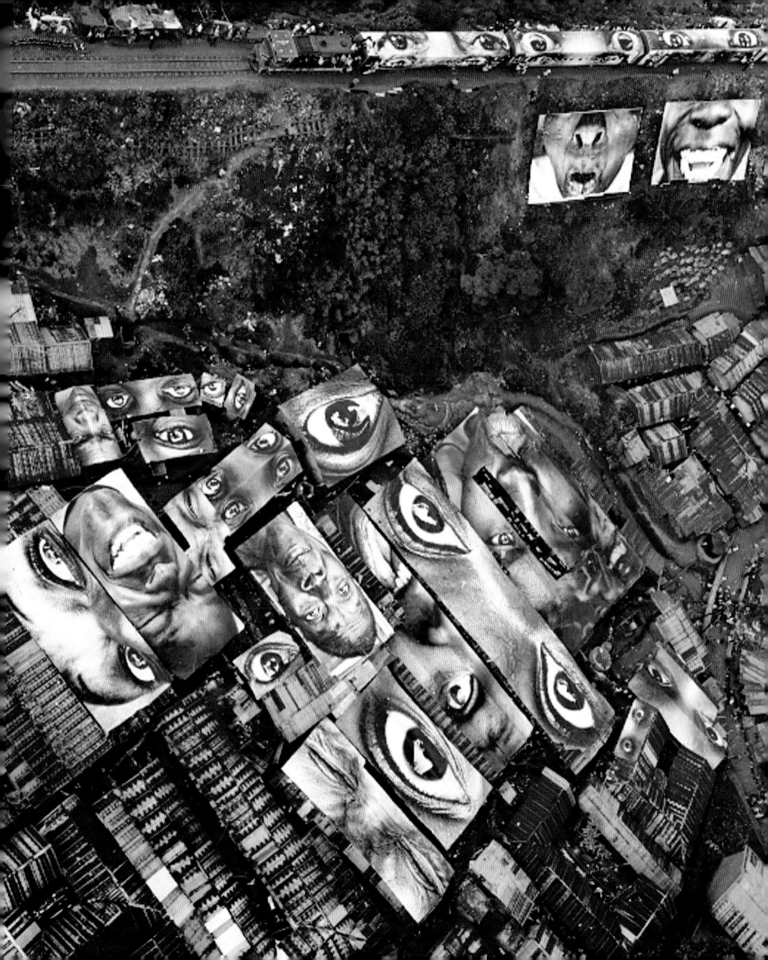

GLOSSARY

A

abstract expressionism: a modern art movement that flourished after World War II until the early 1960s characterized by nonrepresentational and improvisational art

abstraction: the visual simplification, distortion, or rearrangement of a recognizable image

acanthus: a plant whose thick, fleshy leaves are used as a model for the carved ornamentation on the lower portions of the Corinthian capital

adobe: sun-dried (i.e., unbaked) brick predominantly used in buildings and structures throughout Africa, South America, and Central Asia

aluminum: a silvery-white, lightweight, corrosion-resistant metal that has highly conductive and thermal properties

amber: a hard, translucent yellow, orange, or brownish-yellow fossil resin primarily used for jewelry and ornamental objects

analogous colors: a set of colors created from adjacent colors on a color wheel that possess minimal chroma differences

animatronics: a technology that animates puppets or figures by means of electromechanical devices

anthropomorphic: characteristic of having human form or attributes

applied arts: the application of design and aesthetics to objects of function and everyday use, such as in the fields of architecture, graphic design, photography, industrial design, fashion design, interior design, and furniture design

apse: a semicircular area at the east end of a church or sanctuary, first applied to a Roman basilica, which originally contained an altar

arabesque: a surface decoration, fanciful in character, using flowing lines and geometric patterns

arch: a curved structure composed of wedge-shaped elements used to span an opening

argon: a colorless, odorless, inert gas used in incandescent and fluorescent lightbulbs and other types of gas discharge tubes, such as neon

art deco: a decorative style of the 1920s and 1930s using elements characteristic of modern technological developments of the machine age; also known as Art Moderne

art nouveau: French for "new art;" also known as Jugendstil, German for "youth style"; an international movement and style in art, architecture, and applied arts that was popular from 1890 to 1905 and characterized by organic, floral, and plant-inspired motifs

Arts and Crafts movement: an international movement that originated in Great Britain during the late 1800s through the writings of William Morris (1834–1896) and John Ruskin (1819–1900) and was characterized by simple form and a medieval style of decoration

ascender: the part of the lowercase letter that rises above the body of the letter, or x-height, as in a, b, d, h, l, or t

asphalt: a brownish-black solid or semisolid mixture of bitumens used in road paving, roofing, and waterproofing

assemblage: a sculptural composition consisting of an arrangement of miscellaneous objects

avant-garde: the development of new, experimental, and innovative concepts, especially in the areas of the fine and applied arts

B

balance: a state of equilibrium in which visual forces of equal strength pull in opposite directions

balustrade: a series of pillars or columns supporting a handrail or coping

barrel vault: a continuous vault of semicircular sections; also known as a tunnel vault, wagon head vault, or wagon vault

bas-relief: a sculptural carving in low or shallow relief, on a background

base: the lower portion of any built structure or architectural feature

Beaux-Arts: an architectural style developed at the French school of art and design in Paris, the École des Beaux-Arts

billboard: a large-scale panel display for advertisements in public places, such as alongside a highway or on the sides of buildings; also known as hoarding

blackletter: a heavy typeface based on medieval script and gothic minuscules with very broad counters and thick, ornamental serifs

bronze: a metal alloy composed of various proportions of copper and tin

burlesque: a comic or parody performance, often including striptease

buttress: a projecting support built into or against the external wall of a building, typically used in Gothic architecture. A flying buttress is an arch starting from a detached pier and abutting against a wall to take the thrust of the vaulting.

Byzantine: an architectural style dating from the fifth century in Constantinople (Byzantium, now Istanbul) and characterized by masonry construction around a central plan, with domes on pendatives, typically depicting the figure of Christ

C

calligraphy: the art of fine handwriting

capital: the topmost feature of a column

capitalis monumentalis: Roman capital square letters used primarily in inscriptions

Carrara marble: a snow-white marble from the Carrara district of Tuscany; the favored medium of Michelangelo, also known to the Romans as Luna

cast iron: iron shaped by pouring into molds and used to a rapidly increasing extent in buildings and structures from the late eighteenth century until superseded by steel in the mid-nineteenth century

catwalk: a narrow, elevated walkway found on either the sides of a bridge or above a theater stage

chevron: a zigzag molding first used in Romanesque architecture

chrome: a hard, lustrous, steel-gray metal resistant to tarnish and corrosion

cladding: an outer veneer of various materials applied to a building facade

classical: an architectural style originating in ancient Greece and Rome, and largely revived in the Renaissance in Europe and elsewhere

classicism: a tradition of Greek and Roman antiquity, distinguished by the qualities of simplicity, harmony, and balance

collage: an artistic composition of materials and objects pasted over a surface

colonnade: a row of columns, usually spaced equidistant from one another, supporting an entablature or arches

color: a visual property of an object that depends on a combination of reflected and absorbed light from the spectrum, as well as hues found in light and pigment

column: a circular, vertical support consisting of a base, shaft, and capital

condensed typeface: a typeface with characteristic form or proportion that is compressed to a narrower width than is normal; its opposite is extended (or expanded)

constructivism: an art movement, originating in Russia in 1919, that rejected the idea of "art for art's sake" in favor of art as a practice directed toward social purposes and needs

Corinthian: see *order*

cornice: the upper part of an entablature, extending beyond the frieze

cubism: a twentieth-century avant-garde art movement, pioneered by Pablo Picasso (1881–1973) and Georges Braque (1882–1963), characterized by objects that are broken up and reassembled in abstract forms

cuneiform: a system of writing developed in Mesopotamia (2500 BCE), in which wedge-shaped pictograms were impressed using a square-ended reed, into the smooth surface of wet clay tablets, which were then baked. The name comes from the Latin word *cuneus*, meaning "wedge."

cupola: a spherical roof or small dome and its supports that crown a structure

curtain wall: the logical outcome of skeleton-frame construction, in which the external walls serve no load-bearing purpose but are suspended on the face of the building like a curtain

cyclorama: a large, composite image on the interior walls of a cylindrical room that appears in natural perspective to a spectator standing in the center of the room

D

descender: the part of the lowercase letter that falls below the body of the letter or baseline, as in g, j, p, q, and y

de Stijl: a Dutch art movement (also known as neoplasticism) founded in 1917 and characterized by pure abstraction as well as an essential reduction of form and color

dichroic: a visual characteristic that appears to show different colors at different concentrations

digital: a term for electronic technology that has taken over print and image manipulation systems since the 1980s

dome: a convex covering, usually hemispherical or semielliptical over a circular or polygonal space

Doric: see *order*

dormer: a vertical window in a sloping roof, with its own roof and gable

E

Elementarism: a conceptual art movement founded by Theo Van Doesburg (1883–1931) characterized by diagonal lines

entablature: the upper horizontal part of a Greek or Roman order, composed of an architrave, frieze, and cornice

F

facade: the external face of a building or structure

faience: glazed earthenware, originally made in Faenza, Italy (ca. 1300), used for pottery and building

Fascism: a system of government marked by a centralized authority under a dictator with stringent socioeconomic controls, suppression of the opposition through terror and censorship, and a policy of belligerent nationalism and racism

fauvism: an early-twentieth-century art movement in characterized by vivid colors and distorted forms

fiberglass: a resin-based plastic made from polyester resins and reinforced with glass fibers

flying buttress: see *buttress*

forecourt: a courtyard located in front of a building or built structure

form: three-dimensional derivatives of basic shapes, such as a sphere, cube, or pyramid

fresco: a wall painting made on wet plaster with water-based pigments

functionalism: a design movement where the function of an object determines its physical design and materials

futurism: an Italian art and design style of the 1920s featuring movement, mechanization, and speed

G

gangway: a passageway along either side of a ship's upper deck

gargoyle: a projecting waterspout, carved in the form of a grotesque figure, human, or animal

glass block: a translucent and durable rectangular-sided construction material comprising two halves of glass joined together; also known as glass brick or cellular glass

glyph: a simplistic form or element of writing

Googie architecture: a modern, futuristic architectural style influenced by car culture and the space age

Gothic: a medieval European architectural style (1400–1600), originating in twelfth-century France, characterized by high stone vaults, pointed arches, towers, and flying buttresses

graffiti: a contemporary form of writing or drawing scribbled, scratched, or sprayed on a wall surface

granite: a hard, coarse-grained, igneous rock composed of quartz and mica; primarily used in monuments, buildings, and other structures

Great Depression: the longest, most widespread, and deepest depression of the twentieth century that occurred throughout the world in 1929 and lasted until the early 1940s

grid: a modular system composed of a set of horizontal and vertical lines used as a guide to align type and image and create a uniform composition

grotesque: a classification of sans-serif lineale typefaces with characteristic form and proportion that is uniform and upright

H

hieroglyphics: an ancient Egyptian system of writing in which pictorial symbols were used to represent meaning or sounds or a combination of the two

hoarding: see *billboard*

Huichol: a native American culture in the Sierra Madre mountain range of western central Mexico

human factors: the study of designing equipment and devices that fit the human body, its movements, and its cognitive abilities; also known as ergonomics

humanist: a classification of sans-serif lineale typefaces with characteristic form and proportion that is reminiscent of Roman inscriptional letterforms and calligraphic writing

I

incandescent: the visible light emitted by an object as a result of being heated

inlaid: a design created by setting materials, such as wood, stone, or metal, into a surface, usually at the same level

International Style: a twentieth-century architectural style based on function, without ornament, and characterized by flat roofs and large glass areas

International Typographic Style: a graphic design style developed in Switzerland in the 1950s and characterized by clean, readable, asymmetric layouts and use of the page grid and sans-serif typefaces; also known as the Swiss School or Swiss Style

Ionic: see *order*

isometric: a drawing projection method where three visible surfaces of a form have equal emphasis, all axes are simultaneously rotated away from the picture plane at 30 degrees, all lines are equally foreshortened, and angles between lines are always at 120 degrees

J

Jugendstijl: see *art nouveau*

L

LED (light-emitting diode): a semiconductor diode that emits light when voltage is applied to it

limestone: a sedimentary rock commonly used in the construction of buildings and structures

lintel: a structural element over an opening that supports construction above

logotype: a word set in a specific typeface, designed as a cohesive unit, and functioning as a graphic identity for a product, company, or service

M

marquee: a rooflike structure, often bearing a signboard, projecting over a building entrance such as a theater or hotel

medieval: a period of European history that follows the fall of the Roman Empire in 476 until the fifteenth century, preceding the modern era; also known as the Middle Ages

megalith: a huge, irregular stone used in various prehistoric architecture and monuments, especially during the second millennium BCE

mercury vapor: a gas discharge glass lamp that utilizes an electric arc through vaporized mercury to produce illumination

minaret: a high tower, usually attached to a mosque, from which Muslims are called to prayer

Moderne: a French-language term for modern or modernistic design

modernism: a twentieth-century architectural and design style based on function and structure

Moorish: a Spanish architectural style (900–1700) characteristic of the horseshoe-shaped arch and decorative ornamentation

mosaic: a surface decoration for floors and walls, consisting of small pieces of stone, marble, or glass set in cement, mortar, or mastic

motif: a repetitive figure or design element found in architecture or decorative ornamentation

Mughal: a architectural style that is an amalgam of Islamic, Turkish, and Indian architectural styles with symmetrical and decorative characteristics

mural: a large image, such as a painting or enlarged photograph, applied directly to a wall or ceiling

N

Nautical Moderne: see *Streamline Moderne*

Nazism: the ideology and practice of racist nationalism, expansionism, and state control of the economy

neoclassical: the last phase of late-eighteenth-century European classicism characterized by the sparing use of ornamentation and a strong emphasis on geometric forms

neon: an colorless, odorless, inert gas that glows reddish-orange in an electric discharge tube

New Deal: a series of policies and programs introduced during the 1930s to promote economic recovery and social reform during the Great Depression

New Typography: a twentieth-century design movement, influenced by both the Bauhaus and Russian constructivists, that celebrated abstract modernist principles such as asymmetrical compositions and sans-serif typography

O

obelisk: a tall, tapering shaft of stone, square in section and pyramidal on top

oculus: a window or opening at the apex of a dome or other structure

onyx: a semiprecious cryptocrystalline consisting of silica and quartz in parallel bands

op art: an abstract art movement characterized by the use of geometric shapes and brilliant colors to create optical illusions

order: a term applied to the three styles of Greek architecture—Doric, Corinthian, and Ionic, referring to the style of columns and their entablatures; the Doric order is unique in having no base to the column. Its capital is plain; the shaft is fluted. The Ionic order is lighter and more elegant than the Doric, with slim columns, generally fluted. It is principally distinguished by the volutes of its capital. The Corinthian order has a bell-shaped capital, from which eight acanthus stalks (caulicoli) emerge to support the modest volutes. Its shaft is generally fluted.

organic architecture: a style of architecture having direct form and economy of materials common to natural organisms

ornament: an architectural embellishment or decorative element

P

pagoda: a tiered temple or building in Chinese or Japanese culture, usually pyramidal, forming a tower with upward curving roofs over the individual stories

parapet: the portion of a wall above the roof gutter, sometimes battlemented; also applied to the same feature, rising breast high, in balconies and bridges

pattern: the combination of lines, shapes, and/or colors in a consistent, orderly, or repetitive motif

pavilion: a prominent structure, generally distinctive in character, marking the ends and center of the facade of a major building

pedestal: a support for a column, statue, or vase that usually consists of a base, die, and cornice, or cap mold

pediment: the triangular gabled end segment of a roof above the entablature

petrogram/petroglyph: a prehistoric rock carving or line drawing

piazza: a public open space, surrounded by buildings that may vary in shape and in civic purpose

pictogram: a picture or symbol that represents a word or group of words

pier: a large pillar used to support a roof

pilaster: a rectangular feature in the shape of a pillar projecting only slightly from a wall

plaza: an open area in a city, usually surrounded by buildings or streets, and paved and landscaped

polychrome: a term originally applied to the art of decorative painting in many colors, extended to the coloring of sculpture to enhance naturalism, and used in an architectural context to describe the application of variegated materials to achieve brilliant effects

pop art: a twentieth-century art movement that depicts objects or scenes from everyday life and uses commercial art and popular illustration techniques

porcelain enamel: a glasslike coating for metal fused to the surface using high temperatures

portal: a large doorway, entrance, or gate to a building or structure

portico: a structure usually attached to a building, such as a porch, consisting of a roof supported by piers or columns

postmodernism: a twentieth-century architectural and design style succeeding modernism and characterized by historicism and decorative elements

pounce: a fine powder, such as pulverized charcoal, dusted over a stencil to transfer a design or image to an underlying surface, such as a billboard or hoarding

Prairie School: a late-nineteenth- and early-twentieth-century architectural style, common to the Midwestern United States and characterized by pronounced horizontal lines, flat roofs with broad eaves, and an integration to the natural landscape

prism: a transparent geometric form whose two ends are similar, equal, and parallel and whose sides are parallelograms; used to separate white light into a spectrum of colors

propaganda: an organized program of publicity and visual information used to propagate a doctrine or practice

pylon: a masonry tower with a central opening, forming the entrance to an ancient Egyptian temple

pyramid: in ancient Egypt, a quadrilateral masonry mass with steeply sloping sides meeting at an apex, used as a tomb

Q

Quakers: a Christian movement, formally known as the Religious Society of Friends or Friends Church, devoted to peaceful principles and eschewing formal doctrine, sacraments, and ordained ministers; members are known as Friends or Quakers

R

rationalism: a philosophy where reason rather than religion is a guiding principle in life

relief: moldings and ornamentation projecting from the surface of a wall

Renaissance: a design style in the fourteenth to sixteenth centuries that adapted ancient Roman elements and motifs

rivet: a metal bolt or pin with a head on one end, inserted through aligned holes of metal pieces to be joined and then hammered on the plain end so as to form a second head

rococo: a style originating in France in the early 1700s that developed out of the baroque style and is characterized by lavish ornamentation of shell work and foliage and its refined use of different materials, such as stucco, metal, or wood

S

sandstone: a sedimentary rock formed by the consolidation and compaction of sand held together by a natural cement, such as silica

sans serif: meaning without serifs; see *serif*

scaffold: a temporary structure or platform, either supported from below or suspended from above, that allows workers to perform tasks above the ground

scrim: a transparent fabric or screen used as a drop in the theater to create special lighting or atmospheric effects

script: a classification of typefaces that is calligraphic based with characteristic form and proportion imitative of fine handwriting

semaphore: a visual signaling device with flags, lights, or mechanically activated arms

serif: the beginning of an end of the stroke, arm, leg, or tail of roman letterforms drawn at a right angle or at an oblique to the stem or stroke

serigraphy: the art or process of printing an image by means of silk-screening

shaft: the part of a column between the base and the capital

Shaker: a reserved and simple style developed by the American Shaker religious communities

silk-screening: a process, similar to stenciling, with ink forced through a prepared sheet of fine material, such as silk; see *serigraphy*

skyscraper: a very tall building or structure composed of many stories or levels

space frame: a frame that is three-dimensional and structurally stable in all directions

spandrel: the triangular space between the curves of adjacent arches; in modern architecture, an infill panel below a window frame in a curtain wall

spire: a tall, tapering structure rising from a tower or roof and ending in a point, as in the top of a steeple

stainless steel: a steel alloy containing chromium that is highly resistant to corrosion and rusting

Streamline Moderne: a late development of the art deco style that emerged during the 1930s and characterized by curving forms, long horizontal lines, and sometimes nautical elements; also known as Nautical Moderne or Art Moderne

stucco: a fine quality of plaster, composed of gypsum, lime, and sand and used in Roman and Renaissance architecture for ornamental modeled work in low relief

Suprematism: a Russian abstract art movement that focused on fundamental geometric forms such as the circle and the square

swash: the flourish that may extend a stroke or replace a serif on a letter

Swiss Style: see *International Typographic Style*

symbol: a visual element used to represent or identify a product, company, or service

symmetry: a state of visual balance (also known as formal balance or reflective symmetry) in which all compositional elements are identical, equally balanced, and can be divided into two equal parts that are mirror images of each other

T

tension: a principle of visual perception in which the forces of balance or imbalance, stress, action, and reaction exist between the elements of any composition

terminal: a stem or stroke ending other than a serif

terra-cotta: a building material that is earth baked or burnt in molds for use in construction and decoration; harder in quality than brick

terrazzo: a floor surface composed of small chips of marble embedded in cement and polished smooth

trademark: see *logotype*, *symbol*

trompe l'oeil: a realistic painting technique creating an illusion of reality (literally means "fools the eye")

turret: a small tower, usually starting at some distance from the ground, attached to a building such as a castle or fortress

U

Usonian architecture: a term coined by Frank Lloyd Wright (1867–1959) to describe his approach to American architectural design

V

vault: an arched brick or stone structure forming a ceiling over a building; the simplest form is the barrel vault, a single continuous arch; the groined vault is two barrel vaults joined at right angles; a ribbed vault has diagonal arches projecting from the surface

veneer: a thin surface layer, as in finely grained wood, adhered to the surface of an inferior material

Vienna Secession: a group of Austrian artists, including Gustav Klimt, Koloman Moser, Josef Hoffmann, Joseph Maria Olbrich, and Max Kurzweil, who resigned from the Association of Austrian Artists in 1897 to form their own independent artists union; also known as the Union of Austrian Artists

vitreous: resembling glass in either color, composition, brittleness, or luster

W

wainscot: a lining for the lower part of an interior wall surface

WPA Moderne: an architectural style of the 1930s projects of the American governmental agency characterized by stripped classical forms

wrought iron: an easily welded and forged iron that is a mechanical mixture of refined metallic iron and siliceous slag

Z

ziggurat: a mud-brick stepped pyramid in Mesopotamian sacred architecture

BIBLIOGRAPHY

BOOKS

Albrecht, Donald. *The Mythic City: Photographs of New York by Samuel H. Gottscho*. 1925–1940. New York: Princeton Architectural Press, 2005.

Albrecht, Donald. *Paris/New York: Design/Fashion/ Culture/1925–1940*. New York: Princeton Architectural Press, 2008.

Albrecht, Donald and Broikos, Chrysanthe, ed. *On the Job: Design and the American Office*. New York: Princeton Architectural Press, 2000.

Aldersey-Williams, Hugh. *New American Design*. New York: Rizzoli International Publications, 1988.

Ambasz, Emilio. *The Architecture of Luis Barragán*. New York: The Museum of Modern Art, 1976.

Apeloig, Philippe. *Jean Widmer: A Devotion to Modernism*. New York: The Cooper Union for the Advancement of Science and Art, 2003.

Arup in Beijing: Solutions for a Modern City. London: Black Dog Publishing, 2009.

Ault, Julie. *Come Alive! The Spirited Art of Sister Corita*. London: Four Corners Books, 2006.

Baljeu, Joost. *Theo van Doesburg*. New York: Macmillan Publishing Co., 1974.

Benevolo, Leonardo. *The History of the City*. Cambridge: MIT Press, 1975.

Benevolo, Leonardo. *History of Modern Architecture*. Cambridge: MIT Press, 1977.

Bergdoll, Barry and Dickerman, Leah. *Bauhaus 1919–1933: Workshops for Modernity*. New York: The Museum of Modern Art, 2009.

Blackwell, Lewis. *20th Century Type*. New York: Yale University Press, 2004.

Blotkamp, Carel, et al. *De Stijl: The Formative Years 1917–1922*. Cambridge: MIT Press, 1982.

Bock, Manfred, ed. *De Stijl: 1917–1931, Visions of Utopia*. New York: Abbeville Press, 1982.

Booth-Clibborn, Edward and Baroni, Danielle. *The Language of Graphics*. New York: Harry N. Abrams, 1980.

Braybrooke, Susan. *Print Casebooks 3, 1978/79 Edition, The Best in Environmental Graphics*. New York: Watson-Guptill Publications, 1979.

Braybrooke, Susan. *Print Casebooks 4, 1980/81 Edition, The Best in Environmental Graphics*. Baltimore: RC Publications, 1980.

Braybrooke, Susan. *Print Casebooks 6, 1984/85 Edition, The Best in Environmental Graphics*. Baltimore: RC Publications, 1984.

Braybrooke, Susan. *Print Casebooks 7, 1987/88 Edition, The Best in Environmental Graphics*. Baltimore: RC Publications, 1987.

Burke, Christopher. *Paul Renner: The Art of Typography*. New York: Princeton Architectural Press, 1998.

Busch, Akiko. *Print Casebooks 8, 1989/90 Edition, The Best in Environmental Graphics*. New York: Watson-Guptill Publications, 1989.

Carpenter, Edward K. *The Print Casebook, First Annual Edition, The Best in Environmental Graphics*. New York: Watson-Guptill Publications, 1975.

Chermayeff & Geismar Associates. *Designing*. New York: Graphis, 2003.

Chermayeff & Geismar Associates. *Trademarks*. New York: Chermayeff & Geismar Associates, 2000.

Cohen, Arthur A. *Herbert Bayer: The Complete Work*. Cambridge: MIT Press, 1984.

Cohen, Barbara; Heller, Steven; Chwast, Seymour. *Trylon and Persiphere: The 1939 New York World's Fair*. New York: Harry N. Abrams, 1989.

Constantine, Mildred. *The Ubiquitous Sign*. New York: American Institute of Graphic Arts, 1970.

Craig, James and Barton, Bruce. *Thirty Centuries of Graphic Design*. New York: Watson-Guptill Publications, 1987.

Crosby, Fletcher, Forbes. *A Sign Systems Manual*. New York: Praeger Publishers, 1970.

Desilets, Deborah. *Morris Lapidus: The Architecture of Joy*. New York: Rizzoli, 2011.

de Noblet, Jocelyn, ed. *Industrial Design: Reflections of a Century*. Paris: Flammarion, 1993.

Diamonstein-Spielvogel, Barbaralee. *The Landmarks of New York: An Illustrated Record of the City's Historic Buildings*. New York: The Monacelli Press, 2005.

Diethelm, Walter. *Form & Communication*. Zurich: ABC Verlag Zurich, 1974.

Eskilson, Stephen J. *Graphic Design: A New History*. New Haven: Yale University Press, 2007.

Feldman, Edmund Burke. *Varieties of Visual Experience: Art as Image and Idea*. New York: Prentice-Hall, 1971.

Finke, Gail. *You Are Here: Graphics That Direct, Explain, and Entertain*. Cincinnati: ST Publications, 1999.

Fletcher, Sir Banister. *A History of Architecture*. London: Butterworths, 1989.

Follis, John. *Architectural Signing and Graphics*. New York: Watson-Guptill Publications, 1979.

Friedman, Mildred, ed. *De Stijl: 1917–1931, Visions of Utopia*. Minneapolis: Walker Art Center, 1982.

Friedman, Mildred. *Graphic Design in America: A Visual Language History*. New York: Harry N. Abrams, 1989.

Gardner, Louise. *Art through the Ages*. New York: Harcourt, Brace & World, 1970.

Gaur, Albertine. *A History of Writing*. London: The British Museum, 1983.

Gossel, Peter. *Modern Architecture A–Z*. Cologne: Taschen, 2007.

Gray, Nicolete. *Lettering on Buildings*. London: Architectural Press, 1960.

Grossholz, Andrea, ed. *Who's Who in Graphic Design*. Zurich: Benteli-Werd Verlags AG, 1994.

Heller, Steven and Cohen, Elaine Lustig. *Born Modern: The Life and Design of Alvin Lustig*. San Francisco: Chronicle Books, 2010.

Heller, Steven, ed. *I Heart Design*. Beverly: Rockport Publishers, 2011.

Heller, Steven. *Paul Rand*. London: Phaidon Press Limited, 1999.

Heller, Steven and Fili, Louise. *Stylepedia*. San Francisco: Chronicle Books, 2006.

Henrion, FHK. *AGI Annals*. Zurich: Alliance Graphique Internationale, 1989.

Herdeg, Walter. *Archigraphia*. Zurich: The Graphis Press, 1978.

Hess, Richard and Muller, Marion. *Dorfsman and CBS*. New York: Rizzoli International Publications, 1987.

Hughes, Robert. *American Visions: The Epic History of Art in America*. New York: Alfred A. Knopf, 1997.

Igarashi, Takenobu. *Igarashi Space Graphics*. Tokyo: Shoten Kenchiku-sha Co., Ltd., 1983.

The Institute of Graphic Designers. *Graphic Design, San Francisco*. San Francisco: Chronicle Books, 1979.

Jackson, Kenneth T., ed. *The Encyclopedia of New York City*. New Haven: Yale University Press, 1995.

Kinneir, Jock. *Words and Buildings: The Art of Public Lettering*. London: Architectural Press, 1980.

Kostof, Spiro. *America by Design*. New York: Oxford University Press, 1987.

Kostof, Spiro. *The City Assembled*. London: Thames and Hudson, 1992.

Kunstler, James Howard. *The Geography of Nowhere*. New York: Simon & Schuster, 1993.

Leggio, James, ed. *Vienna 1900: Art, Architecture, and Design*. New York: The Museum of Modern Art, 1986.

Lemmen, Hans van. *Tiles: 1,000 Years of Architectural Decoration*. New York: Harry N. Abrams, 1993.

Lin, Mariah. *This Way Please*. Beijing: Sandu Publishing, 2009.

Lin, Maya. *Boundaries*. New York: Simon & Schuster, 2000.

Lodder, Christina. *Russian Constructivism*. New Haven: Yale University Press, 1983.

Lynch, Kevin. *The Image of the City*. Cambridge: The MIT Press, 1960.

Masaaki, Hiromura. *Space Graphysm*. Amsterdam: BIS Publishers, 2003.

Mattie, Erik. *World's Fairs*. New York: Princeton Architectural Press, 1998.

McCullough, David. *The Greater Journey: Americans in Paris*. New York: Simon & Schuster, 2011.

Meggs, Philip B. *A History of Graphic Design*. New York: John Wiley & Sons, 2005.

Middendorp, Jan. *Dutch Type*. Rotterdam: 010 Publishers, 2004.

Middleton, William D. *Grand Central . . . the World's Greatest Railway Terminal*. San Marino: Golden West Books, 1977.

Miller, J. Abbott. *Signs and Spaces*. New York: Rockport Allworth Press, 1994.

Miller, R. Craig. *Modern Design 1980–1990*. New York: The Metropolitan Museum of Art, 1990.

Müller-Brockmann, Josef. *A History of Visual Communication*. Zurich: RR. Weber AG, 1986.

Neuhart, John. *Eames Design*. New York: Harry N. Abrams, 1989.

Ovenden, Mark. *Transit Maps of the World*. New York: Penguin Books, 2003.

Parissien, Steven. *Pennsylvania Station: McKim, Mead and White*. London: Phaidon Press, Ltd., 1996.

Parissien, Steven. *Station to Station*. London: Phaidon Press, Ltd., 1997.

Pevsner, Nikolaus. *Pioneers of Modern Design: From William Morris to Walter Gropius*. New Haven: Yale University Press, 2005.

Phillips, Lisa. *High Styles: Twentieth-Century American Design*. New York: Whitney Museum of American Art, 1985.

Pile, John. *A History of Interior Design*. New York: John Wiley & Sons, 2000.

Powell, Kenneth. *Grand Central Terminal: Warren and Wetmore*. London: Phaidon Press, Ltd., 1996.

Rees, Helen. *The Dutch PTT: Design in the Public Service 1920–1990*. London: Design Museum, 1990.

Remington, R. Roger. *Lester Beall: Trailblazer of American Graphic Design*. New York: W. W. Norton & Co., 1996.

Remington, R. Roger and Hodik, Barbara J. *Nine Pioneers in American Graphic Design*. Boston: MIT Press, 1989.

Riley, Terence. *Frank Lloyd Wright Architect*. New York: The Museum of Modern Art, 1994.

Rouard-Snowman, Margo. *Museum Graphics*. London: Thames and Hudson, 1992.

Roussel, Christine. *The Art of Rockefeller Center*. New York: W. W. Norton & Company, 2006.

Rudofsky, Bernard. *Streets for People*. New York: Doubleday & Company, 1969.

Rydell, Robert W. and Schiavo, Laura Burd. *Designing Tomorrow: America's World's Fairs of the 1930s*. New Haven: Yale University Press, 2010.

Sharp, Dennis. *Bauhaus, Dessau: Walter Gropius*. London: Phaidon Press, Ltd., 1993.

Shaughnessy, Adrian. *Supergraphics*. London: Unit Editions, 2010.

Shaw, Paul. *Helvetica and the New York City Subway System*. New York: Blue Pencil Editions, 2009.

Silver, Nathan. *Lost New York*. New York: Weathervane Books, 1967.

Smith, G. E. Kidder. *Source Book of American Architecture*. New York: Princeton Architectural Press, 1996.

Smith, Whitney. *Flags and Arms across the World*. New York: McGraw-Hill, 1975.

Society for Environmental Graphic Design. *SEGD Design Annual 1987/1988*. Tokyo: FP Books, 1989.

Solomon, Nancy B., ed. *Architecture: Celebrating the Past, Designing the Future*. Washington, DC: American Institute of Architects, 2008.

Sprigg, June. *Shaker Design*. New York: Whitney Museum of American Art, Norton Publications, 1986.

Sprigg, June and Larkin, David. *Shaker: Life, Work and Art*. New York; Stewart Tabori & Chang, 1987.

Stern, Robert A. M. *New York 1930: Architecture and Urbanism between the Two World Wars*. New York: Rizzoli International Publications, 1987.

Stern, Robert A. M. *New York 1960: Architecture and Urbanism between the Second World War and the Bicentennial*. New York: The Monacelli Press, 1995.

Stern, Rudi. *Let There Be Neon*. New York: Harry N. Abrams, 1979.

Sutton, James. *Signs in Action*. New York: Reinhold Publishing Company, 1965.

Taylor, Lisa. *Cities: The Forces That Shape Them*. New York: Cooper-Hewitt Museum, 1982.

Taylor, Lisa. *Urban Open Spaces*. New York: Cooper-Hewitt Museum, 1979.

Tell, Darcy. *Times Square Spectacular: Lighting Up Broadway*. New York: Harper Collins Books, 2007.

TwoPoints.Net, ed. *Left, Right, Up, Down: New Directions in Signage and Wayfinding*. Berlin: Gestalten, 2010.

Uebele, Andreas. *Signage Systems & Information Graphics: A Professional Sourcebook*. London: Thames and Hudson, 2007.

Van Hoogstraten, Nicholas. *Lost Broadway Theaters*. New York: Princeton Architectural Press, 1991.

Varnedoe, Kirk. *Vienna 1900: Art, Architecture & Design*. New York: The Museum of Modern Art, 1986.

Varnedoe, Kirk and Gopnik, Adam. *High & Low: Modern Art and Popular Culture*. New York: The Museum of Modern Art, 1990.

Venturi, Robert. *Complexity and Contradiction in Architecture*. New York: The Museum of Modern Art, 1977.

Venturi, Robert. *Learning from Las Vegas*. Cambridge: MIT Press, 1977.

Vigne, Georges. *Hector Guimard: Architect, Designer 1867–1942*. New York: Delano Greenidge Editions, 2003.

Vignelli Associates. *Vignelli Design*. New York: Rizzoli International Publications, 1990.

Watkin, David. *A History of Western Architecture*. London: Thames and Hudson, 1986.

Yew, Wei, ed. *The Olympic Image: The First 100 Years*. New York: Quon Editions, 1996.

Younger, William Lee. *Old Brooklyn in Early Photographs 1865–1929*. New York: Dover Publications, 1978.

Zim, Larry. *The World of Tomorrow: The 1939 New York World's Fair*. New York: Harper & Row Publishers, 1990.

PERIODICALS

Aldersey-Williams, Hugh. "PTT: Studio Dumbar Flexible Geometry." *Eye*. London: Autumn 1990, pp. 54–61.

Baines, Phil. "A Design (To Sign Roads By)." *Eye*. Winter 1999, pp. 26–36.

Bassi, Robert A. "Chicago: Still the City of 'Firsts.'" *Print*. 1968, pp. 26–33, 114, 118, 121.

Berry, John D. "Legible in Public Space." *Eye*. Spring 2008, pp. 18–25.

Brandon, Kelly. "The Writing on the Wall: A Conversation in Two Languages." *Identity*. Summer 1993, pp. 68–72.

Braybrooke, Susan. "Fling Out the Banner!" *Print*. March/April 1978, pp. 37–49.

Canty, Donald J. "Beyond Writing on the Wall." *Architectural Record*, May 1992, pp. 44–45.

Carpenter, Edward K. "What Goes on Here: Messages in the Environment." *Print*, March/April 1976, pp. 37–49.

Cembalest, Robin. "Apocalypse Then." *Print*. March/April 1997, pp. 130–133.

Chermayeff, Ivan. "Graphic Design in Public: How Important Is It?" *Immovable Objects: Urban Open Spaces*. 1979, p. 47.

Dean, Andrea O. "Graphics in the Environment." *AIA Journal*, 1975.

Drummond, Scott. "Monumental Endeavors." *Dimensions*. Vol. 3, No. 1, pp. 14–16.

Dugdale, Juanita. "You are here." *ID* magazine. November 1993, pp. 66–73.

Dugdale, Juanita. "Landmarks and Milestones: Building an Environmental Graphic Design Time Line." *Dimensions*. Vol. 1, No. 1, 1993, pp. 5–13.

Dunlop, Beth. "Interview: Timothy F. Rub on the Work of Joseph Urban." *The Journal of Decorative and Propaganda Arts*. Issue 8, Spring 1988, pp. 104–119.

Elliman, Paul. "City of Words." *Eye*. Summer 2001, pp. 62–66.

Gandee, Charles K. "Missed Connections." *Architectural Record*, March 1987, pp. 128–139.

Kennedy, Randy. "Award to Artist Who Gives Slums a Human Face." *New York Times*, October 20, 2010, pp. C1–C2.

Kennedy, Randy. "Underground Renaissance Man: Watch the Aesthetic Walls, Please." *New York Times*, August 3, 2007, pp. C33–C34.

Knapp, Pat, ed. *SEGD Design 25*, No. 25, 2009.

Lahr, John. "New York Is New York—Alas." *Print*, 1968, pp. 50–57, 122, 130.

Lees, John and Farman, Melvin. "The Sign along the Highway." *Print*, 1968, pp. 58–61.

Linn, Charles. "Signs of the Times." *Architectural Record*. June 1997, pp. 85–91.

Lukach, Joan M. "Design in Transit: Boston's Revitalized Subway System." *Print*, 1968, pp. 62–67.

Margolies, John. "New Amsterdam Theater." *Architectural Record*. June 1997, pp. 113–119.

Meggs, Philip B. "Peter Behrens: Design's Man of the Century?" *Print*, March/April 1991, pp. 70–79.

Murphy, Jim. "A Grand Gateway." *Progressive Architecture*. November 1987, pp. 96–105.

Ohlson, Kristin. "Farmer Turns Geneticist on Quest for Black Kernel." *New York Times*, May 11, 1998, p. A10.

Pearson, Clifford A. "Five-Star Motel." *Architectural Record*, August 1994, pp. 64–69.

Rodenbeck, Max. "In Search of Lost Time: Snohetta's Alexandria Library." *Architecture*, October 2001, pp. 77, 105–110.

Russell, James S. "VSBA Today." *Architectural Record*. February 1998, pp. 58–67.

Sarhandi, Daoud and Rivas, Carolina. "This Is 1968 . . . This Is Mexico." *Eye*. Summer 2005, pp. 24–37.

Shaw, Paul. "In Praise of Neon." *Baseline*. No. 54, 2008, pp. 22–31.

Shaw, Warren. "The First Subway Line." *Metropolis*. April 1992, pp. 23–27.

Sinclair, Mark. "Disappearing Information." *Print*. August 2011, pp. 65–69.

Stiff, Paul. "The Way Ahead." *Eye*. Winter 2010, p. 42.

Treu, Martin. "Messages from the Past." *Dimension: A Design Journal of the Society for Environmental Graphic Design*, Vol. 1, No. 2, pp. 7–13.

Trieb, Marc. "Alphabets, Building, Cities." *Print*. May/June 1978, pp. 47–53.

Turner, Raymond. "Designing London Transport." *Places*. Summer 1994, pp. 52–79.

Vanderbilt, Tom. "Making the Cut." *Print*. January/February 2005, pp. 65–71.

Walters, John L. "Brian's Signature." *Eye*. Spring 2009, pp. 46–49.

Walters, John L. "In the Thick of It." *Eye*. Spring 2011, pp. 20–29.

Wood, Gaby. "Massive Attack." *New York Times Magazine*, February 27, 2011, pp. 24–31.

IMAGE RESOURCES

Rockport Publishers wishes to thank the institutions and individuals who have kindly provided photographic material for this book. In all cases, every effort has been made to contact copyright holders. Any corrections or omissions will be noted for future editions.

8, 26, 27, 30, 31, 32, 47, 58, 61, 82, 91, 93, 96, 102, 108, 120, 122, 130, 131, 148, 194, 203: Corbis.

12, 15, 29, 61, 87, 88, 92, 102, 109, 116, 121, 127, 132, 161, 172, 173, 194, 203, 214, 225, 234, 239, 241, 243: Poulin + Morris Inc.

16, 19, 180, 198, 199, 211, 213, 230: Sussman/Prejza & Company.

22, 30: Vatican Museums.

26: Anatoly Pronin/Art Resource, NY.

28: British Museum.

33: Alinari/Art Resource, NY.

34: Government of India Tourist Office.

34: Hancock Shaker Village, Pittsfield, Massachusetts.

35: City of Mitchell, South Dakota.

35: Craven Dunhill & Co. Ltd.

38, 45: Manuel Cohen/The Art Archive at Art Resource, NY.

41, 59, 60: U. S. Patent Office.

42: French Government Tourist Office.

43, 44: Brown Brothers.

46: The Brooklyn Historical Society.

48: Wisconsin Center for Film and Theater Research.

48, 100: Museum of the City of New York.

49: Theatre Historical Society of America, Ben Hall Collection, Elmhurst, Illinois.

50: The Pennsylvania State University, Historical Collections and Labor Archives.

50: Collection of the Margaret Herrick Library, AMPAS.

51: Museum of the City of New York, Photo Archive, Gottscho-Schleisner Collection.

52: © Photographs: Paul Shaw.

52, 104, 113: New York Transit Museum.

53: Picture Collection, The New York Public Library, Astor, Lenox and Tilden Foundations.

54: Buffalo and Erie County Historical Society.

55: Photograph: James Stringer.

56: Photography Collection, Miriam and Ira D. Wallach Division of Art, Prints and Photographs, The New York Public Library, Astor, Lenox and Tilden Foundations.

57, 58: © Photographs: Andrew Bordwin.

60: Let There be Neon.

62: RIBA Library Photographs Collection.

63: © Tfl from the London Transport Museum collection.

64, 74: Netherlands Architecture Institute.

67: Historiches Museum der Stadt Wien.

68: AEG Aktiengesellschaft Offentlichkeitsarbeit Firmenarchiv.

69: Van Abbemuseum.

70: © Photograph: Kaoru Akiyama.

71: © Photograph: Jan Derwig, RIBA Library Photographs Collection.

72, 75, 77: Bauhaus-Archiv Berlin, Foto: Hermann Kiessling.

76: Museum of Modern Art, New York.

78: © Photographs: Jan Middendorp.

79: Luc Boegly/Artedia.

80: Lust, The Hague.

85: Neil Setchfield/The Art Archive at Art Resource, NY.

86: © V&A Images/Victoria and Albert Museum.

90: Museum of the City of New York, Gottscho-Schleisner Collection.

91: © Photograph: Robert Leaper.

92: Milstein Division of United States History, Local History & Genealogy, The New York Public Library, Astor, Lenox and Tilden Foudations.

94: Museum of the City of New York, Byron Co. Collection.

89, 95: © Photograph: Wally Gobetz.

97: Los Angeles Public Library, Photo Collection.

98: © J. Paul Getty Trust. Used with permission. Julius Shulman Photography Archive, Research Library at the Getty Research Institute (2004.R.10).

99, 111: Teague.

101: © Photograph: John Vachon.

103: Syracuse Research Library, Special Collections.

106, 112, 123, 124: © Library of Congress, Prints and Photographs Division.

107: © Chicago Tribune Photos Archive.

108: Steven Heller.

110, 150: © Photographs: Ezra Stoller, Courtesy of ESTO. All rights reserved.

119: City of Los Angeles.

121: © Photograph: Peter Beaumont.

125: Alvin Lustig Archive, Courtesy of Kind Company.

126: InterContinental Hotels Group.

128: Jian Chen/Art Resource, NY.

129: McDonald's Corporation.

135: CAVS Archive, Massachusetts Institute of Technology.

136: © 2012 Barragan Foundation, Switzerland/Artists Rights Society (ARS), New York.

137: © 2012 Artists Rights Society (ARS), New York/ProLitteris, Zurich.

138: © 2012 Artists Rights Society (ARS), New York/ProLitteris, Zurich.

139, 140: Kinneir Calvert.

141: International Paper Corporation.

142, 143: Paul Rand Papers, Yale University Library.

144, 145, 147, 159, 160, 166, 167, 170: Chermayeff & Geismar.

146: Photograph: Charles Eames, Courtesy of Vitra Design Museum.

149: IBM Corporation Archives.

151, 152, 153, 154: Lou Dorfsman.

152: Getty Images, CBS Photo Archive.

155: © The Museum of Modern Art/Licensed by SCALA/Art Resource, NY.

156: Barbara Stauffacher Solomon.

157, 158, 206: Vignelli Associates.

162, 163: Lance Wyman, Ltd.

164: © ABC-CLIO LLC.

165: © Photograph: Robin Johnstone.

166: Herb Lubalin Study Center of Design and Typography at the Cooper Union.

168, 169: Photographs: Florian Aicher.

170: Mayers & Schiff Associates.

171: © The University of Texas at Dallas, McDermott Library, The History of Aviation Collection, Department of Special Collections.

174, 175: AIGA, AdamsMorioka Archives Vault, New York City.

176: Pei Cobb Freed & Partners Architects, George Cserna/Avery Architectural and Fine Arts Library, Columbia University.

177: Pei Cobb Freed & Partners Architects, John Naar; George Cserna/Avery Architectural and Fine Arts Library, Columbia University.

178: Armin Hoffman.

179: © 1979 by Watson-Guptill Publications, a division of Random House, Inc..

183, 184, 185: Venturi Scott Brown and Associates.

186, 187: James Wines/SITE.

188, 189: Richard Haas.

190: © Photograph: Robert Fiehn, Courtesy of Rogers Stirk Harbour + Partners.

191: Milton Glaser.

192: Dan Reisinger.

193: Gregotti Associati International srl.

195: May Lin Studio.

196, 197: © Photographs: Mitsumasa Fujitsuka, Courtesy of Takenobu Igarashi.

200, 201: Schenker, Probst & Barensfeld.

204, 205 222, 223: Communication Arts.

207: Debra Nichols Design.

208: Gensler.

209: Studio Dumbar.

210, 211: Carbon Smolan Agency.

215: Murphy/Jahn.

216, 217: Edenspeikermann.

218: Alan Fletcher.

219: Donovan & Green Inc.

220: Barton Phelps & Associates.

221: Whitehouse & Co.

224: The Jerde Partnership, Inc.

228, 242: © Photograph: Zhou Ruogo Architecture Photography, Courtesy of Arup.

230: Selbert Perkins Design Collaborative.

CONTRIBUTORS

Arup
www.arup.com

Carbon Smolan Agency
www.carbonesmolan.com

Eric Chan Design Co. Ltd.
www.ericchandesign.com

Chermayeff & Geismar
www.cgstudionyc.com

Donovan & Green Inc.
www.donovanandgreen.com

Edenspiekermann
www.de.edenspiekerman.com

Emery Studio
www.emerystudio.com

Gensler
www.gensler.com

Milton Glaser, Inc.
www.miltonglaser.com

Gregotti Associati International srl
www.gregottiassociati.it

Hiromura Design
www.hiromuradesign.com

Igarashi Atelier
www.igarashistudio.com

The Jerde Partnership, Inc.
www.jerde.com

JR
www.jr-art.net

Maya Lin Studio
www.mayalin.com

Lust
www.lust.nl

Bruce Mau Design
www.brucemaudesign.com

Murphy/Jahn Architects
www.murphyjahn.com

Debra Nichols Design
www.debranicholsdesign.com

Pei Cobb Freed & Partners
www.pcf-p.com

Pentagram (NY)
www.pentagram.com

Barton Phelps & Associates
www.bpala.com

Poulin + Morris Inc.
www.poulinmorris.com

Dan Reisinger
www.danreisinger.com

Rogers Stirk Harbour + Partners
www.rsh-p.com

Selbert Perkins Design Collaborative
www.selbertperkins.com

Sense Team
www.senseteam.org

Site
www.siteenvirodesign.com

Snøhetta
www.snoarc.no

Barbara Stauffacher Solomon
www.barbarastauffachersolomon.com

Studio Dumbar
www.studiodumbar.com

Studio of Richard Haas
www.richardhaas.com

Sussman/Prejza & Company
www.sussmanprejza.com

Teague
www.teague.com

Two Twelve
www.twotwelve.com

Venturi Scott Brown and Associates
www.vsba.com

Vignelli Associates
www.vignelli.com

Whitehouse & Co.
www.wandco.com

Lance Wyman Ltd.
www.lancewyman.com

INDEX

ACKNOWLEDGMENTS / ABOUT THE AUTHOR

ACKNOWLEDGMENTS

This book is dedicated to Doug Morris . . . my partner in life, work, and love who has always given me the time, freedom, and support to pursue my dreams.

This book would not have been possible without the assistance, support, and generous contributions of so many people.

I would like to thank the following designers, architects, photographers, and colleagues for generously contributing examples of their work— Florian Aicher, Jeroen Barendse, Michael Bierut, Andrew Bordwin, Margaret Calvert, Ken Carbone, Ivan Chermayeff, Greg D'Onofrio, Michael Donovan, Lou Dorfsman, Gert Dumbar, Garry Emery, Alan Fletcher, Richard Foy, Tom Geismar, Milton Glaser, Richard Haas, Steve Heller, Armin Hoffman, Takenobu Igarashi, Maya Lin, Rebecca Maloney, Jan Middendorp, Abbott Miller, Shizuko Yoshikawa Müller, Debra Nichols, Jonathan Posnett, Robert Probst, JR, Dan Reisinger, Paula Scher, Clifford Selbert, Paul Shaw, Barbara Stauffacher Solomon, Erik Speikermann, Erica Stoller, Massimo Vignelli, Roger Whitehouse, James Wines, and Lance Wyman.

A special thanks to Jim Polshek and Deborah Sussman for taking time out of their busy schedules to provide me their wonderful forewords to this book. Their support and friendship over the years, as well as their inspiring work, has been a tremendous influence to my evolution as a designer, author, and educator.

To Winnie Prentiss, publisher; Emily Potts senior acquisition editor; and John Gettings, managing editor at Rockport Publishers for their continued encouragement and support throughout this entire process. And to Regina Grenier for her patience and collaborative spirit in realizing this book.

To Andreina Carrillo, my former student and colleague at Poulin + Morris Inc., for her invaluable insights and contributions to the design of this volume.

And, as always, to my students—past, present, and future, who continue to inspire and challenge me.

ABOUT THE AUTHOR

Richard Poulin is cofounder, design director, and principal of Poulin + Morris Inc., an internationally recognized, multidisciplinary design consultancy located in New York City.

His work has been published in periodicals and books worldwide, is in the permanent collection of the Library of Congress, and has received awards from the American Institute of Architects, American Institute of Graphic Arts, *Applied Arts, Communication Arts, Creative Review, Graphis, ID, Print*, Society for Environmental Graphic Design, Society of Publication Designers, Type Directors Club, and the Art Directors Clubs of Los Angeles, New York, and San Francisco.

Richard is a fellow of the Society for Environmental Graphic Design (SEGD), the organization's highest honor for lifetime achievement; and past president and board member of the New York Chapter of the American Institute of Graphic Arts (AIGA). He is also a recipient of a research grant in design history from the Graham Foundation for Advanced Studies in the Fine Arts.

Since 1992, Richard has been a faculty member of the School of Visual Arts in New York City and was formerly an adjunct professor at The Cooper Union. He has also taught and lectured at Carnegie-Mellon University, Maryland Institute College of Art, Massachusetts College of Art, North Carolina State University, Simmons College, Syracuse University, University of the Arts, and University of Cincinnati.

Richard is the author of the *The Language of Graphic Design: An Illustrated Handbook for Understanding Fundamental Design Principles* (Rockport Publishers, 2011) and the coauthor of *Typography Referenced* (Rockport Publishers, 2011).

He lives in New York City and Clinton Corners, New York, with his partner of twenty-two years.

COLOPHON

Graphic Design and Architecture: A 20th–Century History was designed and typeset by Poulin + Morris Inc., New York, New York. Digital type composition and page layouts were originated on Apple G5 computers, utilizing Adobe InDesign CS5, Version 5.5.5 software.